NICOLA VIVIAN

MY WILL

A Portrait of Love
and Addiction

Z

First published 2019

by Zuleika Books & Publishing

Thomas House, 84 Eccleston Square, London, SW1V 1PX

© 2019 Nicola Vivian

British Library Cataloguing in Publication Data

A catalogue record for this book is
available from the British Library

ISBN: 978-1-99-962326-5

Typeset by Euan Monaghan

Printed in Great Britain by Clays Ltd.

Dedication

I dedicate this book to everyone whose mental chaos and self-judgement negatively impacts their daily life, and to all who are lonely, fearful or unhappy – to everyone who is walking the road of addiction, or who is trapped in the agony of grief.

Disclaimer

This is my story told from my perspective although I fully appreciate that the perspectives of others may be different.

Since the main theme of my book is addiction, I have chosen to change some of the names and a few minor details in order to tell the story more freely.

Acknowledgements

I thank Rachel Kelly for her support and for introducing me to Tom Perrin of Zuleika, whose infectious enthusiasm, bright mind, humour and dedication has made this book possible.

For editorial advice, I thank Lynn Curtis for her clear vision and sense of flow, Louise Naudé and Hannah Burke-Tomlinson for their meticulous precision, and my son Theo for his blistering corrections.

I thank David, my brilliant writer friend, for his priceless encouragement, Laurence for her belief in me, John and Nicole for their constructive guidance, and Oliver for humouring me. I thank Marcelle for her inspirational teaching, Sara for the motivation she has given me, Hugo for his expert counsel, and Susannah for her commitment to its promotion.

Lastly and perhaps most importantly, I thank my darling mother for her unwavering love and my beloved Dad and Will for all the lessons they unwittingly taught me.

Addiction

The word 'addiction' is derived from the Latin *addictus*, a past participle *of addico*, which means, among other things, 'to devote' or 'to surrender'; but the state of addiction is multi-layered, mobile and mysterious. Bound to the pursuit and understanding of its origins, for thirty years I have gone back time and again to the excavation of my own experience and used writing as a vehicle to throw light on it. Quickly discovering the discomfort of candour, I flirted at first with vague portrayals of myself and others in my life, but over time I knew that in order to make sense of it all, I had to confront the truth and significance of the condition. 'The truth hurts' is the old saying, but it was only through addressing the truth that I had half a chance of changing myself.

There is nothing pretty or soft about addiction; its very nature is clawing and shameful, creating a domino effect that falls on everyone related to it. A common tendency amongst its 'relatives' is strategic ignorance, overwhelmed as they are by the confusion of their pain and their visceral urges to cover up the distasteful. Yet even when they know that their reactions are a form of make-believe or even brainwashing, they persist for they know no other way.

By the time I got to my mid-twenties I was stuck in the rut of duping myself. Aiding and abetting my delusions, I could make neither head nor tail of what was truth and what was invention, or why I was so unhappy. But so determined was I to escape from it that my pursuit of wisdom and change was relentless – addictive, even. With guidance from books and psychoanalysts, I asked myself a thousand questions. I double-checked my reactions ad infinitum. I talked myself in and out of relationships and situations as many times as there were days in my life. I examined addiction from every angle and dug under its cover, into the broken core of the human spirit from which it grows.

I am fifty-five now and a divorcee, with a towering twenty-two-year-old son who has integrity and a smile that cracks my heart. Into the mix of experience since my divorce, I can throw a few more relationships, several house-moves, deaths and suicides of people close to me. Even with my hard-earned knowledge, I have continued to fall into the same old patterns of addiction in my roles as a mother, lover, or just as myself, but thankfully over time they've become less extreme, and have shifted direction towards good health and a good environment. Daily I remind myself of the instructions given by airlines to put my own life jacket on before helping anyone else with theirs. I monitor how intensely I care, aiming to be more moderate and balanced about it. 'Be a leaf on the breeze!' I tell myself. 'Go with the flow, see what happens.'

I can't help wondering, however, for whom my learning has been. Surely it wasn't all just for me? Do I not have an obligation to testify to my experience, to bear witness to it, for the benefit of others in similar situations? After all wisdom and fables have been passed down to younger generations since time began. I feel as if I have been studying addiction for fifty years and, even if I am still learning in a quiet way, I think I have graduated beyond my teacher training now and can finally put what I know to use. As a writer, giving voice and form to the state of being human is a productive way to release the stress that comes from the fermentation of bottled-up feelings. For a reader, it legitimises *and* liberates them as relatable words can explain what was hitherto misunderstood. When all is said and done, we are still tribal people who are hard-wired to share and seek like-mindedness.

The current revolution of self-exposure fuelled by social media, reality television, and celebrity confessions tries many people's patience, particularly when faced with another memoir. But to me it seems to be a turning of the wheel away from the lingering Victorian stiff upper lip and the repressed mental trauma brought home from the world wars. In spite of the glory awarded to stoicism then, I have read that the emotional wounds from those wars often bled out through silence, depression, anger, and alcoholism, which subsequent generations absorbed in different forms: guilt, self-contempt, fear, and anxiety.

Wheels turn and bring change, and each cycle has a beginning, a middle, and an end – the latter of which generally brings a levelling of the crescendo in the middle. Maybe now is the 'middle' moment of this cycle, when mankind needs to shout about these issues in order to bring change? Change is uncomfortable and slow, but with it consciousness does shift, and new attitudes become the norm.

The wheel has already moved considerably. Depression and suicides – in young people particularly – are now at the forefront of our consciousness. This is a vast improvement on the culture of my youth, in which 'nerves' were treated with Valium, depression was regarded as a weakness and an embarrassment, and you navigated your emotional life through instinct, prayer and luck, which seems as rash to me as driving a car without ever having been taught how.

Being connected to nature and having rewarding relationships, worthwhile work and status, a past you can make sense of and a future you can look forward to are now being recognised as having greater anti-depressant benefits than medication that alters brain function. So, if the popularity of the revelatory memoir irritates, remember that it won't last forever; nothing ever does, and once the psychological needs of mankind are met it may just balance out.

My personal wish for change is in the lives of children. Emotion is often too complicated to be held in the head, but if a child of the future had the skills to give it voice, its inner compass might point it to a world of limitless possibilities. In my fairy-tale existence, emotional education in the school curriculum would be taught alongside a child's first language so that the two merged seamlessly togeth-er. A child would learn to identify and communicate its emotions, perceptions, responses, and needs as naturally and frankly as debating its choice of ice cream. It would learn compassionate ways to relate to itself and its peers, and to decipher beyond what others do and say, so as to avoid assuming that they're cruel or censorious. It would understand its childhood influences and learn to manage them with clear boundaries. It would learn to roll with the punches, bear grief without abandoning itself, and, instead of being crushed by fear or failure, it would understand that its mind, not its reality, is usually the cause of its emotional suffering. It would learn confidence and its unique value in the world and would learn to take full responsibility for its choices. It would know the strength of support and accord-ingly would never have to feel alone. Its core would there-fore have a greater chance of being strong and remaining unbroken; this core could direct the child to lead a fruitful life, make wise decisions, and avoid the mental chaos that strikes so many of us in our thirties and forties.

To have to unlearn everything we learned growing up is a slow and difficult process, and a waste of time when we could be doing more useful things with life. So, if our perception of the outside world is shaped by inner inter-pretation, is it not prudent to educate our children on this topic first?

Although I am aware that my dream is a small cog in the big wheel, and that there are countless other factors that at-tribute towards mental well-being (like genetics, a healthy gut, and minimizing the input of environmental stressors such as crowds, noise, radiation, and chemicals) I still maintain that, regardless of race, sex, status or class, you are still one step closer to overcoming the thorny pains of life if you hold the ability to articulate your mind in a safe environment. Storing malaise keeps you turning inwards and stuck in its darkness; opening the door and releasing it frees you to find your true value. It is in the forgetting of yourself that you blossom, and by and by so will those around you; a point reiterated by the safety regulations given on aeroplanes.

It seems clear that neither society nor the earth can flourish with damaged cores. A house collapses if built on a broken foundation. Cracks develop in the walls. Depression, phobias, and addiction are those ever-widening cracks, which time and time again topple the house.

Wreckage

What if I removed the hard build-up of grief
creaking like a shipwreck in the pit of your belly
that forgiveness has failed to soften
and disperse like a dandelion head?
What if I nudged you to recognize that,
like a gestating mammal, it is you who holds onto
the decaying foetus that spawns
your wounded child identity?
What if I stilled your self-centred noise
and removed the glass of red
that briefly lightens the weight of your shadow
till the moment of slurred speech?
What if I dared you to peel back the shield of loss,
set free your wounded child, and find who you really are?
For you are there, somewhere, hiding in the rotting boughs
of the wreckage;
waiting, waiting, waiting to breathe.

Reasons to Breathe

1988

Chapter 1

Cigarettes. I need cigarettes. But there are none left. I've searched all his usual hiding places: his cupboards, desk, and chest of drawers, but I found not even a single escapee, mangled in a jeans pocket. There are plenty of lighters, in drawers and down the sides of armchairs. Bic lighters covered in promotional images of 007 films.

No cigarettes, though.

I'll have to go to the shop.

Oh God.

I can't do that. It's too scary. I can't leave his flat. What if he came back when I wasn't here? He might come back – quickly – for a second or two. I can't go out. No. I would miss him coming home.

It's been two days now. I've alternated between hiding under the duvet and cleaning his flat. The day before yesterday I hoovered the floors; then, to suck up cobwebs, I did the walls as well. Pushing it up them, the hoover sounded like an aeroplane taking off, and regrettably, made a dirty smear above his bedroom door that I couldn't reach to wipe off. Instead I bleached every other surface and the whole flat now has the disinfected smell of my old school loos. I also ironed his shirts. I ironed every one of them, some of them two or three times. I ironed his boxer shorts. I ironed his jeans. I thought of ironing his suits. Then I emptied the fridge, freezer, and cupboards, and made lasagne, shepherd's pie, prawn cocktail. I've been baking potatoes, ready to eat with grated cheddar, keeping them in the oven on low, just in case he walks through the door, hungry.

The day runs into night without my knowing. The curtains are drawn shut. They've been shut since it happened. They're brocade and heavily-lined, and without electric light it's too dark to distinguish even the silhouettes of furniture.

My mother stayed with me last night. Emma stayed the night before. Both tried to open the curtains, but I protested. Mum said it would make me feel better.

'Nothing will make me feel better, for God's sake!' I shouted. 'Sorry, Mum. Sorry. Didn't mean that.'

I wipe my nose with my sleeve, and to stop the tears I press my hands into my eyes until sparkles fizz in the blackness. She's tired, my poor mum. Looks like she's aged ten years since Sunday. She spent last night propped up in the armchair in the corner of the bedroom. Like a guard dog, she jerked awake every time I moved, her eyes wide with alarm.

She hates that I smoke but she urges me to go out.

'Good to get out, Nix,' she says, picking up her book. 'I'll go now too. Get this back to the library. Maybe stop at Mr Tibbs' for some fruit. Sends you his love, by the way. I'll call in an hour to see how you've got on. Okay?'

I open the clothes cupboard. The inside light displays hangers of ironed shirts and neatly folded sweaters: my handiwork. I put his blue jeans on. They fall off me, so I thread one of his ties through the belt-loops and knot it tightly around my waist. I roll up the hems. It's the first time I've looked in the mirror in the last few days, and I see a girl I don't really recognise. Or is it the lens through which I now look that's distorted? Like a stranger without knowledge of my history, roots, or what makes me *me*, I observe my face as if it is no longer mine. My eyes are darker than usual. There's a static, stage-fright look about them. Black circles make them look like deep holes, helped by mascara which has run and dried. My skier's tan has faded to a dirty yellow although the pale goggle marks are still apparent, and my hair is dull. I am thinner too.

It occurs to me that I should wash, but I don't have the energy and I am too cold to undress. Squalls of shivers rush across my skin, down my back and around my waist, like the onset of flu.

Mum must have used my pink t-shirt as a pillow, as it is crumpled behind the cushion on the chair. I smooth out the creases with my flattened palms once I have it on. It's my favourite. I bought it in Val d'Isère when he and I were there a couple of weeks ago. He liked the appliqué frog above the bosom and picked it out from the rail on the pavement outside. As he was handing it to me, he slipped on the slushy snow and we giggled at how silly he looked, dissolving quickly into hysterical laughter under the shop girl's watchful eye. In deliberate slow motion, she totted up my items on the cash register and he, knowing that he couldn't keep a straight face, bolted for the door snorting, while my ribs and shoulders shook from repressed giggles, and I thought I might explode.

I bought faded blue jeans to go with the t-shirt, with an appliqué flower and hummingbird on the back pocket.

'Pretty Billy-goat,' he said when I wore them that evening. He ruffled my hair.

I've been wearing them for three days now. They're glued to my body with sentiment and superstition. If I am dressed as I was when he last saw me, the invisible thread of recognition might bring him back. Like a homing pigeon, he might need markers to indicate the path back to his nest. But tracking me down when I'm away from his flat is a different matter. I decide that *his* jeans, not mine, will be the stronger magnet. Yes. He'll find it simpler to find me in *his* jeans.

Sunshine blinds me as I open the door. I hesitate, immobilised on the doorstep, on the edge of worlds between dark and light. My brain slows and judders, like the ill-matched cogs of two wheels – unable to figure out what's happening. Outside there is a sense of ceaseless motion in the air, even if here, in the corner of the square behind the church, it is less obvious. I feel it though, in the rustle of the leaves, the hum of traffic, the fly that bombs into the darkened hall, the Wrigley's paper lifted by the breeze, the muffled thud of a door, a telephone's distant ring, and the fresh dog excrement in the lee of the pavement. I sense busyness behind the tall bay windows: Rice Krispies popping under streams of milk, coffee percolating, briefcases snapping shut, watches being checked, ties being tied, teeth being cleaned, stamps being looked for at the back of deep drawers.

Yet the world inside my head is frozen in time and drab, since light from the sun doesn't reach it. Like a pencil drawing that captures a moment of shocked impact, it is breathless.

The contrast takes me aback. I feel thrown into a parallel universe, and the story of Narnia darts into my mind. It hadn't occurred to me, I realise, that the world outside would contradict my interior one. Its lack of sympathy and defiant disregard feels like a personal attack. It renders me disoriented, and at a loss to know how to manage myself.

Shall I go back upstairs again? Forget about going out?

I move from one foot to the other, swaying back and forth between the two worlds.

But cigarettes... What will I do about them?

Leaning forwards, I look down the street.

It's the same as it always was. But brighter. My heart races and I put my hand up to it, to stop it bolting from its starting stall. Or that's what it feels like.

I make the decision. I'll brave it. I have to.

With tentative steps I turn towards Redcliffe Gardens.

Focus on the ground, I tell myself. Be mindful of my feet on it – feel how the heel, the arch and then the ball are set down onto the pavement.

I look up at the blue sky where there's not a cloud in sight, and at the blossom on the tree by the church. Blossom? It strikes me that it must be new and fresh. It wasn't there three days ago, was it? I really don't remember. In any case, it reminds me of bubble-gum candyfloss, and candyfloss reminds me of being young. Birdsong filters down through its branches. My ears single this out above the moan of a motorbike, as if I had a volume control inside my brain. A woman approaches, pushing a pram, and her head is cocked as if she too hears only their chirping. But as she turns towards the gate of the gardens, I see that she's humming a song to her baby. Passing them I notice her serene smile, and I glance inside the pram at the small, plump arms folded tenderly around a doll in blue gingham.

The world carries on, it seems, regardless of how it has stopped for me. I am a stranger in it, and so cut off that I could be watching a movie at the back of a cinema. The confusion makes me dizzy. I remember to breathe. Breathe! That's what my doctor keeps telling me. 'Breathe, darling. Drop the shoulders. Fill the lungs.' Are there others whose worlds have stopped? I wonder. Are they as shocked as I by the mundane normalcy around them? And do they wear their shock so that it's visible? Do *I*?

I scan the passers-by, but at this hour it's mainly city boys striding towards the tube station. They swing their briefcases and look purposeful. A jacket blows open and a streak of red silk lining flashes against pin-stripe. On the steps of the entrance to number 14 is Jimmy's cardboard box which he sleeps in. He wriggles out from under it. I know his name from when he'd gashed his cheek and I'd called an ambulance. He sits up, sees me, and cocks his head. He always does this; today, though, his smile seems dimmer. Or am I just imagining it? I quicken my steps to avoid a chat. The thought of sympathy brings tears to my eyes.

The door of the shop is open. A light breeze follows me inside, dirt from the pavement caught up in its whirl. Mr Patel winks at me as he takes change from his customer, and the bell of the till, more emphatic than usual, dings piercingly through the ambient noise. From the radio next to the red cash box comes Duran Duran, and in front of me a skinhead jigs to the music. Knuckle-duster rings adorn his fingers and his right ear is pierced. He wears a leather waistcoat and tight leather trousers. The back of his head is bumpy, and a vein is prominent.

The air in the shop is still and warm. I feel impatient. Why is the queue so slow?

I must get a new pen, I remind myself. Mine is running out with all the writing I'm doing. While Mr Patel makes small talk about football hooliganism with the man ahead of the skinhead, I reach for a pack of biros, and think of my writing. I mull over the way it comes to me in urgent bursts, how my pen rushes across the lined paper in a feverish way, discharging every thought – like vomit – whilst cigarette smoke from the ashtray twists across my vision. I sit at his desk to write, and use one of my old A Level notebooks, empty until now, except for an essay on Georgia O'Keefe. Beside it is his white t-shirt, rolled up like a scroll, which I touch from time to time as a superstitious gesture to rally his presence. On the other side is his neatly-organised address book, two lighters, a now-empty pack of Marlboro, and an ashtray made of jade. It is full of cigarette butts and makes me feel seedy, but still I fill it, squishing another one down into any available hole in the mounting pile. Although I would like to, it feels just too arduous to rise and walk the few steps to the kitchen to empty it. I picture the way my tears pucker the paper while my words cover it, and how my facial muscles ache from a prolonged grimace. Why, I wonder, why am I doing it? Why am I so insistent on unravelling and recording every passing moment, memory, and thought? After all, facing them throws me into a state of paralyzing bewilderment like a rabbit caught in headlights.

It's my pursuit of truth, I think; the truth of events and my response to them, new ones, old ones, the visible and invisible. Won't truth make sense of my chaos? Truth. I am hungry for it. When a recollection feels twisted or biased by my use of words, I blacken it out, erasing any influence of falsehood, and start again. It doesn't come easily. I struggle to find the right word and meaning and light another cigarette to distract me from the process. Climbing down into the feeling, making sense of and expressing it with an accurate eye is hard to do, and it hurts.

The light from the door is momentarily blocked by another customer, and it snaps me out of my reverie. He has thick hairy forearms covered in builder's dust, which I notice when he reaches for a newspaper. I pick up a tabloid from the same pile and, leafing through it absentmindedly, I quickly do a double-take. A shock wave rushes through me, and what feels like a punch in my solar plexus. My forehead prickles. My eyes sting with tears. Frantically, I flick back to find what I think I just glimpsed, the rustle of paper noisy in the small, stuffy shop. It was a familiar picture, I am sure of it. Yes, sure of it. Yet maybe my mind was playing tricks on me? It does keep doing that at the moment. In my excitement some of the pages fall like dead butterfly's wings onto my feet and handbag. The skinhead turns around to look at me. Mr Patel's conversation freezes, and the builder swears under his breath. The song is suddenly louder. My breathing is heavy and I feel sweaty. The paper is torn and crushed now from my frustrated grasp. But finally, I have it! There in my trembling hands is the picture I thought I had seen! Yes! And it's the exact same one that I have in my wallet! A picture of him! Yes, *him*! I scrutinise it up close until I am cross-eyed, questioning the accuracy of my sight, but it *is* a picture of him. It *is* him! My Will! A headshot. He is in black tie, looking shy, with his bottom lip drawn in. I press it against my chest and hug it, stifling a desire to wave it around and shout, 'Look! Look, everyone! Look at this beautiful man! He's mine! Isn't he lovely?'

My teeth chatter. I am cold. My mouth is dry.

A small voice inside my head whispers, 'But he's dead.'

***

In that moment I know that the writing I am doing is my attempt to keep him alive.

Every moment, thought, and memory that I write about is tied to him. Capturing them in words and creating pictures with them, keeps him present and stops him slipping away from me. There can be no detail overlooked in my documentation. They must be registered – and quickly – to arrest time's shifting of their shape. I have the impression that I am racing against time, as if the heavy downpour of today will burst the riverbanks tomorrow, and the waters will spill onto the floodplain, rushing away from me, forever out of reach. I must create a new encyclopaedic body. Like the Bayeux Tapestry, it must testify – stitch by stitch – to the truths of my old-world order and the forever-changing new one. I must assemble this history for us with clarity, and I must learn it by heart. It must be tangible and accessible for instant recall, just as if he were here and bound to me by layers of self-knowledge.

I must not forget. Him. It. Us. I must not forget.

***

Ignoring the crumpled mess and the stares of Mr Patel and customers, I page through other papers to find more pictures. There are several. Agitated, I scoop them up, possessive and craving, as if they were aid parcels dropped from a helicopter and my life depended on them.

I don't know why I am so shocked, as journalists have been calling the flat incessantly since it happened. Initially

I had picked up the phone when it rang, but now their speculative sensationalism feels like an incendiary device in my mind. Once I understood that 'fallen aristocrat', or 'poor little rich boy', was the only copy they wanted, I left the phone to ring.

The name of the song suddenly comes to me: 'Rio'. That's it. Yes. It had eluded me before. At the chorus, the skinhead's hips swing and he drums his hands against them. I stare at the dancing tattoos on his biceps and at the rise and fall of the folds of his neck. Reminds me of an accordion.

A conversation outside attracts my attention. Is that Will's voice? I turn quickly to look. No. Of course not. It doesn't even sound like him. God. What's wrong with me?

The skinhead brushes past me on his way out and lightly clips my right shoulder. Suddenly I feel my body give way, and my limbs and torso crumble. I try to keep myself upright, my head high, as if I am being sucked underwater. But I lose focus… stumble… then fall. Just before my head hits the shelf, I think to myself, 'But *I'm* not a fainter! No!'

There is a weight on my chest when I regain consciousness. I try to sit up and sweep away the papers. Mr Patel is yelling.

'Momina! Ambulance! Quickly, now!'

I hear soft footsteps running down stairs. I think of the yellow ball I'd had when I was little, which had sounded similar bouncing down the stairs at home, and I remember my Mum's panicky shouts from the kitchen when she'd mistaken the thumping for me.

Momina has a kind face. She has a deep red bindi on

her forehead and is draped in pink cloth flecked with gold. With one hand she lifts my head, and with the other trickles sweet spicy tea into my mouth. She talks to me in Hindi whispers, and tears run from my eyes. Mr Patel paces behind her, hissing from the corner of his mouth.

'She's breathing, yes? Yes?'

He welcomes in customers, steering them around us.

'Come in. Come in. How can I help? Everything's fine. Yes. Yes. What can I get you?' He's smiling broadly.

'Momina? She alright? Can we move her now? – Two packets of Silk Cut? Of course. Of course. How are you today?'

When there's a lull in business, he comes over to me with three packets of Marlboro in his hand.

'Here, love. Take them. And the papers.'

He hurriedly shoves them into a plastic bag, pulls me up and walks me to the door.

'Look after yourself, huh?' His hand on my back is firm as he pushes me outside.

It is mid-morning. The street basks in warmth and sunshine. A red open-top car roars past and from it comes a blast of George Michael. The driver brakes at two young girls in tiny skirts with bare midriffs on the other side of the street. He pulls up adjacent to them, and whistles with his tanned arm slung over the passenger seat. They flick their thick fringes and giggle.

My face crumples. I swallow hard to hold back tears, but they pour down my cheeks again.

I have to get home.

Laughter. Movement. Freedom. Sunshine. They should make me feel happy, not crazy. But I am a stranger to them. Alone. Isolated. I can't relate to them. No. Of course I can't. They're not happening in my world. My world is disengaged from the world outside, my reality separate.

Chapter 2

Back on home territory, in front of his door – number 44 –
I regret not having bought food. I could at least cook some
more.

I turn the key, wondering what else I could make with
what's left. But there is nothing left. As I dump the news-
papers on the table and open a pack of cigarettes, I think
of how much Will loved my cooking, but I realise at that
moment, that it was also my go-to thing in a crisis. A
home-cooked lunch and dinner – eaten at the kitchen table – painted a wholesome picture of normal life like other
people have. It created the illusion of stability which had
the knack of temporarily erasing – from our minds at least
– the chronic disorder of our lives. Even when things were
really bad, we could still convince ourselves that all was
well on some fronts because, after all, part of normal life
was sitting down to home-cooked meals. And we *did* that.
Even so, he was playful and teasing about it.

'What are you doing to me, my funny little Billy-goat?

Fattening me up? Want me hooked on your delicious nosh so I'll never leave you?'

'Ah, is that what you're thinking of doing? Leaving me?'

'Course not, silly. I'd never leave. Why would I?' He would dunk bread into my chicken stew and point at his bowl. 'Mmm...too damn good. I couldn't'.

I am reminded of the drawings I do for my dad and although I hadn't realised it before now, I see that they carry the same intention as my cooking. They aim to pacify him, humour him, convince him of false realities. Each illustration hopes to smooth out current wrinkles, and usually they're sequential – tending to follow an incident, drama, or outburst.

As he gets older, I prefer not to meet my dad in restaurants – but he enjoys feeling like a bon vivant. He enjoys the exchange with waitresses and the assumption that his charm still works.

When I last saw him, he chose La Famiglia. My local Italian. His speech was slurred when I kissed him hello, but he managed, with some effort, a show of conversation. Once he started winking indiscriminately, I knew the evening would quickly deteriorate. He became distracted by the loss of his napkin, and leaning down to look under the table, went with it, crashing noisily to the floor in the path of the waiters. Riccardo shimmied over with excitable hand gestures and rapid broken English. I waved it away as a medical complaint. Dizziness, you know. Blackouts. Often happens. So sorry. He'll be up in a minute. We'll go – don't worry. Riccardo, I'm sorry. And the bill. I'll pop in tomorrow and pay then. Is that alright?

I tried lifting him and saw that his cheek was cut. Damn. Take a deep breath. All is well.

'Okay, Dad, time for bed. Up! Come on – up!' The volume in the restaurant lowered to a murmur, and eyes bore into my back as I crouched down to whisper to him. I tried rolling him onto his side, but my heel – caught in the hem of my dress – tugged me back down. I toppled forward onto his head, feeling the tear in the fabric as it was released. Still he didn't move. With my cheek to his mouth I checked his breathing, but what with the noise and activity around me it was no use. He was motionless, his face slack. Could be dead, even. With that thought, his well-honed funeral lists tore through my mind like a police siren.

'Daddy! Breathe! Daddy, please! Come on! Breathe, I said!' Alarm raised my voice more than I wanted. I pinched his waist.

He groaned. It was barely audible, but I heard it. An irascible protest tempered by whisky.

'Please get up, Dad! Please. Come on, Daddy! Oh, for fuck's sake – get up! Now!'

Nervous of his caustic tongue, being tough with him was a risk I took only when he was smashed. Instead I tended to humour him in order to counter his mercurial temperament.

Draped heavily around me, he staggered up and out, muttering obscenities at fellow diners who were in his way.

'Wha'-are-you-looking at, hmm?' he challenged a woman in padded shoulders. 'Sssh…should be in a boxing ring, you should. Not-iiiiin Giovanni's nice restaurant.'

I tugged his elbow. 'Riccardo, Dad, not Giovanni. Come on. Keep walking.'

He had little awareness of his meeting with the floor, but he knew that the evening was cut short.

Tears would inevitably precede his apology the next morning. 'Maybe the men in white coats should take me after all, darling. Or better still, the Grim Reaper. It's time, isn't it? There'll be no restaurants left for me to visit soon.'

'It's okay, my Dad. Don't cry. They believed the dizzy thing. All is well.'

I had to protect his dignity. I couldn't stand for him to know how everyone had stared, smirked and moved away as if he were contagious. I couldn't stand for him to know his full humiliation. Downplaying it to him helped to soften the awfulness of the memory. At least for a second or two.

I sketched for him: a picture of a dashing bon vivant with a gaggle of girls around him. Cleavage. Wine. Smiles. He held it in one hand and jabbed it with the other. With misty eyes he said, 'Still got a *smidgeon* of charm, haven't I?' A false memory was imprinted in his mind. All was well. All was well.

Chapter 3

Once I concede that he'll never again wear the shirts I ironed, nor eat the dinners I cooked, I wrap myself in Will's unwashed t-shirt and crawl like a defeated animal into bed, burying myself in his smell. There, under the duvet, I find him – sort of – moving and laughing on a screen behind my eyes. His lean frame and square shoulders swing lazily; blue jeans, blue shirt, his smile teasing – always teasing; and with the evening sun behind him, there's an aura of light around his blond head. I can even smell the pine forest on the warm evening air and the dry dirt kicked up by his scuffing feet. Cicada song, like shaking maracas, muffles his laughter. It's a throw-the-head-back laugh in response to me running ahead.

'You're like a greedy child, Billy.'

His breath is short and his step listless as the hill gets steeper. He lights another cigarette and draws on it deeply. His mood shifts. I can sense it from where I stand. He grumbles tersely about needing a Coke. Speckled light through the branches of the pine tree dances all over him. Then, lost in thought, he bites his bottom lip and with his free hand starts to twiddle his hair.

'Our table's booked for eight, Will. Come on!'

I hesitate to keep calling. I don't want to wind him up. He might get angry and the evening will be a mess. Then what will happen? It could ruin everything between us. Everything! We could be finished before we even properly begin.

He keeps twiddling that forelock, and the cigarette in his left hand burns close to his folded elbow. He doesn't appear to notice the heat from it, and I can tell that his eyes are out of focus, as if he's spellbound. Even at twenty yards, his tension is palpable.

Take a deep breath. Pretend that all's well.

I take the risk. I call him again. On the fourth time he looks up and begins to drag his feet towards me, reluctantly, still twiddling. A frown is etched deep between his brows now.

Cut!

Without warning, an image of him in the morgue moves abruptly across my screen. And my breathing, moving Will – in the dappled light of the trees – dissolves, and vanishes from view.

***

Him dying is beyond the realm of belief. If belief were an island, this fact would lie far out in the ocean on unreachable waters. My brain is unable to grasp it. I find this strange, because, like a whiff of poisonous gas, I had often detected a presentiment of just this scenario in my mind. It had been present but hidden, like a creepy, reclusive neighbour lurking in his overgrown garden.

I am twenty-four years old. Death doesn't intrude at this stage of life, does it? Death happens to other people. Even the word 'death' barely crosses the horizon of my personal vocabulary. And Will's death? No. I can't allow it entry into my world. I won't.

So, I cling – madly and desperately – to a cinematic version of my life 'before it happened,' as if it were a raft on a merciless wave. Yet I'm thrown into the truth of the present moment, into the wave itself, all the time. His autopsy results are re-examined. They find that he had hepatitis, and now I must be tested for it. His funeral must be organised, and I must go with his mother and sister to visit the vicar, florist, and funeral director. I'm tossed from the wave to the raft, and my moods swing.

There is nothing virgin in my sight, nothing unrelated to Will, nothing inextricable from the loss of him. Suffering has hijacked me. It storms through my bloodstream and haemorrhages into every corner of my vision and mind. It fills every fold in the sheets, every particle of dust, every smear on the mirror, every thread of clothing, every drop of water, every colour, glass and drawer. I whirl around it as if circling round a compass of cardinal points, in search of a scent, a touch, a taste – anything that is familiar to me. I wheel from numbness to sorrow, from clarity to confusion, and as days pass, I recognise them as landing strips to which I return over and over again.

Numbness is a place that saps me of sentiment and thought. I sit in a heap, unable to feel, unable to do. It is a desert with far horizons, where the spirit of apathy rids me of all sense of being. I am conscious that I should retain some normalcy, some routine, some discipline. But when I think about it, I wonder what that means. My mind is blank. And then through the blankness comes a flash, a thought: I must eat! Yes! Daily life includes eating. I am dimly aware that my stomach is empty and my hipbones sharp. Cooking is now a chore since there's no one else to eat it. I cut up an apple instead. I accidentally slice the flesh at the base of my thumb. The rush of blood from it makes me recoil, but puzzlingly, I feel no physical pain – just irritation at myself and the inconvenience. Anyway, the apple is old and fluffy and not even worth eating.

In this vacuum of numbness Will's features tend to blur, then fade from my mind's eye. I fight against this happening. Squeezing my eyes tight, I try to reclaim his face from amongst the rush of sparkles in the blackness. Where is it? Where are his green eyes and wide smile, the burst blood vessel next to his nose and that vertical vein in his forehead? Where are his long collarbones and lean chest, and where are his scars? Where are *they*? His scars – etched by his needle and tracking the length of his body – were, I thought, indelibly scorched on my mind. But they too have now vanished. Oh, his scars! Symbols of his history that had cruelly reminded me during our love-making how vulnerable I was to love him, and how flimsy was the shell of our union.

Without the ability to recall his image I am lost and frightened, my past out of reach. I almost prefer – if that's the right word – the shadows of despair into which I swing. The truth there is a plain-speaking truth, and although it undoes me, I appreciate its honesty.

A primitive howling echoes around my head, and abdominal contractions force my body forward. I fling up the loo seat and hurl my head over the bowl. A roll of paper falls to the floor. It reels across the moss-coloured carpet towards the bath in a clean white line. I reach for the end of it with my left hand and pull, but it unravels even more. I gasp for breath between sobs. Then I vomit. I vomit anguish. I vomit anger. I feel like an animal ridding itself of illness in order to survive.

Survive? Do I even want to survive? The question surfaces in my mind dozens of times a day. I think of being with Will again. I picture what that would mean. How he would look. Would we be able to touch each other? Hear each other? Kiss each other? My imagination is sparked by biblical images from childhood: pearly gates, God on his throne, a land awash with light and 'new bodies without the curse of sin'. I think of the act of closing my eyes. Forever. The simple act of closing my eyes is the one thing I can do without effort. Everything else – washing, eating, even moving – requires physical and mental exertion, and above all *courage*. Closing my eyes, well, is so painless. Uncomplicated. No heroism is needed, no valiant bravery to face this new world. No grit, no backbone to stand up to its challenges. The act of closing my eyes is an act of surrender, to peace. I can do that.

Then I think of my mum, my dad. I couldn't leave them. I couldn't. I could *not* make them feel as I'm feeling now. My stomach heaves again. I crush the pile of loo paper and think of the unravelling of a ball of wool or the ribbons of a corset – or me. Is that what I am doing? Unravelling? Feels like it. At what point will it stop? And when it does, will there be anything left of me?

Already I feel like a dried husk. Hollow and nothing without him. There are days when despair swallows me whole. I can't even feel the ghost of who I was. Instead I find another way of feeling. With a pumice stone in scalding bath water I grate the skin from my legs and watch the escaping blood turn the water red. Often, numb to the pain, separate from it, I swirl sketchy abstract patterns in the reddish water with my index finger, as if I'm painting. Other times I feel the soreness acutely and panic. What the hell have I done? Have I lost my mind? What if I bleed to death? I let the water out. I run the cold tap on the wounds. It's freezing. I shiver. I reach for the loo paper and wind it again and again around my shins and pat it, willing the blood to stop. I sit on the floor and snip up bandages that I tie tightly round my legs. Just as Will had done with his tourniquet.

Focusing on nursing my injuries diverts me from torment. Acts as a pause – a breather for air within the spinning maelstrom. It's a relief to actively do something and, in the doing, force myself to be calm.

Shame also serves as a useful diversion.

I retire to his armchair, certain that I merit the punishment. I close my eyes and adopt his pose: hands cupping my chin, legs stretching out, feet crossed, and I feel him with me, in me, part of me. His laugh and big sighs escape on my breath. The twitch of his left eye needles my own, and the ache in his hip transfers to mine. I wear his sloppy sweaters and tweed jacket. I inhale his cigarettes deeply, as he had done. I feel that he is there, everywhere – in the mirror holding my breasts, cross-legged by the fire, peering over his glasses, or leaning against the doorway, his limbs loose and knees buckling. When my shoulders and hips lie in the hollows of the mattress made by his, it is as if he envelops me.

Clarity. It feels like clarity. Calm, clear, comprehensible.

I can't help myself. I go to him. I speak his name. I lift my hand to take his. And in that instant, my meditative bubble bursts. He disappears. Gone. In one fell swoop I fall back into the harsh reality of confusion.

The doorbell rings. It's a long persistent ring. They hold their finger on it without release as if they're trying to stir me from the dead. Is it real or am I dreaming it? I'm not sure. I remain in my chair and listen to it for a bit longer. It doesn't ring, it buzzes. It makes an aggressive buzzing noise which reminds me of an injured hornet, spinning on its back on a stone wall under the southern sun. Its wing is broken. It can't fly. It buzzes in a circular motion until it exhausts itself and dies, its legs in the air, rigid and still.

The bell though… it still buzzes. It must be real. I still

don't get up to answer it. My limbs won't move, as if I'm glued to the chair. I'm nervous. Who is it downstairs? Why the urgency? I don't want intrusion. I'd like to remain alone. Alone to retrieve Will. Alone to manage my madness.

I am making the move to get up when the buzzing stops. My attention is drawn to particles of dust caught in the sunrays streaming in through the window. When did I open the curtains? I've no recollection of doing that. Did someone else do it? They can't have done, no one else has keys, I don't think. I can't remember who, if anyone, does have a set. My mind is blank. Not working. Out of order. What's happened to it?

The bell again. Louder than ever. 'Metropolitan Police,' they say. I open the door and hear beeps, scratches, and chatter from radios coming up the stairs. The police were here the day it happened, so why have they come back? There are two of them this time. Both heavily built in ill-fitting black uniforms, carrying bobby helmets under their arms. I recognise one from before. The other is new. They both wear that expression common in the presence of someone who's grieving: furrowed brow and lips drawn together, mimicking sadness. The learned look of compassion.

'Just a few questions for you, if that's okay.' It's the one I recognise.

'What about a cup of tea?' I ask.

They both shake their heads.

'Well. Come in! Sit!' I gesture to the sofa.

They sit side by side and the one I know 'ums' and 'ers'. He looks at the coffee table, then at his hands. The other looks around the room as if something salient to their investigation might be sitting on a bookshelf. Their helmets are now on the floor beside their feet like black terriers.

'Um… well, there are a few things we'd like to tie up.'

I raise my eyebrows.

'Can you help us with the names of his dealers, by any chance?'

It's as if a black screen descends behind my eyes. Like the house curtain of a theatre signalling the end of a play and blocking access to everything happening backstage.

I shake my head.

They ask about telephone numbers. If there are any I recognise on this piece of paper?

I shake my head.

What were the last calls he made and received? What were his last movements and what were mine?

I shake my head.

They ask me to go over and over that last night. They ask if I have come across anything suspicious. Suspicious is a word they use a lot.

'Like what?' I suddenly hear myself say, but of course I know. Heroin is what they want to hear.

I remember the hard ball in silver foil that fell from the coffee jar into my mug yesterday morning. How my heart had raced. How I'd spooned it out, and, as if competing in an egg and spoon race, dashed to the loo to flush it away. It had fallen as I'd opened the bathroom door, and, terrified of leaving my fingerprints, I'd flicked it against the skirting board and hooked it up again onto the spoon. It had taken several flushes before it had gone down. I'd been drenched in sweat and my breath was so short that I'd worried I was choking.

Afterwards I'd wondered why I had panicked like that. Why had I not opened it before chucking it? It might have been nothing incriminating. And if it had been? So what! It was Will's, not mine, and he was dead. So stupid. What the hell had got into me?

But I know what it was. Into my cup had fallen his killer. My physical response to that thought had been nausea. How could I even have brought myself to handle it? Touching it would have implied association with evil. Connection. For my sanity's sake, it needed to disappear, so I could refuse to acknowledge its existence.

I keep shaking my head. I apologise for not having answers for them. The policeman who's asking the questions pats his knees and says, 'I understand, miss.' He has dark stubble on his face that covers a red rash. He grimaces often, a sort of puckering of his nose and mouth. I feel a pang of sympathy as I presume his skin is sore. It makes me feel guilty that I am not more helpful. He's only doing his job. But still... he's a policeman. The enemy. Will's enemy and now mine. They're encroaching on my sacred space, the only space in which I'm safe. He asks to search the bedrooms, but before I answer I hear his squeaky rubber soles in the corridor. I hear the other one opening drawers in the kitchen.

''Course she knows who they are. The dealers. She'd have used them herself. We weren't born yesterday!'

It's a whisper from one to the other but it's amplified in my ears.

'I heard that!' I shout. 'I heard that! Are you insinuating that I take drugs? Are you?' I am running towards him. My anger surprises me, and for a second I hesitate. I hear my mother's voice from the past. 'Brace up, Nix! Be good!' But I can't. I can't be good. I won't. I burst open the door and scream.

'Get out of his bedroom! Out!'

'Now calm down, miss!' He has my wrists in his hands and I am beating his chest.

'I will not calm down! How dare you imply that I take drugs! How dare you! The most I have ever fucking taken is Aspirin! Get out of his room! Get out of his flat! Enough! I've had enough!'

Chapter 4

Friends drop by on their way home from work. Up until now I've had several jobs, most recently with an interior designer, but my role in Will's life quickly replaced that. My friends are working in the City, or in advertising agencies, auction houses, estate agents, and catering. When I open the door to them, they wrap me in tight squeezes, and chinking bottles of Liebfraumilch knock against my spine.

They bring faded Kodak Instamatic shots of themselves and Will as teenagers, clowning around on windswept pebble beaches, at fancy dress parties, and in dingy digs, surrounded by cigarettes and LPs. In dungarees, rugby shirts, and towels around shoulders, they're either in a boat cutting through the sea, licking ice creams at the marina, or lying in sunny gardens on tartan rugs, with wicker baskets, foppish jackets, panama hats; boys and girls cuddled together, a lipstick-y mark on a cheek, a wink at the camera, a hat tip, a silly face.

'Oh, look at this!' Marcus says, laughing. 'Look at Will

tossing Amy over his shoulder! Don't know which of them has the most hair!' He pulls another from his pocket. 'And where were we here? Is that Speech Day, do you think?'

'Probably. Can't remember exactly,' says Pete, flicking through them like a pack of cards. 'Oh, and here he is with Soph! Look! Obviously had a thing for that old hat of his. He's got it on in all of these. Suited him, actually.' He taps the picture against the edge of the table. 'But then again, a plastic bag would have suited Will.'

Janey slides another one out. 'Yeah. Even here in fancy dress, in these silly sunglasses, he still looks brill. See? It was that smile, I think. Yup. Always made my knees buckle, that smile.'

'Ooh, we were jealous, us chaps.'

'Jealous? Were you, Pete? Really?' I ask, surprised.

'Not jealous in a horrid way. Loved him. But he was just so handsome. So... I don't know... languid... and cool. Got all the pretty girls, of course. You included!' He shrugs. 'Bastard!'

Marcus's eyes well with tears. We all light another cigarette. We're grouped around the kitchen table. Photos are strewn amongst packets of Silk Cut and Marlboro, ashtrays, and Walkers crisps. Two empty bottles of wine with used glasses are piled in the sink.

I'm enjoying listening to them. Enjoying the solidarity of shared memories and contagious tears.

There is a heavy pause. I go to the record player and put on David Bowie's 'Wild is the Wind'. Janey puts an arm around my shoulders when I sit down. I look at her and say, 'He used to play this over and over again, like all his favourites. The same track, thousands of times.'

Peter mumbles over me, his eyes fixed on another photograph that he holds in both hands. 'God, this was only about six years ago – I can't believe he's not here anymore. I've known him forever. Can't imagine life without him.'

'Yup. Was just thinking that too,' says Janey. 'It's not right. Not fair. He had everything going for him. Especially recently... ah... poor, darling Will – he'd so wanted to be clean. Remember all those times when he would call to tell us he was okay?' She lights another cigarette.

'But each time lasted five minutes.' Marcus says. 'Trouble was he always looked so good. He didn't look like a junkie. Was hard for us to know. When he didn't show up for dinner, *I* assumed he was just fucking me around again. I didn't put two and two together. Didn't realise he was back using again.' He sighs and puts his head in his hands. 'I feel so guilty. He must have thought I was such a shit.'

'Ah, Marcus, don't think that.' I stretch across the table and stroke his arm. 'He was out of it most of the time, come on, you know that. He wouldn't have really registered that you were cross with him.'

'Well. I hope that was the case. I feel badly about it. And I did love him. Really, I did. Remember how shy he was when we were all kids? Remember, before his dad died? Before he had the nose job?'

Pete starts laughing. 'God, yes, his nose! That was funny. *And* sweet. Remember the bandages around his head? Said he'd had a motorbike crash, didn't he? Then all of a sudden

– it was in that pub down the road where we met before going to Carey's party, I think – there was a brand-new nose on his face! And perfect it was too! Thought we wouldn't notice!' He shakes his head, still giggling. 'At least he was good at having his leg pulled about it. On the other hand, being blessed with a divine face without that big honker probably made it quite easy to laugh at himself, huh?' Pete elbows me.

My mind wanders. I think about Will's self-deprecating humour, and how much I'd teased him. It was one of the things that made him loveable. And he really was loveable. People always wanted to be his friend and forgave him things that other guys didn't get away with. There was a quiet sort of modesty about him, even after inheriting at such a young age. Maybe it was that that made him withdraw and become so anxious - the sudden responsibility. Was it then, I wondered, that things started to go downhill for him?

'After that, his reputation was sealed. Known for always having a girl in one hand, and of course a cigarette in the other.' Pete's face crumples and he drops his head.

The hang-up about his nose had run deep. Our late-night conversations replay in my mind, and I think how, even in telling me about it, he would squirm with embarrassment. 'I was so self-conscious, so ill at ease, that I could only talk to people front-on. Could never let anyone see my profile. Ever. Imagine how hard that was at a party?' He laughed. 'Drinks parties were out of the question. They caused too much anxiety. And dinners were exhausting. I would arrive late, timing my entrance for when everyone was sitting down. Then, to talk to each girl either side of me, I adopted the habit of leaning back in my chair, far enough away for them to avoid seeing me sideways, but close enough to avoid seeming aloof. Drinking of course was also an issue. Had nightmares about getting my nose stuck in those silly skinny wine glasses! I could never enjoy myself. Was too busy wondering what distance from other people was most flattering. Later on, I heard on the grapevine, that a few had presumed they had bad breath! Tsk! Awful! If only they had known!'

Pete sniffs. 'God. In my mind he's so alive. It seems like yesterday that he was racing his car up the King's Road. Was a bit of a risk-taker sometimes. Competitive, too. It always surprised me, that, 'cause, you know, he was sort of reserved in a way. Wasn't really a party-goer, was he? Just liked hanging out. Quietly, with a friend or two. But then he did love dancing, didn't he? Remember that Roger Daltrey look he had for a while – tight white jeans, open neck shirt, long wavy hair?' He looks into the distance. 'Tsk. So full of life. What'll I do without him?'

We all start crying. Then giggle at how silly we must look. I am conscious of feeling envious that I hadn't known him all his life. That I hadn't got the complete jigsaw in my heart. I feel cheated not to have known the Will they had. My love for him suddenly feels less creditable.

'How's his poor Mum, Nix?' asks Janey.

I wipe my eyes and think about Louise. We were always close and in the last week have become even closer. Like me, she wants to talk about him all the time. When the rest of the world sleeps and we can't, we telephone each other, late into the night or in the early hours of the morning. We resurrect him in words, sharing him. She, her child and teenager – and I, her adult son. We quiz each other, hungry to share every crumb of him that hadn't been ours at first. She asks if he had had normal friends, not just junkie ones. 'He did used to have when he was a child, you know. Nice ones. I liked them. They had fun together, I think. In London and the Isle of Wight and… oh dear, when do you think it started to go wrong? Was it at that Crammer? Or after that, in London? My poor William… he would have been easy prey. But he and Flora were at least close to each other, which was nice. Did him good to have a little sister around. He did love his family, didn't he? I always felt he loved me. And you, darling, was he kind to you? I always wondered if he had a temper. Did he? And, this is strange to say, but I hope he was a considerate lover?'

She talks about when his father died – 'alcohol-related, you know' – and how much she'd worried about him then. 'Alcohol-related' was an expression at which Will and I poked fun. Both our fathers suffered problems referred to then as 'alcohol-related'.

'Fuck that,' Will would say. 'Sounds like alcohol's just a distant relation when they say it like that… *induced* is more like it, no?'

Louise continued, and I let her talk. 'See, he inherited too much money for a teenager to deal with. I was always worried about that. Worried a lot about it. He bought a mews house in South Ken – had nothing in it for a while apart from a bed. And ashtrays. I wish he hadn't smoked so much. Awful how much he smoked. Hmmm...' Her voice faded, as if she was thinking out loud. 'I think he felt that he had to suddenly be the man of the family when his father died. Duty, yes. A big sense of duty, he had. You know – to do the right thing. Maybe I leaned on him too much. What do you think? Did he mention it to you, darling? Of course, my divorce from his father also affected him. Him *and* his sister. Being a bit taboo at that time made it harder. He was a sensitive chap, and none of it was easy. Still.' She paused, and a soft clink sounded down the telephone; it was the noise that came from a photo frame being placed back onto the glass table beside her bed. 'I keep thinking about his work. At the auction house and then the bank. How did he manage to hold down those jobs? Was he smashed *all* the time? He always looked okay, didn't he? So immaculate he was, and such a beautiful boy. Too thin, of course, and tired, but other than that...'

'His Mum?' I say. 'Shattered. Poor Louise. She's such a gentle person. Wants to see the good and beauty in everything. She must be so shocked. For all these years she seemed, on the surface at least, to be in denial about his drug habit. But who knows if that was really the case. Was awful, really. She would make lunch for us every Sunday. You know, proper roast with Yorkshire pudding. And even before we ate, Will's eyes were heavy and his speech slurred. From time to time he would nod off until I prodded him under the table. But poor Louise, she would stroke his head and say, "Darling, you're burning the candle at both ends. You *must* sleep more. Eat properly. Aren't you exhausted at work?" That sort of thing. Used to kill me to watch her. I hated the deceit. But maybe I would have hated it more if she'd really known. Anyway. For all her frailty she is surprisingly strong.'

'Dreadful. Poor woman. Can't imagine what she's going through now.'

***

Some friends are unable to face me. I'm on my way to the florist to order flowers for his funeral when I pause at the window of Luigi's. I am hungry. My mouth waters at the wheels of crumbling Parmesan stacked up on top of each other like pale earthenware pots. I look for the dates of production stamped on their skins – I always do this – and start an internal debate about whether it would be too extravagant to buy some just for myself. If I've given up cooking what would I eat it with? Silly question! Why do I need to eat it with anything? I rummage around in my bag for cash. They won't accept a cheque for a piece of cheese. Luigi strolls out and stands in the red doorway. He looks at the cloudless sky and then greets me. '*Ciao, bella! Come stai?*'

'Drooling over your Parmesan, Luigi. As usual.'

Across the street I see a friend of mine leave a bookshop. Our eyes meet. I am about to wave or call but she turns hurriedly away. I watch her run down the road. She checks her watch as if she is late for something. She does it a little bit too much. She's not late for anything, I am sure of that. She's avoiding me. I wish I could go to her, to tell her it's okay. Tell her she doesn't need to say anything. Tell her that ignoring me is, on the other hand, terrible, and that her fear makes me feel like a leper.

Without Will's presence to dispel my doubts, I start persuading myself that I might be fabricating my relationship with him. Suspicion criss-crosses my mind like a wire grill, fencing in all other thoughts. Am I blowing it up into a fairy-tale? Is it my magical thinking that's warping reality? I know I am prone to that. Maybe our love was entirely one-sided, and everyone but me knew it. Have I become a laughing stock? Am I embarrassing myself with inappropriate displays of grief? My doubts churn, reaching my stomach in waves of nausea. I search frantically in my mental archives for *any* kind of affirmation.

In the dark there I find a burst of memory. Far from being an endorsement of our union, it at least makes me smile. One of our initial encounters.

Due to his laidback manner, his good looks and his string of girlfriends, Will's celebrated reputation amongst our friends distanced him from us – at least in our minds – and his sporadic participation in our social scene boosted his enigmatic allure. Nonetheless, when he did show up, he was so affable, so candid, so child-like – he would fling his arms around everyone with guileless affection as if they had been long lost to him – that his aloofness would be forgiven. To me, he was perfect. I liked that he was discerning and didn't go to every party. I liked his mystery. I liked how he moved in that loose swinging way, as if Lou Reed's music ran in his veins. I liked the gravelly layers of his voice and how his eyes shone. A friend once said with a catch in her throat, 'God, if he were mine, I would put him on a pedestal and just gaze at him all day long.'

Although he and I had met fleetingly in the past, I don't think I had registered on his radar. Whilst I had blushed in his presence, he seemed not to have noticed me.

A couple of years after that he arrived at a house in Hampshire where I was staying for the weekend. It was a hot summer day. I had just helped myself to a jug of elderflower cordial and was watching a game of tennis when he sauntered lazily through the orchard in my direction. His arm was slung round the naked shoulders of a girlfriend called Jessica, with a mane like Farrah Fawcett's and stretches of tanned skin broken by a high-cut bikini.

I was eighteen at the time. My self-image was precarious, my mental landscape bleak. Inadequately covered in borrowed boxer shorts and a bikini top, I wished that the world would swallow me whole as Jessica unravelled her long limbs and lay seductively at Will's feet.

It had all happened very quickly, but as Will sat down he swivelled to hug me hello with surprising enthusiasm, and out of jittery disbelief I leapt up at the same time to shoot behind the bench, and my chin knocked his forehead hard.

'God. Sorry! You alright?' He was rubbing it and laughing. 'Oops! That was tough love, that was!' He looked round at me. 'What are you doing back there? Sit!' He patted the seat next to him, while Jessica stroked his ankles. She turned onto her side and with one hand rolled up the hems of his loose cotton trousers. 'Get some sun on your legs, darling,' she said. The curve of her hips and sharp shoulders gave her the silhouette of a guitar. She looked like burnished mahogany.

While he stretched out his legs, he tugged at my hand, badgering me to sit down. If only he would stop! I was happier behind the bench, not wanting to reveal my whole self. I pulled my boxer shorts down a bit more, to cover my thighs. At least my tummy was flat, I thought.

'Come on, Nix! Do sit! What are you worried about? I'm not going to bite...' He laughed mockingly, and I felt so foolish that I snuck around and sat while he turned his head to watch Lulu serve. In my haste and nervousness, I sat too close – directly on top of his hand. But before I could spring up again, he had pushed me down, then put his finger to his lips, all the while with his other hand still in the same place, under my bottom.

There was a break in the tennis. James and Lulu had lost a set. 'Hey, Will! What you up to? Hands off Nix, okay?' He called.

'Watching you lose, Jimbo – mind your own business!'

'Sssh, darling,' Jessica sighed. 'I'm sleepy.'

Trapped under my bottom, his hand wriggled. Embarrassment made me hot and flushed.

Thoughts of him filled my dreams after that. Hours were consumed by them. I wrote his name all over my exercise book, joining it up with my own. I learned that the meaning of William is 'strong-willed warrior', and that it became a popular name after the Norman Conquest, after William the Conqueror. If only he'd conquer me, I dreamed. Oh, if only. If only. I played back – minute by minute – the hour by the tennis court and in my mind it lengthened in time and deepened in meaning. His throaty laugh echoed in my ears and I wondered what prompted it. I wondered what prompted that frown that flitted like a shadow across sunlight, and I puzzled over his worries, his thinking and his aspirations. I wondered about his days. What did he like doing? Did he wake when I did? And was he grumpy, or did that smile spread like sunshiny butter just as his eyes opened? What did he eat for breakfast and lunch? Did he eat? He was so slender that he looked in need of a good meal. I could do that for him, I thought. I could do that every day. I dreamed of kissing his full mouth and imagined how it might be, and when I saw his face in my mind's eye, I blushed. My heart beat quicker. It beat so hard that sometimes I thought I could see it, bursting from my chest.

It was a while before I saw him again. He was asleep on a table in my local pub, The Phoenix, and had no inkling I was even present. I couldn't understand how anyone could be asleep amidst such noise, and I kept checking over my shoulder, to see if his head had risen from the crook of his elbow. But it never did, and I left to go home, disappointed. Another missed opportunity! Maybe 'we' were never meant to be. As I walked back past the cricket pitch, I found myself wondering if the stupor was drug-related – or, I thought, perhaps he was just terribly tired.

Chapter 5

Roz, a cousin of Will's and my friend, had family living in France. Together we planned a summer there, firstly visiting her grandmother, and then renting a studio of our own in the hills above St. Tropez. I was, at the time, hand-painting silk – a form of batik – principally for cushions, but for our trip Roz and I created a swimwear collection, aiming to peddle it on the beaches. Coincidentally, she had decided that Will and I would be a perfect match, and she invited him to stay. If that fails, she said, a stint out of London would at least do him good. She had heard that he wasn't in great shape.

Heroin use was the talk of the town then, but its underground image meant that, unless you were directly acquainted, your personal knowledge of it was sketchy and removed, as if it were being done in a neighbouring country. We thought of it as cocaine's sister. You either did one or the other, but with both, dope would have been your springboard. But there were no governmental warnings about heroin, nor any informative leaflets and posters. No adverts depicting the corruption and the deaths it caused. Campaigns against it came later, at the end of the eighties. Word had it that it was much more dangerous than cocaine. It was definitely touted as a 'bad' drug, but since no one was yet coming to calamitous harm, we had no concept of how bad 'bad' was, *or* what that really meant. Still, I heard the stories on the grapevine, and they tended towards unhappy endings of prostitution, theft, and being cut off from society. I didn't know how much of it was Chinese whispers or how much was true. Dealers got a very bad rap. The rumours were of rough, hardened criminals with little value for life. They carried guns. And they didn't care. This distinction hampered many a would-be heroin user from even starting. But since we had no proximity to them, they remained nebulous – mere whispers – and as with all victims of gossip, there was a gulf between you and them. Most of my friends took cocaine, but my fear of drugs and its culture meant that I never joined in. I didn't even drink.

Being ignorant of the facts, I was more daunted by the social division between 'them and us' that heroin's underground reputation forged, and the elite status it gave to its users. Immediately recognizable in their drainpipe jeans, winkle pickers or stilettos, and loose, crumpled jackets, with their hollow cheeks and unkempt hair, they looked sexy, hard-edged, and sinister. It was the look of the moment, and fashion applauded it.

The sky was cloudless when Will showed up in Le Plan-de-la Tour. The scent of thyme and pine hung in the still heat, and the dust thrown up by his taxi hovered a while before settling. The cicadas' grating chorus, loudest in the afternoons, blotted out all other sounds. He jumped out looking healthy and tanned – surely this boy couldn't be a junkie – and his breezy manner and wide smile washed away my nerves. He joined us in our morning routine of leaving early to buzz down to St. Tropez on our mopeds, avoiding the traffic that jammed the coastal road later on. Our swimwear collection was folded in straw baskets that we strapped to the backs of our bikes. It was warm already by the time we got to the old port, but the air was still fresh. Fishermen were unloading their catch. The sea sparkled. Jean, a waiter at Sénéquier, had served us croissants and café au lait every day for the last month.

'*Et alors?*' He nodded towards Will. '*C'est ton copain qui est arrivé, huh?*'

I blushed, shook my head, and gave him a wide-eyed glare to say 'Shush!' I hoped that Will hadn't understood.

Enjoyment of our café ritual was enhanced by daily people-watching. With envious curiosity we scrutinised the breakfast tables on the anchored yachts opposite. While girls in leopard-print bikinis and gold high heels appeared with tousled hair and long bronzed legs already glistening with sun oil, their boyfriends, resembling ageing Armani models in tight t-shirts, clubbed together against the guardrails on deck, dragging on Sobranies, and sniggering about what seemed to us like in-jokes.

Afterwards, we meandered under medieval arches, following the twist of the narrow streets. The pink render peeled decadently from the walls, while pots of geraniums bright-ened balconies. From inside open windows came the clat-ter of breakfast plates, a child's whine, a mother's impatient response. In the Place des Lices the plane trees cast mottled sunlight onto the market stalls. Around them, boutiques were opening up, and from inside one France Gall sang on the radio while a tanned lady with jangling bangles wheeled rails of kaftans onto the pavement. The market already bus-tled with elderly women carrying straw baskets stocked with baguettes, and chatter amongst the stallholders softened the whine of a Vespa. We bought peaches and pains au chocolat before heading to Graniers beach. It was quiet still at that hour, with plenty of mattresses and parasols to hire.

I was unable to meet Will's eye and became tongue-tied and giggly if I accidently did. 'When are you going to let me into your bed?' he whispered as I locked my bike. With my eyes fixed on the padlock, I pretended it was stuck. 'Billy? *Are* you going to?' He lifted my chin towards his face. I shivered. My skin was alive and tingly, and under its sur-face a rush of heat surged up to my head. Still I couldn't look at him. I would take off, I thought. Up, up, and away I would go, like a hot air balloon. Did he not feel the burn emanating from me like heat shimmer? Did he not notice my trembling hands, blazing eyes, and shy smile? Could he not read my mind, which felt as revelatory as an open book? 'Course he could. I was captivated by him. His eyes stripped me bare, challenging me, daring me to surrender. In every snatched moment that Roz's attention was turned, he whispered against my neck.

'Billy… you know I want you, don't you?' 'What am I going to do about it? Hmmm?' 'How long will you torture me? Billy?'

Billy was the nickname he had given me when he caught me Sellotaping a cracked coffee pot handle in the kitchen of our rented studio, his first morning there. 'Oh, Billy Billionaire!' he'd said. 'Come on, you silly billy! I'll buy you a new pot.'

Torture? It was *I* who felt tortured; exquisitely so. I didn't know how to manage its intensity – what to do with it. It was as if the contours of my body had melted away, and I was open – wide open – and everything inside me was spilling out in an aching torrent towards him. Wanting, wanting, wanting.

Roz and I took it in turns to hawk our swimwear along the beach through the lapping waves. I wore one of my bikinis and carried the others, along with swimming shorts, in a basket in the crook of my arm. They were hand-painted in Seurat-style pointillism, in yellow, khaki, petrol-blue, and orange – colours I liked against bronzed skin. We were asking a hundred francs for each. To make our bikinis, Roz had sewn triangles and threaded them with ribbons – two for the top half and two for the bottom. The silk puckered up under the breasts in baby-doll style, and ties on the hips held the bottom bits together. They were cute and sexy to look at, but lacked practical requirements when swimming, tending to slip off your bottom and float to the surface like jelly fish. We had previously sold some yellow and blue shorts to a guy with oiled hair and medallions around his neck, but when we spotted him the following day, his shorts were green, for the paint had run in the sea.

My walk through the water gave me time out from the build-up of tension between Will and me. Like beams of light, his eyes bore into my back, sweeping over me and through me as I walked away. I shook my head to free it from the pulse of longing, but however far I wandered, it hovered, encapsulating me in fuzzy warmth. I lay down next to him on my return. He rolled onto his side, and with his fingers wrote feathery messages on my tummy, across my bikini line. My stomach lurched with the same sharp whoosh you get from driving over a hill too quickly. He sensed it – of course he did, it was as obvious as a tidal wave – and he edged closer, his gaze so intense that I thought I was drowning. When he lowered himself on top of me, it felt as if we were dissolving into one another like honey into milk, and I surrendered completely. I was his, and he could do with me whatever he wanted. With cupped hands around our heads he made a shady pod, flecked with sunlight from the chinks between his fingers, and in it our noses touched, our breath fused, and his tongue traced my lips.

'Your heart, Billy. It's knocking against my chest. Bang, bang!' Trying to get in.' With his soft lips around mine, the surrounding drone of voices and waves was suddenly muted, and my body arched spontaneously to his.

'Yes,' I whispered into his mouth. 'I want in. Right in.' All else evaporated as my ache to blend with him flared like the burner of that hot air balloon. Later that night, after we danced at the village fete, I succumbed to my dragging desire, and to the unmistakable beat of love. Our eyes locked, and our fingers intertwined. I longed to stay fastened together like that until the end of time. 'Don't move. Don't ever move. Stay inside me forever, Will. You've conquered me, you have.'

I didn't question the reason he gave for the green liquid he reached for every morning and drank as if it were Coca Cola. He said it was medication for his throat. Then, at dawn, Roz and I woke to a bloodcurdling din like the howl of a wolf. We rushed to the sofa bed to see his limbs thrashing, his muscles in spasms. He was doubled up, holding his stomach, trembling all over. We had no idea how to deal with something like this, or what it even was. We started by restraining his legs, and because he was drenched in sweat, we sponged him with a cool damp flannel. Even then, he showed no recognition of us and continued to make eerie, whining noises. Imagining the worst, we whispered frantically over his head.

'Who do we call?'

'Do you know the number of an ambulance?'

'No idea, no.'

'What the hell should we do then?'

'Fuck, it's scary!'

'Will! Listen to us. Your name. Tell us your name? The day. What day is it? Breathe!' I rinsed the flannel in cold water and wiped his head to bring down the fever. His nose was running. Goose bumps rushed across his skin. 'Will, breathe! Please!'

Finally, he responded. The awful noises died to a

murmur, his eyelids fluttered and closed, and his body lay motionless. Yet his inertia was even more worrying. Was he *dying* now? We were peering at his eyes, our ears close to his mouth, when a sputtering burst of laughter sent us jumping suddenly back.

'Fuck you, Will!' Roz screamed.

He was laughing so hard he held his tummy.

'I'm sorry. Sorry. I don't mean to laugh, but you looked so funny and sweet, the two of you. So dramatic...'

'God! Were you having us on?' I asked.

'No! 'Course not. No – really, I wasn't,' he protested. 'No. Believe me!' I stomped to the door. 'Billy, come here!'

'So, what's so damn funny then?' I shouted with my back to him.

'Sssh… Calm down, Billy! Come on! Come here! I'll explain. It's withdrawals, Billy. Nothing to worry about. Okay?'

Withdrawals? I stopped in my tracks. It took a few moments for me to register what he'd said. Withdrawals. The word felt like a punch in my gut. Withdrawals were for serious addicts, everyone knew that. Roz was hanging up the towels over the balcony railing. She shook her head, warning me not to comment. The cool dawn air slipped in through the open door and over my feet. I stretched the bottom sheet of his bed taut and picked up the upturned bowls. I took them to the kitchen, still silent. Processing what he'd said left me devoid of words. There was too much circulating my brain: my new, fresh passion for him and my dream to live 'happily ever after'; my mum's warnings about drugs; the gossip about addiction at home; and now this wake-up call – the mention of withdrawals. I was placing the bowls in the sink when I heard a suppressed giggle, like the spluttering of a garden tap, quickly muffled with a pillow.

Anger was the only emotion I could acknowledge. I turned on him.

'How dare you come here with your drug problems and then laugh at me? How dare you! Fuck, Will! It's not on!'

I slammed the door behind me and ran down the hill. The scent of pine was strong, and it reminded me of Badedas, the bath stuff my Mum soaked in. Helped her unwind, she said. A picture of her dark head slipping beneath the bubbles came to mind.

'Sex'n'drugs, sex'n'drugs.' Mum's hoarse whisper with its tremor of forewarning echoed around my head. I felt sick.

Be calm. Breathe. All will be well.

The earth between the twisted vines was scratchy under my skin, and the knobbles made by the plough acted like a deep tissue massage for my shoulder blades. I pulled off a handful of grapes and let the juice run from the corner of my mouth like I did when I was little. An ant traced a tickly passage over my shins. The low sun pierced through the leaves, and behind my eyelids rainbow colours danced. A woodpecker's intermittent drumming was the only sound beside the distant chatter from the village boulangerie. After a while, I slipped through its beaded curtain and stood in line behind patterned dresses, woven baskets, and busy hands. The sing-song gossip and sweet, doughy air with traces of chocolate raised my spirits as effortlessly as would a bunch of roses.

I had got into the habit of playing table football with Georges in the café in the main square. Georges and his cronies met at the bar for Pastis at any time of day. His skin was weather-worn from a lifetime in the vineyards and his hair lustrous and steely grey. Black bushy eyebrows danced above heavy-lidded eyes, similar to a Labrador's. He had taken to watching me play with Roz, and one evening had suggested we have a game. I didn't drink Pastis and I was half his age. I was quicker, more agile, and my desire to win was fiercer.

As I had passed the bar that morning Chrissie Hynde's sultry voice had been loud: 'Gonna make you, make you, make you notice – I'm special, so special...' Fifteen minutes later, George's hands, which were thick and square, had twisted the handle with such force that the ball shot down the table and slammed angrily into the goal like a bullet.

Will was coming down the hill as I walked back to the studio.

'I wanted to be with you,' he said. An apologetic look crossed his face. 'You're upset, Billy. Distant. Talk to me, darling.'

Coral-pink brushstrokes tinted the sky and butterflies flitted like musical quavers in roadside flowers.

'It's okay. I'm fine...' I sounded terse. I bent down to clip a twig of thyme, rubbing it in my hands to release its scent. 'Shall we have moules and frites again at lunch today? They're so yummy, aren't they?'

'Tsk – Billy… you're not fine. Don't change the subject.' He swung me to him with that smile. And what a smile it was! He put his nose to mine, his eyes twinkling and reassuring, hands tight around my waist.

He tickled me and said, 'Always thinking about this little tummy, aren't you?'

I squinted into the sunlight and smiled at the halo of light framing his blond head.

'There's nothing to worry about, Billy.' He said. 'When I stop using, they always happen – withdrawals. Every nerve ending feels open and raw. And crawling.' He kissed me.

When I stop using.

'When I stop using' were the only words I heard. Wanted to hear. Chose to hear. They made me hopeful enough that he had stopped. For good. They convinced me to restrict his limbs, mop his brow and hold him during his seizures. I was proud of him, after all. It showed courage to overcome such physical distress.

The seizures continued. In the mornings Roz and I staged shows imitating them. Farce dispelled my anxiety almost entirely.

By now, I understood that the green liquid was Methadone, and once I started to watch him, I saw that he reached for it the moment he woke.

***

Back in London and alone to explore each other, Will and I spent days in a cloud of dizzy elation. Hours passed as I stared at him. I marvelled at his beauty and fell into it as if drugged, our naked bodies intertwined, my heart so open I felt as if I could embrace the world in it. We tumbled out of bed when we wanted music. Tina Turner or Dire Straits. 'Better Be Good To Me' and 'So Far Away From You' we left on repeat. I danced around his sitting room, strutting and pouting as she did, and he leaned against his bookshelf and sang. We ventured out only for cigarettes, cereal, pita bread, and taramasalata, but often we forgot to eat. We were still wearing our scanty holiday clothes – me in pink silk harem pants, him in beach-dried white t-shirts – yet the cool autumn air barely touched us. We moved down the street joined at the hip, and as if it was too far to travel without kissing, we would stop to do so every twenty yards.

After a couple of days, I noticed bits of silver foil and a tub of vitamin C powder in the kitchen. I was confused. Where had they come from? We hadn't bought them in the last two days and I had seen the contents of the cupboards and drawers when looking for cutlery, coffee, washing-up liquid. They'd been quite empty with no sign of any product. My antennae sent out alarm signals, but I wasn't sure why. It was only silver foil and vitamin C after all.

Why the fuss?

All is well. Just breathe. It will go away. Love will make it go away.

What I knew for certain was that I lacked the courage to disrupt our intimacy, and even as my mind told me that I should, the words wouldn't come. He was under my skin, as if we had blended together to make a whole. I felt as he did, and saw as he did, and was caught in the web of loving – the high it granted intoxicating me. My anxiety that a confrontation would rock the status quo and he'd run off with someone else in a shot, curbed all thoughts of speaking up.

It'll go away, I thought. It'll fade. Yes. If I don't think about this, it will go away.

After all, I am grown-up now. I mustn't be anxious or over-react as I did when I was little. I mustn't anticipate catastrophe, or reasons to be fearful. I must relax! This is too important. He's the best thing ever to happen to me. The light in my life – my conqueror! We must be happy. I must be positive. Make it good. Make it perfect!

Love Conquers All

1970

Chapter 6

I followed my mum down the narrow corridor of the Calais to Nice sleeper train and squinted into the four-berth couchettes. In one, a boy in shorts and brown lace-ups sat on the top bunk, and in the net pouch on the wall was a crumpled copy of *The Beano*. A half-eaten Crunchie in its shiny wrapper balanced on the edge of the bed. His mum had backcombed hair like my stepmother Caro, and she was unpacking a small suitcase while his dad, in braces, studied a road map. In the couchette next door were two girls playing cat's cradle in matching smocked dresses, their thin fair hair in bunches. Others were unoccupied, the bunk beds pristine with white sheets folded back over grey woollen blankets. The corridor was crowded with passengers carrying tickets, traveller's cheques, and suitcases. I was jolted, bumped into, my feet trodden on, my face scratched by a ring on someone's finger, and I lost my mum's hand when a man shoved her aside. I had noticed him in the distance a little while before when Mum had picked me up, for he had towered above everyone else. More than that, though, it was the way he had looked at me which made me remember him. He had fastened his gaze onto mine and, aware of the sudden heat in my head, I had at once turned away. He wore a blue and white striped shirt with a starched white collar. His black hair was greased back from an M-shaped hairline – its two points reminding me of horns – and his face was ruddy with a greyish hint of stubble on his jaw. His size gave him the authority to barge through the crowds. Like a vast predator, his shoulders swung and his hands, like paddles, pushed people from his path. Just as I lost sight of Mum he was there, right in front of me. Piercing blue eyes, unblinking and joyless – like a shark's. He stopped, and my heart beat so hard I thought I might pass out. Radiating sinister undercurrents, his gaze rested on my head, and mine on the tufts of black hair that crept from his white shirt cuffs onto his knuckles. His fingers were swollen, reddish, and his nails long. Passengers jostled with impatience. 'Can you hurry up, please? What's going on?' they called. He cupped his crotch and squeezed it several times, slowly and deliberately, then patted my head with that hand.

Thereafter, a sense of foreboding colonised my mind, like a rampant pernicious vine. He would come for me, I thought. He would torture me. And the most harrowing way to do so would be to kidnap my mum. I had to protect her, to protect *me*.

In the hills above Bandol, flashes of him kept cleaving through the gladness I felt at being there, injecting me with a sense of dread that flipped my stomach. It dirtied the gold of the sunshine and bruised my sense of connection to the land, which felt deep. I sat between knotted vines and dry dirt dusted my legs. While the sun burned the jagged parting of my hair, I closed my eyes to lose myself in the cicadas' rhythm. I pulled dark cloudy grapes from the branches and juice dripped over my thighs, over the dust. The tacky smears made when I rubbed it away looked like strokes of tribal paint. I tried to forget, but those icy blue eyes followed me and made me shiver in the heat. The malevolence behind that smile of his was, I felt, a forewarning of what was to come, and like a black cloud it extinguished my delight.

My attention was caught by a bell that rang out across the hillside. Next to the chapel, high above the house, stood a giant cross. At night I lay on the terrace floor and gazed at its starry illumination in the midst of the pine forest. I wondered for how many centuries it had stood there, and about its healing draw for the black-clothed villagers who climbed the hill for pardon. I wondered if its power could protect me and Mum from the evil of the man on the train. In the early mornings, when the clean, woody scent of pine was sharpest, I climbed the hill and prayed to it, wrapping my arms around its base.

We went to the beach for lunch. The sun cast slatted light through the bamboo awning of the restaurant and onto its shabby metal tables. Sasha Distel and Francoise Hardy sang from a crackly radio. Waiters, mimicking Alain Delon in tight faded shorts and deep tans, greeted us with kisses, while women in huge sunglasses and cone-shaped bikini tops swung past. Printed tote bags slipped from their shoulders as they leant over to greet their boyfriends, already seated. '*Salut, Yves, ça va?*' they sang, the last syllable rising girlishly. My flesh tingled from sea salt on sunburn. I gazed at the bare brown limbs, crossing and uncrossing themselves, reaching for dewy glasses of wine and plates of steak tartare, wiped clean with chunks of baguette. Laughter filled the restaurant, and with each burst, thick, Latin hair was tossed over nut-brown shoulders. Afterwards they settled on the raft, not far out to sea, where they frolicked like children, then lay languidly intertwined for the duration of the afternoon.

Moving in and out of these abundant visions was the sinister flash of the stranger on the train, of those hairy swollen fingers curled around his crotch. I ran to the water and dived in, opening my eyes wide so that they stung, and when I got out, they were so cloudy and sore that my mum, still at the table, was a blur.

Much later, back in grey, ossified England, with no diverting escape to the generous freedom of the Mediterranean Sea, home suddenly felt at high risk of threat.

Leaving Mum alone for more than two seconds reduced me to hysteria; my body shook, my heart raced, my hands trembled. I tailed her around the house watching her every move, suspicious and alert like a bodyguard, from the kitchen to the sitting room, from the bedroom to the bathroom. My sight and hearing amplified. I picked up every noise and movement – even the flutter of a leaf against the back door was perceived as danger. Every rustle, click, creak, and bang was him. He was either on the roof, or picking the locks, or scaling the wall, or already inside, about to pounce, as stealthy and soft-footed as the Milk Tray man in all those adverts. While Mum slept, I lay awake next to her in bed. My eyes strained to see though the darkness, and my ears filtered familiar sounds from unfamiliar. I got up regularly to peer through the break in the curtains. As if I had laser vision, I scanned the blackness outside for the flash of an eye or some unexpected movement. Avoiding the loose floorboard, I padded to the door to verify that it was still locked, doubting my own memory of the last time I checked. We were never safe. Night-time rendered me sightless, and thus powerless: its blackout added an extra layer of foreboding. Once the grey light of day began to cut through the curtain, my acute state of alarm blunted. I would see him coming – although I did wonder what good that would ultimately do. If he got us, he got us. Me *seeing* his approach wouldn't stop that. But the illusion of control that came with daybreak made me feel useful, and routinely I checked cupboards, corners, and behind curtains, while Mum sighed and leant against doorframes with a mug of coffee and a cigarette. I worked my way down from the attic, convinced he could slide like a ghost through the tiles of the roof. I checked under rugs for secret trap doors about which only he knew.

The telephone too posed a threat: its intrusive ring was the signal of his imminent materialisation. Only I was permitted to pick it up. Only I was able to shield us. I fancied

I heard his heavy breathing and whispery allusions to intimacy in the handset and slammed it down before discovering the caller's identity. Ring, ring, ring. It would start up again.

'For crying out loud, Nix,' Mum shouted, 'you've got to let me pick it up!' Ring, ring, ring. My head hurt. The ball of pain pushed so hard against my skull that I thought it might burst it. I yawned all the time, and then scolded myself; I had to be canny and vigilant, for goodness' sake. No matter what, I couldn't let my guard slip. I shook my head and scrunched up my eyes before stretching them wide. The smoke from Mum's cigarettes caught in her throat and made her cough. She bent over, patting her chest, and when she stood up again she was crying and laughing at the same time, saying, 'We can't live like this, darling. It's barmy!' I couldn't let her pick it up though. She didn't believe that we were in danger. She was too unsuspecting. Too vulnerable. Too polite. She would do her normal thing of inviting him to tea. And he was so clever that he could foresee that.

The threat level from other unsavoury individuals was also, over time, raised to critical in my mind. Home became both refuge and prison. When television adverts for Christmas toys were aired on our fuzzy black and white screen, Father Christmas was my only concern. In anticipation of his visit I fell ill, the somersaulting activity in my tummy raising my temperature so that the doctor was called.

'Silly girl,' he said. 'Father Christmas brings gifts to little girls like you. *If* you behave yourself, of course. Never heard such nonsense!' He gave Mum a packet of pills. 'Valium. For you, my dear. You need it. Even a small corner for her, from time to time, won't hurt. Good luck!'

Why did no one else understand what was happening? Being completely alone in reality increased the weight of responsibility on my shoulders. I cried buckets over how they trivialised my battle, how they dismissed it. It was hard work, for goodness' sake, with no rest. I would willingly forgo Father Christmas' presents – all presents – if it kept him away from me. He was a big, bearded, unfamiliar man in heavy boots and a suit the colour of blood. Could I welcome him into my bedroom? *No!* I just couldn't do that.

Even his title of 'Father' made me dubious. That, I believed, was just a lure, to affect familial cosiness. I, for one, wasn't going to be fooled.

Mum persisted. We compromised. She hung a stocking from the banister on the landing but promised to leave him no food or drink by the fireplace. But she told me I was uncharitable, that he would be cold and hungry with his tireless travel round the world. I didn't understand her. He was a stranger, after all. She'd told me all my life never to talk to strangers, and if one should approach me, to run straight to the nearest bobby. Why, in that case, was it okay to welcome him into our house, have him lingering around to eat mince pies, and possibly even rifle through our things? It was a long night, the night before Christmas. I lay in bed rock-still and held my breath to pretend that I wasn't there. If I breathed, I was present. Not breathing absented me.

I was so used to living in a state of high alarm that

the vine of foreboding kept growing, twining its tendrils around one social norm and then another, shifting the shape of the threat from the man on the train to the catastrophic consequences of my own inadequacies.

We had some family who lived over an hour away. There were five children in all, and in terms of age I came somewhere in the middle. Mum would receive a letter from them every so often inviting us to Sunday lunch in a month's time, and her acceptance would throw me into a spiral of panic. They lived in an imposing house with a tennis court and a walled swimming pool. The atmosphere was high-spirited, with lots of voices vying to compete above soaring classical music. There were high ceilings, heavy silk curtains, a grand piano, stone floors, fine art hanging on striped wallpaper, several knives and forks at each setting laid for lunch, and book cases lined with old leather-bound books.

What if I ate with the wrong fork in front of them? Or wasn't able to eat because of being sick? What if I refused to let go of Mum's hand again? Refused to make eye contact with them? Or if I blushed when they asked me how school was? What if I couldn't speak again? Or what if I did speak, and, like last time, words tumbled out in a stammering rush, making no sense at all? What if... what if?

God, how I'd wished just to melt away the last time we went, and not to have had to stand there as if I were an exhibit in a science museum, my humiliating display of anxiety under scrutiny. Why couldn't I have hidden it better? The very last thing I wanted was to be the focus of attention, and stupid me – that's what I couldn't stop being.

They probably dreaded the lunch as much as I did, and particularly the moment when their mother, with wide, coaxing eyes, said, 'Take Nix off to the garden. I'm sure you'll find something to do until lunch. Go on, now.'

As the 'three days away' mark approached, I would fall ill, increasingly so as Sunday loomed. Fever, sickness, migraine.

'Sorry to cancel again, love. Can't make lunch this weekend. No. Yes. Hmm. Don't know. She's not ill, no. Just highly-strung, according to the doctor. Says it'll pass in time. It'll finish me off before then, though!' Mum's lowered voice was audible above the buzz of the television, where there was no programme showing.

Chapter 7

Other than Benson and Hedges cigarettes, church on Sundays was my mum's one regular habit. During the service, she would elbow me as I fidgeted, but the collar of my woollen coat aggravated the skin of my neck, and yew tree needles pierced its hem. I had crouched under the tree beforehand while she'd chatted to neighbours, and my coat had brushed the ground. Picking them out without tearing the wool occupied my attention for much of the sermon. The air was cold inside, and I tensed my body against it, but the atmosphere of solemnity cooled it further. I never understood why God should intimidate everyone. Why the vicar had to spread his word with accusatory threats of divine vengeance against us sinners. I wasn't a sinner. And God's word was love, I thought. And love, well – wasn't love welcoming and safe? I was confused.

It was an unnecessary event, as far as I was concerned. I understood Mum wanting to be with her family or friends, but the vicar and congregation... well, why should they matter so much? God, on the other hand, was everywhere. I didn't need to go and stand in a freezing church to communicate with him.

'For goodness' sake, Nix, it's only an hour. Surely you can do that for me?' She was irritated by my weekly opposition.

'But Mum, why church? Why can't I just talk to him here, at home, from my bedroom?'

I told her that I did that anyway. That I had too many requests during the week and couldn't wait until Sunday to ask him. In any case, in church he'd never hear me over the din of all the other prayers. Chatting to God was simple, I said. As simple as making a telephone call. You just had to know that he was there at the other end.

Being the only child in the small congregation I felt obliged to conform, convinced as I was that thirty-odd pairs of eyes were homing in on me in anticipation of the echoing double clunk of my hymnbook as it first hit the kneeler, then the floor. My tension resulted in fits of nervous giggles which compounded my anxiety, and their displeasure. Before the spluttering escaped my mouth and my shoulders began to heave, I had to make myself stop. I put my chin to my chest, squeezed my eyes tight, and diverted my mind to the lingering scent of a recurring nightmare that was butchering my sleep at the time.

In it, my mum was prey to armies of savages wielding knives, axes, and arrows. My role as her protector had me hiding her behind rocks, down holes, in caves; and when there was nowhere else to go, I would stand in the line of fire until her disappearing back was far enough away to be safe. Usually I woke before they got her, but once or twice I failed. Her death cries haunted my consciousness after that, and the fear of them became like a shadow: life-like and permanently stitched to me. I couldn't let her die. Without my mum I knew I'd be lost.

My dad had already left me. Only once or twice had he come back from Kenya, where we had lived as a family, and played with me in St. James's Park. He stayed with friends, whose house off Walton Street had pale blue carpets that swept up the staircase to a drawing room furnished with striped chintz and swags. Otherwise, time spent together involved driving around the country visiting yet more friends. Once there, I was allowed to watch a new sitcom called 'The Liver Birds' while they 'took the dogs out', although the task was a mysterious one to me, as it was always dark by then.

He drove a Jaguar. Dark green. Its smooth ride and smell of leather made me nauseous. We stopped frequently for a 'Scotch egg pit-stop'. The law, I understood, prohibited young children from entering pubs.

Pulling up in line with the pub door, he'd squeeze my cheek between his thumb and index finger.

'Won't be a sec, darling – I'll grab a Scotch egg and then we'll be off again.'

But hours later, it seemed, I was still locked in the car.

This was it, I thought.

I reached for the tin of travel sweets, chose a yellow one covered in soft powdery sugar, and rested my feet on the glossy wooden dashboard. I yanked at the wool of my white tights until a small hole appeared, high up on my leg. He didn't like me 'looking tatty', as he said, so I did it where he couldn't see.

This time he's gone forever. This was it.

I gently pulled the yarn and watched how the tiny loops of wool were freed.

Yes, this was it.

My face was burning, and my tummy somersaulted.

He wouldn't come back. This *really was* it.

It started to drizzle. I was shivery. Creepy strangers peered in at me through the windows and I held my breath, pulling the wool harder so that the thread ran from the loops and the oblong stretch of exposed skin widened. But when that no longer distracted me, and a man started wiping my window with a wide-palmed hand, I looked up from my tights and fixed my gaze on the pub door. The trickles of rainwater obscured my vision. I leaned closer to the windscreen. Milky clouds of my breath spread out onto the glass, and I had to keep moving my face towards a fresh patch in order to see out. I played a game with myself to keep from blinking. How many times could I count to ten before I blinked? Three, four, five times? I couldn't permit myself to do so, however sore my eyes got. If I blinked, I might miss him. Or miss the one clue essential to explaining his absence.

Did I dare to go in there? Go find him? No, not really. The term 'den of iniquity' had a long way to go before crossing the threshold of my vocabulary, but there were things I knew I shouldn't know – '*pas devant les enfants*' – and as far as I understood, they must all be happening in there. Besides that, Dad would be angry. And besides *that*, it was illegal.

Dad's unsteady figure finally appeared in the doorway, warmly thumping the shoulders of another tweed jacket. My irrepressible relief poured down his neck in tears when he lifted me. I had bolted to him, and he'd disentangled himself from the red-faced gentleman.

'What on earth's the matter, my little African baby? What?' I inhaled his familiar pub breath as he pummelled my back as if it were his horse. 'No boo-hoos, darling, your poor, old Dad's fine. Happy as Larry! Come on – dry your eyes! We've had a good old laugh, me and… uh, er… haven't we? No need to cry – I'm perfectly alright.'

He opened his jacket, tucked me under it, and we ran back to the car. He muttered impatiently as he fumbled for the car keys.

'Get oorn! Gawd! Bloody weather! What a wretched little island it is!'

Chapter 8

My parents' marriage had been short-lived. Raised voices and tears punctuate my memories of dawn in the vegetable garden, or the warm kiss of the Indian Ocean against my skin. I was young when they divorced, and Mum only twenty-three years old. She had lived in Kenya her whole life and her parents were still there. Yet she had decided that the community was too small for both her and my father, and that the gossip about his busy romantic life would inhibit and isolate her. So, she turned her back on Africa and went to England. She took me with her.

The skies in England were low and heavy. I imagined them falling on my head... engulfing me... suffocating me... like a damp grey blanket over my face, stuffing my mouth so that I couldn't breathe. I felt trapped by the cloying humidity and the bleak, lifeless cold there. My eye could travel only so far until it was blocked.

Where had it gone, my former life? Where were my dad, my dog, my rescued zebra? Where were my wide African plains and the snowy peaks of Mount Kenya? Where was the hollow clip-clop of horses' hooves on scorched earth, their rhythm interrupted by Dad's tetchy voice breaking into the English curses that littered his Swahili? Where was his big rough hand cupped around mine? Where were the verandah, the zebra skins, the tatty rose-print chintz, the dark wood, the mosquito nets, and the watercolours of the mountain? And where was Ngary, my guardian? Where was he? Was he still there in his tired khaki clothes and bare feet, holding my horse Conker's forelock, waiting for me to be mounted? Who was I to talk to now? Swahili was my first language and that too had gone.

And why? Why had my daddy gone? Why had he left me? The question circled my brain like a bird of prey. Why? Why? Why?

A small voice in a recess of my sub-conscious hardly dared to articulate the answer. But the words crept out unbidden, drawing closer and closer like a military siege, circumventing the ramparts of my consciousness. I didn't like the sound of them, so I shook my head, trying to deter them. Deaden the noise! Make that answer go away! I ran from the house to my climbing frame. I wrapped my body in and out of the bars, slipping round the cool metal like a dolphin through waves. With bent knees I hung from them until the blood filled my head and drowned out the words, and my dangling arms felt like lead. And still the answer threatened to break free, to make itself known to me. So, I swung myself onto the top bar and flung my concentration into walking its length. Like a trapeze artist, I held my back straight with my arms spread and my chin up; my bare feet gripped the metal, their metatarsal bones white and raised – trembling, then steady, then trembling again – and by the time I reached its end, the adrenaline had temporarily silenced the threat.

Later on, though, the troubling chorus resumed and crushed my barriers like a stampede. It seized control of my mind, and its din drowned all other thoughts.

What if? What if? What if? What if *I* was to blame? What if *I* had driven him away? What if *I* had done something wrong? And if so, *what*?

I listed the things he yelled at me for: firstly, throwing up down his back when he drove too fast; secondly, making a fuss when my ayah forced me to eat vegetables; thirdly, getting in the way when they were milking the cattle; fourthly, looking tatty; finally, crying when he shouted. At my mum, in particular.

I scoured my memories for a time when I might have rankled him enough to prompt him to take off. When he might have thought, 'Oh, to hell with all this!' But even in my embroidered imagination I could find no specific occasion.

So. Was it more generalised than that? What if he'd just had enough of me? Enough of being disappointed in me? And what if, what if – however hard I tried – I just didn't have it in me to *ever* be good enough, clever enough, quiet, nice, or pretty enough for him to *want* to be my dad?

My forehead was suddenly hot, and butterflies flipped in my tummy. It was as if my heart stopped beating as I took in the unavoidable conclusion.

I had the answer: my failure was inevitable, my world doomed. I wasn't worthy of being his daughter.

But. I had another thought. A thought that let light into the dark. A glimmer of hope. What if I worked at changing myself, to be better for him? What if I could mould myself to be just right? Might I then win him back?

As I raced out again across the garden, to the bald patch of lawn under my climbing frame, I willed that to be possible. I would scale that mountain, no matter what – to make myself just right for him.

Chapter 9

Mum gazed searchingly out of the window, as if through the Somerset drizzle she might glean thorn trees, burning dusk skies, or elephant on their way to a watering hole. I watched the almost imperceptible movements of her back as she sighed. Her shoulders lifted, and her ribs filled out slowly, then sank inwards on a shiver. Despite the bravado in her smile I knew it was sadness that was shaking her. I knew that she was dragging the weight of homesickness, that it was tethered to her in the same way that her soul was tethered to Africa.

The tall Gothic window gave onto a majestic copper beech and green hills beyond. Fog and rain clung to them, and its dense grey soup blocked out the sky even from the highest point of the house; the attic. I sat on the Victorian rocking horse in there and waited patiently for a patch of blue to reveal itself.

This was my great-grandmother's house, with turrets and towers and rooms the size of cricket pitches. The carved wood panelling of the hall smelt of Earl Grey, and the dining room walls, lined with William Morris fabric, of sweet doughy puddings. Breakfast was left on the hot plate – a row of gleaming silver dishes with hats. Johnson, the butler, picked me up so that I could lift each one: porridge, scrambled eggs, sausages, kippers. I danced on the table in the kitchens downstairs and chatted in Swahili to the Portuguese cook, relieved to have found another foreigner who I assumed, being foreign, would understand what I was saying. In the hall there was a bronze gong that Johnson struck with a leather-covered mallet to summon everyone to dinner. Occasionally I was permitted to do the job myself. The power of the ricochet threw me backwards as its vibrant tone rushed up the wide circling staircase to the heights of the roof, resonating around the first-floor landing where the ladies were dressing. Marjorie was employed as my nanny while Mum went back to Kenya for a bit to 'sort things out'. She and the staff downstairs became my only companions; as for my great-grandmother, a kindly but imposing woman, I saw her only fleetingly once or twice a day.

We moved again when it was time for me to start school. We went to Suffolk, to another branch of our family, who lent us a little farmhouse on their estate. It was the countryside of Gainsborough and Constable, of big skies, gentle folds, hollows, woodlands, and the wide brown ribbon of the river Stour.

The tall gates and black Tudor cross beams of Sadler's School had a witchy, ominous feel to them. I hadn't yet learned to read or write, so I presumed that I would stick out and be scorned by everyone else who could. 'But everyone is in the same boat as you, my darling. That's why you are all off to school,' Mum said. 'To learn.' Other than a brief spell at nursery, where I had daily wet my pants due to an inability to speak, I hadn't yet been forced into any social interaction with large groups of my own peer group, but even before going I had already decided that I was at a disadvantage.

They were loud and boisterous, the other children, and seemed to all know each other. They shared the same games, stories, songs, and upbringing that I hadn't experienced. Trying to find similarities between them and me – anything in common with which I could break the ice – I observed them from a distance. I watched closely how they interacted – the ways that they selected their leaders and befriended or excluded each other – and I imagined myself copying them. I compared their visible personalities with my interior one, and though I longed to find similarities, I failed to do so. A discomfort with being me came in the wake of that.

I hid in the folds of my teacher's skirt, trying to disappear in anticipation of being spotted and mocked. I moved as she moved, as if I were her shadow. Fade into the background, I said to myself. Fade. No one will notice you that way. I disappeared into her long skirt and into the back row where it was darkest. To avoid all eye contact, I focused on the charred-looking ceiling beams. I dared not speak, and the idea that the teacher might turn her attention to me provoked such terror that often I missed class and spent it in the girls' loo, with my head over the basin.

At break, while Miss Thomas took tea in the staff-room and everyone played games in the courtyard, I peeled away to the refuge of the horse chestnut tree, out of view behind an old flint wall. Leaning against its rough trunk, I wished it would suck me inside so that I could lose myself and no longer attract unwanted scrutiny. I pulled the flesh from between the veins of its palm-like leaves to make them look like fish skeletons, and a niggling feeling of self-contempt jabbed at me. Why couldn't I fit in? Play with the others? Or even try to? I was useless, I thought. Useless. Notwithstanding that, the fear I had of the renowned school bully helped vindicate my harsh self-judgment, and justified, to some degree, my feelings.

Kevin was like the child-catcher in the film *Chitty Chitty Bang Bang*, but fair-haired, with a pasty, lumpy face like a sticky bun, and brown shorts tight over his pale stocky thighs. He ran faster than I did, and when he caught me he would lift my dress and jab my bottom with a needle he'd glued to the end of a twig which stuck in my flesh and hurt, and then twist my arms behind my back, laughing into my ear, his panting breath hot on my neck.

'Doesn't that hurt? Cry! Go on!' Determined to deny him that, I closed my eyes and held my breath until there was a separation between my mind and body, and numbness replaced pain.

'Cry!' he breathed hoarsely.

Let him do what he wants! I told myself. If he hurts

you, you'll have proof to show to the teachers. That way he might be stopped.

But the other girls he caught kicked and screamed, which seemed to appeal less to him. Next time, I thought, maybe I should fight like them.

Chapter 10

My home life looked up with cousins close by. Aunt Vicky
was kind and loving, with a saintly smile and dark, gentle
eyes. She had an instinctive gift for boosting confidence in
us children no matter how insignificant our achievement,
and for wrapping us in a net of emotional safety. When I
was with her all my threats melted away, looming large only
at school.

She and Uncle Hugh lived in a big house between a river
and flat fields that were peppered with old wartime bun-
kers and herds of black and white cows. A vast inglenook
fireplace around which the family congregated filled the
hall and there was a corridor linking two outside doors,
like a mini airstrip, which we used for roller-skating. The
kitchen, which held its warmth because of the old Aga, had
a laundry pulley above the scrubbed table, and on that
there was fresh white bread, strawberry jam, and bottles of
milk topped with yellow bands of cream. The rambling gardens merged with fields, broken by a stile here, a gate there.

There were towering horse chestnut trees, walled rose gardens, mown paths through cow parsley, gooseberries under netting, apple orchards, and outhouses that smelt of freshly-cut grass.

One day I had to go to hospital to have adenoid surgery. The metallic smells, the stretchers, the nurses in blue scrubs, and the patients' moans had already infiltrated my mind, unsettling me long before my admittance there. It had become the subject of nightmares in which I fled from the heavy swing doors, chased by doctors waving needles and other medical paraphernalia. I would sleepwalk and wake, shivering, out of breath, with a galloping heart, outside in the dark, my bare feet on wet grass and my brushed cotton nightdress absorbing the drizzle like a sponge.

They gave me an anaesthetic to which I had an allergic reaction. Consequently, I stopped breathing for a couple of hours, and was put on a life support machine. When I finally came around, woozy and nauseous, with my throat as sore as if it had been chafed with sandpaper, I was alone, and my last recollection flooded back to me: being wheeled away from my mum down an endless corridor whose lights streaked past in a blurred line. Swing doors hit the gurney with force and jolted my body to the side. I fixed my eyes on the ceiling squares. 'Mumma!' I called. Follow the straight line! Keep awake! It was like a spacecraft, I thought. White lights, masked aliens, squeaky soles, and mechanical beeps – they all meshed together, out of focus yet close up, in and out of my vision. 'Mum!' I called again, but no noise came from my mouth. I squirmed. The nurses held my shoulders down. I called again. No voice. Look at the straight line! Keep awake! Keep awake! Then suddenly there was nothing but blankness.

I looked around the room. A big window let in dim light. Where was Mum now? What had they done to her? A nurse appeared at my bedside with a bowl of pink ice-cream. Smiling at me, she scooped it up and put it to my mouth. Then she jiggled the spoon between my closed lips, trying to open them, and the sharp sting of the cold made my nose twitch. She kept coaxing me with reassuring words, but I shook my head and made stifled protests. Not until my mum came back to me, not until I knew she was safe, would I trust the nurse, or do anything she told me to.

When Mum and Aunt Vicky did turn up, the tears I shed were waves of pent-up tension. Aunt Vicky brought me a book. It was a compilation of stories about the lives of fairies and elves. My mum's favourite bedtime story for me at that time was a book about a cat called *The Wait For Me Kitten*, whose exclusion from the adventures of the other farm animals made me cry inconsolably. My dad favoured two books – there was *Little Red Riding Hood*, whose message was to be a good little girl in order to avoid danger, and *Hansel and Gretel*, whose echoes of paternal abandonment were equally tormenting. Aunt Vicky's book, by contrast, had no dark messages in its tales. No character felt left out, abandoned, or lost their innocence to predatory shadows. Instead it was a colourful escape – illustrated in detail – into a magical universe. Illnesses were cured with caresses, and broken wings with wands and prayers. In the blink of an eye

84

grievances, bruises, and worries were fixed with tenderness and jokes. When rains flattened their flower forest and saturated their homes, the elves wove more. Spiders re-spun hanging bridges and playgrounds, and robins spread their wings to provide shelter. Hungry mouths were comforted with poppy seed cakes and nettle tea. The book showed a society founded on safety and nourishment, beauty and cheerfulness, with the simple message that good rewards good. In my mind its approach to life became indistinguishable from Aunt Vicky's, and ultimately developed into the framework for my dream future life. The alternative was one of hyper-vigilance against threat. For me, it was either good or bad, light or dark – there was nothing in between.

I found a way to move between the real world and my fairy world, shifting from the material to the spirit, until the border between them was blurred, and the existence of fairies became unquestionable. Like nomads settling into a new camp, they moved into my consciousness and my reality shifted to incorporate them as part of it. Tuned into their frequency, I saw them in the garden, playing or swinging from leaves. They skipped over my bed to spring-clean my dolls' house. I picked up petals they'd dropped on my pillow, the floor, the stairs, and I rescued a wisp of a fairy child lost on the windowsill. One day I found a chick with a broken wing under my climbing frame. With a fluffy dust cloth, I made a bed for it in a shoebox, and put it in the airing cupboard with an eggcup of water. When it died, a tiny sprite in pink rose petals appeared out of nowhere to pull the cloth over its eyes.

I assumed that everyone drifted between worlds as I did, so I was shocked to discover not only that this was not true, but that they spurned the idea – even mocked it. The teachers at school in particular were dismissive. It wasn't that they said anything outright to me; it was their facial expressions – the drawing in of their eyebrows and concomitant smile – that gave them away. What prejudice! I thought. I cried tears of fury, provoked by humiliation and injustice. Protective of my fairies (and of course my faith in them), I burned to change human nature, in the same way that conservationists want to protect the rights of tribal people.

The river behind the house was our playground. From its banks tumbled weeping willows and swans nested in the bulrushes and under the bridge from which we played pooh sticks. At the end of the school day Tess, my cousin, and I ran to the orchard where Face and Page waited. Face and Page were two little boys, apparently invisible to everyone else, who lived in the boughs of an apple tree overlooking the grass tennis court. Thin with scarred knees, they both had fair hair and pinched cheeks. Page's ears stuck out and he wore a floppy cap to cover them. They had bare feet and wore long ragged brown breeches, matching waistcoats, and oversized shirts. They had neither parents nor a home, and they looked so frail and insubstantial that they seemed transparent, like two diaphanous feathers on a breeze.

We worried about them, and often took a basket filled with bottles of milk, Ribena, and slabs of bread and jam. Sometimes I remembered to save a gobstopper or liquorice sherbet, but their favourites were Curly Wurlies and flying saucers.

Uncle Hugh pretended to disapprove of them – 'They lead you astray, those boys,' he would say, winking. As we left for the orchard Mum would ruffle my head. 'Be good,' she'd call, and she and Aunt Vicky, huddled by the Aga, would laugh as we closed the door.

We took off for the old wooden boathouse after Face and Page had wolfed down their tea. The ledges were slippery and there was an earthy smell of silt trapped inside. The boat rocked as we clambered down into it before pushing ourselves out onto the wide brown river. Mallards, disturbed from dabbling in the irises, shot away from us, and across their wakes we glided downstream under trailing willow branches that reminded me of maypole ribbons. A pigeon's soft cooing followed. Sometimes we ended up circling the eddy the other side of the bridge, and one of us had to jump into the water to pull us back out. My uncle was cross when we lost an oar in the bulrushes. Though I'd tried to rescue it, the water was too deep for me to stand in. Face and Page were out of bounds for a week. A week? That seemed an awfully long time without them.

In the early mornings it was still dark when the postman stopped his van outside the farmhouse. I listened for the creak of the gate, his footsteps on the path, the clang of the metal letterbox, then the mail hitting the doormat. Rameses, my Abyssinian cat, didn't care for him, and miaowed menacingly from the wall under the laburnum tree. Sometimes a parcel was squeezed through the narrow slit, or a box covered in airmail stickers was left on the doorstep to soak up the dew of the dawn. In winter a thin white glaze laced its top and sides as Jack Frost hurriedly left his handprint on it. Inside were pawpaws, avocados, pineapples, and mangos, sent from Kenya a few weeks previously. Giddy with excitement, I would fly downstairs.

His letters were addressed to me as M.L.A.B: Much Loved African Baby. They had a formulaic composition, starting with news about the dogs and horses, then progressing to tit-bits of scandal, interjected with 'tee hee!' and 'serves them right!' He relished scandal, my dad. Fed off it. Said it made him feel better about himself. Finally, he would relay lengthy stories of near visits from the 'Grim Reaper' or 'the men in white coats'. 'BUT…' he'd write triumphantly, 'I outwitted them again, darling! Clever, old Dad!' It usually meant yet another incident that resulted in his finding himself in 'the doghouse' or Emergency Care. Despair lurked within the triumph and 'big boo-hoos' were always noted. Envelopes were signed with S.W.A.L.K in a spidery scrawl: Sealed With A Loving Kiss.

In wafer-thin blue airmail paper, I sent back drawings of encouragement, such as him kicking in a doghouse, or fleeing hospital. It troubled me that my dad had no knowledge of my life – the place where I lived, what I did every day – and that our geographical distance accentuated the widening emotional gulf. 'Out of sight, out of mind…' I'd heard the man in the corner shop say to Mum about cigarettes, when persuading her that she shouldn't smoke. To keep me *in* Dad's mind, I recorded my daily life with pictures as if he were my diary. I drew the river and the boat, the blue-bell-wood, the disused railway along which we bicycled, the hay barn, the dens we made, and the sugar beet pile we climbed. I drew a map of Sudbury, my route to school past the sweetie shop, the terrible dentist's house, Sunday school, and the church. I drew the route to Long Melford, where Mum had an antiques shop. I drew the auction houses that she would take me to after school, where men with nicotine-stained fingers and cigarettes tucked behind their ears would greet her in a rough, manly way. I drew the corridors of heavy brown furniture that rose higher than me, their dusty doors ajar, opening onto shelves that were house and board for spiders, beetles, and woodworm. I drew a little girl with a down-turned mouth. Next to it, a picture of Woolworths and its colourful plastic supplies featured the same girl with a smiley face. I drew the café called Number 4, and its frosted lemon and orange shells filled with sorbet – treats with which Mum bribed me to attend her auctions. 'They must be foreign. Portuguese probably...' Mum would say, referring to the owners, having not before seen such exoticism in England. I drew pictures of the time when the river overflowed into the farm cottages and we had to wade through waist-high water to get to school. I drew one of the most eventful moments of my childhood. Friends of ours lived in Ballingdon Hall, an Elizabethan manor close to the river. When their view was threatened by a new road and development, they had their house jacked up and placed on a giant trailer, and towed, inch by inch, to the top of the hill, over a period of years. I drew the mud, the towering criss-crossing wheels beside me, the shuddering black and white building, its ghosts pressed to the leaded window panes, and crowds in soggy tweed and wellingtons. I drew the excitement on their faces and the worry when rain and mud halted action. I drew portraits of Face and Page, my cousins, some of my favourite fairies, the beastly Kevin, my school uniform, and Mum's little car, a Riley Elf. I drew my Tiny Tears doll. 'No boo-hoos, Daddy!' I wrote in a bubble coming from her mouth.

I worried about him. Wished I could go to him, hold his hand, put my arms round him, make him better. He did get so terribly unhappy.

I'd made a circular clearing in the cow parsley from having lain in it and fanned my arms and legs to batten down the celery-like stems. They made a hard, knobbly surface like a wicker futon underneath me, and the feathery leaves and frothy white flowers swayed above my face with a faint smell of aniseed. Through them, I watched cloud shapes of faces and animals and dragons. Sometimes an aeroplane's white trail cut across them. I thought about the earth that I lay on and the sky above me. How they were the same earth and same sky below and above my dad. Just further away. I wondered if through them we could connect to each other. If I concentrated hard, could I send a message across the airwaves or underground tunnels? I envisaged roots from my head into the earth and through them I transmitted my thoughts and longings. I stared through the sky and pictured them shoot upwards, turn left then south towards Africa. There I visualised Dad, adjusting his stirrups before galloping off, with his stable boy holding the rein – lean, still, and upright like a spear. Dry dirt swirled around his horse's hooves and flies around its face. Suddenly Dad would rise up out of the saddle and put a hand to his ear. I would feel the little stab in his belly when my longing for him flashed across his mind, and his chin jerked upwards in a series of tiny jolts, the facial tic signalling unwelcome thoughts.

Chapter 11

In the summer of 1972 we moved to Norfolk, and I started boarding school there. I was eight. A Palladian house the colour of sand, with tall windows; it was set in wooded parkland scattered with stately cedars and monkey puzzle trees. I went with an initialled trunk, a wooden tuck box, and a leather overnight case. This contained my acrylic photo cube, my teddy bear, my pyjama case and fur slippers, a lockable diary, and a gift from Mum: a pressed four-leaf clover. 'For luck,' she said, when she gave it to me.

My weekday uniform was a grey pleated skirt and a dark red cardigan. We had to wear two pairs of underpants – a white pair underneath, and large grey gym knickers on top. On Sundays we swapped the gym knickers for bloomers under our blue wool dresses, which were coarse and scratchy and made my skin break out in a rash. To quell my fears of boarding, Mum and Aunt Vicky had fed me enticing stories of hijinks like apple pie beds and midnight feasts and had told me that the experience would be 'character building', which I understood to be a good thing. I had been eased into the process by meeting another student a week before term had started, so that 'I wouldn't be alone.'

But it wasn't Mum's jolly japes that I clung to as my stomach somersaulted in the weeks leading up to the dreaded day; it was the kindly face of the headmistress, Miss Read. When we had visited the school, she had welcomed me with tenderness, and even in the strict lines of her powder blue dress-coat and neck bow, she'd seemed homely when she had caressed my head. She was also the art teacher, and the art room had appeared to me like Aladdin's cave, with its pottery, paints, and collages, basket weaving and looms. Once school began, however, I realised that Miss Read's position of authority distanced her from the rest of us. To find her you had to get past Miss Smith, her fearsome secretary.

There was nothing that could have prepared me for the sense of being that alone; not even the abandonment I'd felt when my dad had gone. It was a dark tunnel that I had to pass through before going home for Christmas, the length of which was only momentarily broken by a couple of short exeats and the half-term. A month, at that age, seemed like an eternity. But I knew I had to get through it, that I had to be a good little girl and not be 'difficult', that stoicism had to be conjured up from somewhere, and that I had to surrender to my fate. 'Chin up, darling,' Dad had said when I'd last seen him, and his big hand had cupped my head. A slight tremor conveyed his tension and he'd patted his stomach with his other hand. 'Ah, awful collywobbles, I have. My poor little mite.'

At home we didn't have central heating. But we had blankets to snuggle in and hot water bottles that I fastened under my waistband. What I remember about that first winter term was how freezing I was, and how taxing I found the lack of privacy. We slept in dormitories of six or seven girls, took shared baths of tepid water – two, sometimes three of us in a bath, twice a week only – and on the other five days, had early morning ice-cold 'strip-washes' in bathrooms of ten basins. Our hair was washed by Matron, once every couple of weeks, and then brushed fiercely by her. A hundred brushes per head. The schedule, from the wake-up bell until we filed down to breakfast, had to be met with military precision. Use the lavatory (and hard, waterproof paper made a loathsome chore of that), strip-wash, clip nails, brush hair, tie it back, polish shoes, hide possessions in bedside lockers, and make beds with hospital corners. Like little cadets, we then waited at the end of our beds for Miss Jones' inspection, before the bell for breakfast. She fussed around me with Kirby grips, and complained that I looked like a Pekinese. The only bunches I could muster stuck out at right angles to my head and swung as I ran. On weekends she supervised remedial exercises for our feet and deportment classes in which we had to walk with small piles of books on our heads.

Food was baked beans, tinned spaghetti, digestive biscuits, grey gristly meat, tinned tomatoes on fried bread, bread and butter pudding, spotted dick, custard. Tuck boxes were kept in the tuck room, a windowless space under the ground, the walls of which were shelved at a steep gradient to allow us to climb to the top.

The Christmas before I started school my godmother sent us a circular box of chocolates, the height of me and twice the width, with a red satin bow around its circumference. The chocolates were filled with nuts, caramel, toffee, violet, Turkish delight, and nougat. I had never before seen such richness, and once I removed the lid to study the little menu inside I waded through each flavour, unable to stop. Mum walked in, and my gluttony made her cross. She said I reminded her of Augustus Gloop, from *Charlie and the Chocolate Factory*, who had fallen into the chocolate river and got sucked up into a pipe, never to be seen again. She then added, 'All that sugar, for goodness' sake! Do you want all your teeth to fall out?' There was an elderly lady in one of the farm cottages who kept her dentures in a glass of water. To entertain me, she would slip them in and out of her mouth, gnashing them together to make a rattling noise, like an old skeleton. The thought that I could end up like her was a terrifying one. There and then, and for years to come, I stopped eating sugar. Sweets. Puddings. Cereal. My tuck box was the only one in the whole school that wasn't stuffed full of Cadbury's, liquorice sherbets, Spangles, Marathon bars, Fruit Salad chews, sherbet lolly pops and sugar mice. Mine had crisps, monkey nuts, raisins, Ritz crackers, Tuc biscuits, and bricks of cheddar cheese. Miss Jones wrote messages of concern in every school report. 'It is most unusual.' 'Such a peculiar child.' 'She won't develop properly without sugar.' 'It's very worrying.'

Letter-writing to our parents was limited to Sundays, in a classroom presided over by a member of staff who had the right to veto our letters if she found anything negative about the school. If the message was too affectionate, it was deemed open to misinterpretation by the parents, so 'I love you' was sometimes censored, depending on the supervisor.

After marrying again, Dad had settled in Jersey a few years previously. His new wife was Caro, a vivacious French beauty from Brittany, who was living in London when they met. She had back-combed hair the colour of copper which was wild and curly when she left it to dry naturally, smudgy freckles around her nose, smoky eyes, and painted lips and nails. I thought she was wonderful. She took to me with love and affection and called me 'mon petit chou'. She brought colour and stability to Dad's life, with her innate home-making skills and French cooking. His long car journeys with me stopped, and instead they bought a lovely house with a garden and a Labrador puppy called Taxi.

From his study there he wrote me a letter every day. Occasionally long news-like ones. He had a gift for writing. He wrote as he talked; his voice was strong and layered, translating in a spidery scrawl every nuance and shade of mood. It drew me close to him, even with few words, and every morning as the mail was sorted, I hurled myself down to the post room ahead of all the other girls, craving connection to him.

'How's Colditz? Be good. Work hard. Make your poor, old dad proud while he keeps the Grim Reaper at bay. Big kiss from your halo-less father (and a wag from Taxi).'

Sometimes he relayed gossip or funny stories – at someone else's expense – or even his own – and the racier ones I knew to hide under lock and key. Somewhere in my mind I understood that I shouldn't know about who was sleeping with whom but being his 'chum' was seductive. His letters were medicine to me. They brightened my days and were antidotes to the sense of exile and isolation I felt. Perpetual fear of everything and everyone swamped my mind, forever steering me towards the conviction that I was unacceptably different from the other girls. Judging from their photos and late-night chatter, their family lives seemed to run parallel with each other's but entirely separate from mine. They lived in draughty country houses, where ancestors loomed prominently over sweeping staircases, and above beds were pinned bouquets of multi coloured rosettes – first, second, and third prizes won in weekly gymkhanas. They had sculleries where Barbour and Husky jackets were piled on top of coat hooks. Rows of muddy wellington boots lined the walls. The smell of horse and wet dog hung in the air, and tufts of Labrador hair floated on stone flagging. The girls had apple-red cheeks and grazed knees. The order of their lives revolved around grooming their ponies and collecting eggs for Papa's fry-ups. There was a goat or two, and rabbits and guinea pigs in hutches and runs. They took breakfasts in morning rooms with their distant fathers, and high teas in nanny's rooms: fish fingers, cottage pies, baked beans on toast, an apple, and a choice of Quality Street. Mummy kissed them goodnight on her way to dress for dinner. They slept in flannel pyjamas under floral print eiderdowns, their bedroom windows open wide. They didn't stir when Teddy fell out of bed, nor when the house's ghostly inhabitants paced up and down in the attics. Their personalities seemed to have been shaped by an entirely different God from mine. Like the children of Enid Blyton stories, they were placid, jolly, and plucky.

A long portrait of the Darings hung over the mantelpiece in the common room at school. Lord Daring's gaze followed us to every corner of the room, and legend had it that he refereed the table tennis matches there. The Darings had lived in the house a century before, and stories of a murder during their occupancy fuelled the pupils' imaginations.

My mum had a habit of clearing her throat with a couple of delicate coughs. Thinking I had heard it beside me, I would wake in the night in a wave of relief, as life-affirming as the first inhalation of breath after swimming underwater. But it wasn't Mum, I quickly realised; it was Lottie, one of the six girls in my dormitory, each of them with their own habits of tossing and turning, snoring or coughing. Afterwards, I lay awake and watched the currents of cool air blow in through the window and puff out the heavy curtain. In the cedar tree outside, whose sprawling branches I climbed, an owl hooted low calls that sounded like a transmission of codes – secret messages that I fancied deciphering. The night was so black and dense and otherwise noiseless that they seemed to pierce the atmosphere like darts. An African night was different, I thought. Its air was filled with a rich chorus of chimes and hums and clicks and coos, broken by a lion's low moan or the whooping of hyena.

Where had Mum gone? She had left me in the echoing

hall, with my hand in the firm grasp of Miss Jones. I'd squirmed to be free, and to run down the steps after her retreating form which shook with tears, but Miss Jones, in her white nurse's uniform, was big and stern and had told me, 'It's all nonsense, your fuss.' She had pulled me away from the steps just as Mum had turned the corner round the yew hedge into the car-park. The flickering point of her headscarf was the last piece of her I'd seen, and when that too was swallowed by the big green hedge, a piercing pain had seared my stomach like a red-hot iron.

I longed for her. I longed for the comfort of her arms around me, her smell, her touch, and I longed for home and its safe familiarity. I leant over to retrieve my teddy bear that had, as usual, ended up on the floor.

Under my bed there was a lion. He had come with me from Kenya and had never left. I was never sure if he was friend or foe, but I knew he must be hungry, so when I picked up my bear, I had to ensure that the flick of my arm was gone before he realised its nourishment value. I then slipped my hand under my pillow to touch the photograph I kept there. It was a picture of Ngary and our baby zebra in the shade of an acacia tree. I'd kept Ngary hidden since 'the black man' had become the focus of my classmates' bullying, and by association I had too. I hadn't been able to defend him to begin with, because no words had come out of my mouth. They had stayed jumbled in my throat in a tight and furious ball. When occasionally they did emerge, I told them about him saving me from a mole snake and how I'd tracked giraffe from his shoulders. When they jeered at me for eating eggshells, I told them, 'That's what Ngary does,' – that it was good for the bones, as he'd told me. I built him up into a hero so that their taunts would backfire, or at least shrivel, in comparison to his glory. But nevertheless, he was still black. Their prejudice was stronger than my defence. And as there were many of them against me, they got the majority vote. To be accepted, I thus learned to giggle with them when they hissed his name, whilst simultaneously praying for forgiveness to counterbalance my shame.

I closed my eyes and listened for the call of a nightjar. I imagined the swoop of bats above my head and waves in my mosquito net as their wings fanned the air. I strained to hear Ngary's voice and cried.

Sometimes when I opened them again a lady was by my bed. A creak in the old floorboards alerted me to her presence. I knew it was Lady Daring from the portrait downstairs. She wore the same blue silk dress, gathered at the front with a bustle behind, with her blonde hair piled high and a sapphire at her neck. In the dark of the dormitory she glowed. I looked forward to her visits. I felt as if she knew me somehow, and without either prejudice or sympathy. She was a neutral presence. And a comforting one, convinced as I was by then of my irremediable foreignness, which was creating a flourishing habit of self-reproach. A tremor in the air above my head signalled the movement of her hand, and I fell back to sleep, soothed.

Even when I considered that perhaps I was being melodramatic, I always returned to the facts: I was complicated and dark, and obviously so. No one else was like that. On the contrary, they seemed light-hearted and simple. My shyness was so crippling that often no word could be uttered. Not even hello. No one else had shyness that bad. I had a gap between my teeth. No one else had gapped teeth. And mine was big – wide enough to fit two fifty pence coins, and to foster a complex so terrible that for years I smiled with my lips zipped, and when a rare word escaped, it was from a skinny slice of mouth that revealed only my bottom teeth. I had divorced parents; no one else did. I was an only child; no one else was. Ngary, my nanny, was a black African and male; no one else's was. A lion lived under my bed; no one else had one. I played with fairies; no one else did. To cap it all, I wouldn't eat sugar. And *that* was unheard of. *Everyone* in the whole wide world ate sugar. More than that, they craved it.

Divorce then bore the weight of social stigma. Its association made you tainted and elicited shocked expressions, covert whispers, and the embarrassed shuffling of feet. At my last school, Mum had stood apart from the other mothers outside the school gates, and when we students poured through them, the other mothers had manoeuvred their children around me, as if I had had chicken pox. The only other children to receive that sort of treatment were the poor 'bastards' whose parents weren't married. At that time in rural areas, the words 'bastard' and 'divorce' were spat out like mouthfuls of rotten fruit. In my first year at boarding school I was told that I was the only child there with divorced parents. By the time I left in 1976, most of my classmates were in the same position.

It wasn't just that which set my mum and dad apart. As individuals they seemed different from the others at my school. Money was tight for my mum. She barely had enough to feed us, so she worked in London when she could, taking jobs in shops and florists. Oxfam in Sudbury was where she found clothes for me. The colour mustard was going out of fashion as quickly as it had come in, and Oxfam stocked piles of its cast-offs which ended up in my wardrobe in the form of sweaters, skirts, mittens, bobble hats.

Mum hadn't learned to cook, but with the little money she had she did her best to conform to expectations. Our picnic on Speech Day was a random assortment of Frazzles, sausages, boiled eggs, and Kendal Mint Cake. Other picnic baskets groaned with curried eggs, coronation chicken, and flasks of chilled consommé. For me, my mum's picnic was always the best, regardless of its contents, but I recognised that it was different, that it lacked the wholesomeness of the others, the staple 'pot-stirring-Mum-by-the-Aga' ingredient.

Mum was willowy, with deep dark eyes like pools full of secrets. She had no notion of the impression she made on others, nor how heads would turn whenever she entered a room. She wore no make-up and had never worn nail varnish. But arriving for Speech Day she cut a striking figure, her long legs exposed in yellow hot-pants and knee-high boots, and her dark hair skimming the shoulders of a peacock-coloured shirt. Other mothers resembled the Queen, in headscarves, husky jackets, and flat shoes with buckles. My Dad, suntanned in a pink shirt and spotty blue tie, accompanied her to Speech Day in my first year there, and the other students' curiosity in me was piqued. As we walked around the grounds, I was aware of an ever-expanding escort of older girls – like the Pied Piper's rats – who up until then had never acknowledged me.

Dad had effortless film-star looks. As a small child, I skipped alongside him down Beauchamp Place, the discomfort of my woollen coat, patent shoes, and chapped lips making me feel shabby beside him. His metal toecaps clip-clopped and reverberated on pavement squares. As if bound for Africa, he dressed in khaki – subtle shades of tweed, clinched at the waist, a cap, spotted neckerchief, and pale 'farm trousers'. His straight back, square shoulders, and long stride suggested confidence. A young woman in white knee-high boots and a short coat gazed admiringly at him, and he raised his cap to her, flashing a smile, while she shuffled past with reddening cheeks.

After that first Speech Day I was aware that a sort of exoticism had rubbed off on me due to my parents' glamour and good looks, but I couldn't make up my mind if I should be proud or embarrassed. 'Being different' or the 'odd one out' was the pole around which my thoughts ceaselessly revolved.

Walking into the dining hall was the toughest moment of the day. Though I was neither bullied nor rebuffed, my reality was perceived through the lens of anticipated humiliation – the fear of making a fool of myself hounded my movement through the rowdy throng of girls. I fought against myself. Talk! my inner voice shouted. Be normal! Make eye contact! Talk! Be normal! Imagining myself to be invisible helped for as long as I could hold the fantasy.

Mum had always said, 'Nix, remember everyone's in the same boat. We're all worried that we are different, unpopular, or no good at something. It's human nature to be insecure and afraid of not being loved or good enough.' I understood that the comparison I drew between my inside personality and other people's outside personalities was not only speculative, but potentially way off the mark, because if Mum was right, then maybe their outside ones were just a show. Her advice was conciliatory and tailored to make me feel better. I had focused on it over half-term once, with the pleasing result of feeling a measure of empathy with my peer group. But as soon as I returned to school, I couldn't believe she was right. No one around me appeared to feel the slightest trace of fear. And I was paralysed by it. I tried to pretend otherwise, but my treacherous stomach gave me away.

Before food was even put on the table I was throwing up and, shamed by the vomit running through my fingers and the girls scattering in disgust, I ran as far as I could across the lawn to the fields. Decaying rabbits, stricken by myxomatosis, lay strewn across my path to the monkey puzzle tree.

With every two-footed jump on the hopscotch squares I told myself that it would never happen again. That soon I would be brave enough to talk – to open my mouth and have a few words escape. That maybe then I would have friends and would no longer be alone. One day, I would be fearless. Yes, fearless.

I vowed that once I turned nine all would be fine.

Inevitably, my fear of being sick induced further episodes. Eventually Miss Read, worried at how thin I was getting, had me eat lunch with her in her apartment every day. Lady Daring, always in her blue silk and sapphire, often sat with us there. With an expectant air she gazed through the branches of a crab apple tree at the church, as if waiting for someone to come out from its heavy oak door.

Chapter 12

Once I turned nine my view of school life did indeed brighten. I got a best friend and best marks for netball and tennis, art, English, drama, Latin, French and History. I scooped up cups at the end of each term – 'all-rounder' cups, handwriting, and deportment cups. I got pats on the back and unexpected attention. It was nice. My dad was proud of me and wrote lovingly in his letters. For once his mood seemed stable.

For some years by then I had been flying as an unaccompanied minor to Jersey, to stay with him. A flight there could never be guaranteed. Soupy fog hugged the island and often prevented us from landing as visibility was too poor. We were diverted to Guernsey, to plastic chairs in empty departure rooms for hours into the night. The first time it happened I was five. My fear of abandonment in that foreign airport precipitated uninterrupted bawling, which reduced to sniffles when my attention was drawn to the young woman sitting in the chair beside me. She was pretty, wore a maxi waistcoat of purple suede and square buckles on her shoes, and seemed to be asleep, which marked her out as being the only passenger who wasn't scowling at me. I couldn't take my eyes off her. Her head was tilted back, and her blonde hair fell like a curtain of silk threads. Behind her eyelids her eyeballs quivered, and the up and down of her breathing showed above her low-slung belt. Since she was so calm and silent, it was startling when intermittently she hissed a sort of 'Sssh', and more so when my volume ramped up a gear, and she quite suddenly took my hand in a vice-like grip. The cabin crew, at a loss to know how to deal with me, shunted us prematurely back onto the aeroplane, taking the risk to land in the fog, and she squeezed my hand even tighter. I winced. Was it because I'd scooped up two sherbet lemons from the air hostess's bowl? I knew I was only meant to take one. She squeezed it again. Then, as if there was a dream playing out behind her eyes, she smiled, and the word 'groovy' floated huskily from her mouth.

It was only when she found herself unexpectedly engulfed in my dad's mighty hug with his tears wetting her hair, that she let go of me.

'Darling girl!' His words between sobs of gratitude were barely audible. 'Little saint you are. Tsk... deserve a medal you do.'

She freed herself from him – shaken, I thought – and I noticed his eyes were red-rimmed and his hair dishevelled. I slipped my hand into his as a gesture of comfort to him.

Lingering long enough to watch her retreating back, he smoothed down his hair, replaced his cap and said,

'Strewth! Look at the time! Let's scarper! Been here for bloody hours, I have.' He picked me up, squeezing me so tight that I couldn't breathe, and kissed my chest noisily as I put my arms round his neck. 'Thought I'd lost you, my baby.' He muttered repeatedly under his breath as he walked to the car park.

Returning home to Mum was equally turbulent. Leading up to 'the dreaded day' of departure, Dad worked himself up into a state of agitation. Round the clock, tears streamed down his cheeks like rivers after rainfall, and soaked the back of my nightdress when he hugged me goodnight.

'What will I do without you, my little African child?' he snivelled, 'Don't go. Your poor old Dada needs you. Lost, he is, when you're not here.'

In between the chaotic to and fro, there were some hours spent together doing things that dads normally do with their children. We bicycled down narrow lanes lined with pink granite walls, ancient oaks, a palm tree or two, and steep verges. Daffodils burst to pop amongst drifts of snow-drops, and in the valleys giant ferns rose like prehistoric undergrowth from the banks of rushing streams. Spring quickened the wintery air, its dark light highlighting the wet grooves of ploughed fields. In front of me, Dad's anxious gesturing took my eye off the road, and I hit a rabbit hole, flying headlong over my bike and onto the tarmac. I was unconscious long enough for him to think me dead.

'Gawd! Bloody hell! I thought the Grim Reaper had paid a visit! My nerves are shot. No more bloody bicycles! Always hated them.'

He stuck with horses after that. For Dad, the seat of a horse felt infinitely safer even at thirty miles per hour.

When the tide was low, we would take Taxi to the beach, and while Dad galloped through the surf, I hurled myself into the wind – over the dunes and down the steep rocks where swathes of matted seaweed stretched for miles along the beach. It smelt faintly of rotting eggs, and Taxi dug his nose through the hovering sand flies. He tugged at a piece and, as if it were a bone, pulled it free and bounded off, dragging it behind him. I chased him until I caught the other end, and we whirled around in circles. Round and round and round until my breath was tangled with the wind, the salt, the spume, and I was a mere blink of the eye in the turning of the world, or a pinprick on the map of its rolling history. The weight of my worries ceased to exist. Clouds scudded across the sky and seagulls, like tossed bridal ribbons, circled me. I laughed and joined in with their raucous squawking. Through my open mouth the briny air filled me like a balloon, hoisting me up to join them. I was free. Weightless. Part of the universe. A grain of salt. A drop of water. A wisp of cloud. A star.

'What on earth are you doing, darling? Catch your death like that.' I was spread-eagled on the hard sand, Taxi's hot panting breath over my face and the dark cut-out of Dad astride his horse suddenly above me.

'Gotta shove off now. Mustn't wind Caro up by being late for lunch. Be back in the dog-house otherwise. *Dans la merde... dans la merde....*' He muttered.

On my summer holidays with them, Caro made picnics

for cousins and friends – lots of bread, pâté, cold meat, cheese and 'vino'. She pronounced it 'vano'. We found rocky inlets with steep inclines, and like a line of porters we heaved the baskets down to the half-moon shores, setting up camp on ship-wrecking rocks. Behind me Dad griped to himself.

'Oh, the beach. Always the bloody beach. So bossy. Always have to do her thing. Damned beach. Ugh!'

Caro, in a fuchsia towelling skirt and a bikini held to-gether with white plastic rings, laughed over her shoulder and called jovially, 'Oh *tais-toi chérie*! Moan, moan! *Comme tu m'énerve!*'

In a basin hollowed out at the foot of a rock face there was a deep pool of seawater filled by the tide. The only way in was to dive from a rocky ledge fifteen feet above. I would stand on it, looking down into what seemed like a bot-tomless sinkhole of slatey water, and target a spot between the snaking seaweed into which to dive. There was always that live-or-die question that flashed across my brain as I pushed off, first with my toes, ankles, knees and then hips. And as I arced through the air, Dad's voice carried: 'Gawd! Can't watch! What will her mother say if she smashes her head open? Aargh!'

A glass of vino cheered him up, and he clowned around, telling coarse jokes that made us fall about laughing. Where the waves washed up over the sand, he stood sometimes to watch me climb the stacks of rocks far out to sea or count-ed how many cartwheels I achieved whilst Taxi barked alongside me. My shape was muscular and strong, and he always remarked on it. 'Funny looking little thing you are! And such a toughie!' he would say, squeezing my arm affectionately. These were my snapshots of him as a hero. My attentive and entertaining dad. I clung to those moments, hoping to suspend them like a photograph, and fix them in the weave of his psychological tapestry so that he would never again transmute.

The threat of the 'School Report Drill', however, was the heavy cloud that darkened my time with him. When it finally arrived in the post, he would summon me to his study where I would be judged, and a sentence passed. By and large he was proud of my endeavours, and proud that the teachers were fond of me. Accordingly, his expectations were high, and on those grounds he dramatised the faults. Miss Harrison, a maths teacher, once referred to me as being 'a bit sulky', and his reprimands about that dragged on for days. Arrows of scorn rained down. Hugs were denied to me.

'No. Can't get around me like that.' He said, pulling his hand away from mine. 'I'm disappointed.'

'Sorry....' I grappled to apologise in the pause between his words. But he refused eye contact and continued to carp.

'It's just not good enough. Sulky! Tsk! Awful! Gotta brace up! Sulkiness is just not on. Now get a grip!'

Or he'd mutter repeatedly as he paced around the stable yard, 'A bit sulky!' 'A bit sulky! Tsk! How embarrassing! So un-feminine! Eurgh!'

Unable to bear his disapproval, I vowed to achieve top

marks in everything from then on in. I would also comply – conform – to whatever was expected of me – and would do so forever. In my mind, I signed a contract, between me and my higher self. The 'or else' clause in it – my potential failure – would, I convinced myself, result in the total and irreversible loss of him.

I rose before dawn to help him pick watercress. It grew in the stream that shot through the field like a dart before flowing under the hawthorn bushes. The air was thick and grey. It felt clammy on my tired, unwashed face and cold through my well-worn anorak. Dad wore gardening gloves and handed me bunches to pack tightly into crates. Hauling them back to the Land Rover, we tripped over moist tussocks of grass and fell into squelchy holes made by the horse's hooves. In through the split of my Wellington boot, cold, viscous mud oozed. It seeped through the wool of my sock and down between my toes, its globby texture like the custard at school. Don't complain, I'd tell myself. He hates that. Be cheerful. And smile! Moving in and out of the dark fog, Dad's silhouette, with cap and cinched waist, looked like a character from a Dickens novel, and I told him so.

'Not fucking Fagin, I hope darling?' He laughed at my fanciful comment. 'Hurry up! We'll get these to market before they open, then Yours Truly – effing Fagin – will let you drive. Back roads only. Avoid the goodie-goodie-two-shoes bobbies. Yes. Wretched police! Probably lurking behind hedges waiting to pounce.'

Learning to drive in his Land Rover was rewarding. I was ten when I started – just tall enough to reach the pedals.

All aspects of driving appealed to me, not just his pride in my ability: I liked the freedom and being in control of the car, its rough roll over uneven ground and the laborious manipulation of the spindly gear stick.

'Could have been in the Auxiliary Territorial Service darling! Good old Queen couldn't have done better!' He clapped my thigh and grinned. 'Chip off the old block you are!' With both hands planted around my head he kissed the top of it loudly.

A couple of years later, whilst visiting Kenya again, my Mum and I were driving to see friends for dinner. It was early evening in the middle of the bush. The sun had fallen from the sky and been replaced by blackness, lit weakly by the climbing moon and galaxy of stars. The dirt track was rough and we hit a pothole. A tyre burst. The creak of the rusty doors echoed in the still night. It cut rudely through the insect chorus, low rumblings of elephant, and cracking of wood as they moved across the plain. There were lights in the distance and with a faint torch we set off towards them. Fear caught in our throats; my mouth was so dry I couldn't speak. Mum's voice was low.

'Hold onto me! We'll be fine. Nix? You ok?'

Out of nowhere vicious barking shattered the night. Two male voices shot through the undergrowth – fast and breathless – and with them the flashing fire of their paraffin lamps.

'Night watch-men!' Mum whispered. 'Here. My hand!' She greeted them in Swahili. '*Jambo! Habari gani*? Our tyre. It's burst. Is there someone here who can help us? We're on our way to dine at Bwana Fielden's. I'm with my daughter.'

The lamplight steadied as they slowed down and spread out like fans around us. They murmured softly to one another while they circled us, and Mum chatted, looking for common ground. In the glow, the skin of their shoulders and cheekbones shone, and on the black earth it flickered with the shadows of moths. Once they were confident that we were no threat, they beckoned us with their lamps and their smiles flashed in and out of the light, like crescent moons between clouds. '*Njoo!*' They called.

The barking had briefly ceased only to start up again – louder and fiercer as we neared the house. I gripped Mum's shirt-tail and my heart beat so loudly I worried that I would pass out. Just as she moved to the gate, the pack of dogs leapt out at me and I ran – no, I flew – to a large, dark, and immobile shape: a tractor, which I climbed to the very top of. There was a house to the side of me, and in its lights I saw that the dogs were Dobermans and Alsatians. I saw the white flash of their teeth, their bloodshot eyes, and claws that scraped the metal – a noise that set my teeth on edge – as they sprang up towards me, then slid back down again. Screams of '*Bwana!*' and 'Nix!' were swallowed up in the commotion.

I had reached the highest point of the tractor. There was a cool metal bar under my bottom, over which I presumed went a shade, and where I gripped it the rough, dry sand of rust rubbed against my skin. There was nowhere higher to go, I kept thinking. Nothing left for me to do. Give up, I told myself. Surrender.

Then a sheet of blackness dropped behind my eyes, and

I felt myself separating from the din as if in slow motion. My breathing seemed to stop, and reality became distant and muffled.

My mum's impatient voice tuned me back in. 'Oh, darling, do get down. Come on! How many more times do you need me to tell you they've gone? Nix! Do you hear me? Get on now! We're already so late.'

The owner of the house accompanied us back to the car with a couple of new tyres under his arm. In the light of paraffin lamps, he showed me how to change our dud one. 'You'll have a burst tyre every day on these roads. Better learn now how to change them.' He clipped me on the cheek with his rough hand. 'Easy when you know. Here's a spare for good measure.'

The next morning, we hit another pothole and burst another tyre.

On our return to England, I telephoned Dad and relayed my experience. The part of the story that he begged me to repeat was of me changing the tyre. For months afterwards he would say, 'Just one more time. Please. Oh, don't be a spoilsport. Make your Dad proud. Go on.'

Aiming to please my father brought the added bonus of pleasing my teachers. Paradoxically, though, I regarded each cup and accolade I won as just another stroke of luck; that it wasn't that I merited it, but that those awarding the honour had suffered a lapse of judgement. They had a soft spot for me after all; were touched by how hard I tried to conceal my inadequacy.

That wouldn't last. Couldn't last. It was just a matter of

time. I wouldn't be able to dupe them forever. Sooner or later I would be discovered and seen for what I was: a fake.

Chapter 13

Catastrophic thinking was a trait shared by both my parents in equal measures but applied in different ways. My mum's was directed towards me, and it stemmed from her maternal protectiveness: 'If you go down to the woods today, you're sure of a big surprise…' The 'surprise' shifted from calamity and disappointment to abject failure. The underlying message was clear: disaster lurks around every corner. As a young girl she had lived through the Mau-Mau Uprising in Kenya, and was then sent away to an English boarding school and didn't see her parents properly again for several years. I can only presume that those traumatic events scarred her psychologically and shaped within her an abiding unease and chariness towards life in general.

Dad's sense of catastrophe was applied to himself. 'They' – the men in white coats, the Grim Reaper, or the enemy – were all out to get him, and expectation of their presence coloured his outlook. In his mind his role switched between being a victim of them and hero against them, and for psychological comfort, he attached the presence of guardian angels to counteract his suspicions. *Mungu* (the Swahili word for God) was one of them, and more often than not I was another. Other people would be selected, depending on where he was, geographically or psychologically, or from where the most sympathy for him was coming.

As a sensitive and nervous seven-year-old, he had been sent away to boarding school and was bullied there. It was the harsh era of beatings, power games, and predatory behaviour – often of a sexual sort. He went missing once, for three days, and was eventually found cowering in a cupboard under the stairs into which he had been locked by his tormentors. His father told me how, after his beloved nanny died, he would scrape his hands over the gravel until the bleeding wounds were filled with shards of stone. Then under the spectre of war, to avoid capture by German soldiers, he would run up and down the stairs at night whistling the German National Anthem – a demonstration that, he believed, would make them think he was on their side.

He had a tendency to live life in retrospect, heroizing himself or others from days gone by. I got the impression that as a soldier he had dazzled. It was long before the drinking got hold of him, and his sharp sense of duty, responsibility and personal courage were given their finest hour. He talked little of his war experiences – it just wasn't done to do so – but he threw into a conversation once, the rescue of 'all his soldiers' from a burning boat during the Korean war; a war that by all accounts had been as bloody as any before. His devotion to his military unit blazed mistily in his eyes as he heroized them: 'Wasn't my trumpet to blow, darling– it was their duty and loyalty that got us all to safety.'

I wish I could have known that dad, who'd had a strong purpose and pride in what he did, because once he had met my mum and gone to East Africa, he wove a new set of glories. Being a rancher – breeding cattle – was humdrum compared to war, although he was still, in a sense, in command of a 'unit'. But with his dashing looks and bawdy sense of humour, he fell readily into the warm embrace of the busy social scene there, whilst his horsemanship and shooting skills complemented the long camping safaris into the bush. He shone in that small circle; a little too brightly for a married man. He gained a wealth of kudos from the attentions of other women, which he wore like a badge for the rest of his life. In the wake of my mother leaving him, the catastrophe of abandonment *and* its perpetrators, materialised again. His drinking habit escalated, and effortlessly so in a hedonistic culture of ever-flowing sundowners.

In the present reality, his fears had no substance other than their memory. But his belief in them was real, and it convinced me. The Grim Reaper and men in white coats were his ever-constant adversaries in a power struggle waged around his drinking habits. It was a win or lose, live or die game, and with his increasing age the odds were stacked against him. These characters littered his conversation, usually triggering another glass of whisky.

The enemy lurked at home, and anywhere else he chose,

which again depended on my dad's mood, and who at the time was in or out of his favour. My mum was a constant enemy who, as a result of having abandoned him, was responsible for all other grief – imagined and unimagined. Her desertion pushed the buttons of his childhood abandonments and caused the repeated return to babyish outbursts.

On good days he used this default setting as part of his shtick, turning his eye for the absurd onto himself. On bad days, however, If Caro had hidden his whisky, she would fall under his accusatory stare. And if I, at such moments, shared an unrelated giggle with her, he would lump me into the same camp. If he had received a shock bank statement, it was the bank manager who was out to get him; and even the postman, nervous of leaving his van because of Taxi's bark, was construed as 'shifty' or 'up to no good'.

His world was full of enemies; they circled like vultures. No one should be trusted. Even a pretty hitchhiker was regarded with potential suspicion, convinced as he was of the likelihood of being conned by one. He thought that, to lure 'old fools' like himself, a filthy youth with a knife would plant himself at the side of the road, disguised as a ravishing blonde in wig and lipstick.

We would be driving to the garage with a defunct lawn mower in the back of the Land Rover when he would spot a girl on the verge.

'Give the hands a once over darling.' He would say, swerving to pull over. 'Then tap my shoulder – twice if they're a girl's, once if they're a man's. You can always tell by the hands. Got it?' He came to an abrupt stop, and leant across me with his tanned arm outstretched, his chin down and eyes upturned so that the horizontal wrinkles on his brow deepened. 'Hop up!' He'd call to her. 'Where are you off to?'

My heart raced.

As she opened the door to step in, he patted my thigh urgently, gesturing me to make room for her. 'Quick, quick!' He said under his breath, excitement for a pretty girl quashing his fear for a filthy youth.

I swung myself into the back, swivelling my head to check the hands. While Dad launched into jocular playfulness, I worried about him being mugged at knifepoint, and kept a vigilant eye on any slight movement of her body; always unsure how many times to tap him. Once he started winking at me in the rear-view mirror, I knew we were out of the woods. His apprehension was gone, and he was relishing the ritual of flaunting his self-deprecating charm.

The banter he enjoyed with the hitchhiker would boost his ego and mood for the next few days. Then it would wear off amidst tears of self-pity, as he remembered all his other lost flirtations, jammed up like traffic behind him.

Flirtations, in Dad's eyes, tended to be dramatised into all-out romantic novels with him as the central hero, but when I was young, I hadn't yet learned that.

He would drop his head onto my lap, sniffling while he confided in me.

'Did you see how Leonora looked at me at lunch the other day darling? The hurt in those big blue eyes of hers?' Or, another time, 'She's always loved me, Birdie has... says I'm the one for her. Says she'd leave Bill tomorrow... if only I would...'

He rubbed his eyes.

'It's ok my Dad. It's ok.' I would tell him, brushing away his tears. 'All is well.'

***

Since before I could talk, I viewed Dad as a God. First and foremost, he was shiny, golden and glorious, with a heart as soft as butter, but in the wake of his absence, his shine shone brighter. Like a hunter I chased him, seizing any snatched moment that I could catch. But, for all his glory, I recognised that the magnetic needle of his moral compass wavered from east to west – often dependent on the time of day. At the start, its intended direction was principled and kindly, but sometimes by mid-afternoon it was juddering – loose and blurred – towards disintegration.

It was mainly after lunch that his ethics jarred with mine. When that happened, it tore me in half because opposing him gave me an uncomfortable sense of betrayal. On the one hand I knew it wasn't proper to be disloyal, even if it was just flirting, and that I should be ticking him off in support of Caro. I loved her too, and didn't want her to be unhappy either.

On the other hand, moments together with him were rare, and precious, and I felt like I belonged to him again. What's more, being part of his grown-up conspiracy also made me proud. Felt like a badge of honour.

Besides those things, sticking with him and backing him up were the essential ingredients in the 'Be Happy and Pretend that Everything's Fine' recipe; my coping formula for our mutual benefit. After all, upsetting Dad could result in me being cast away forever; thus, my tiptoeing around him was crucial.

In any case, I reassured myself, they were very affectionate with each other, Caro and Dad. While he made his fry-ups, they would enjoy touchy-feely hugs, often loaded with overt innuendos. Blushing, I would rush from the kitchen with an excuse and count to a hundred before going back in again. Often before a drinks party, I would lie on their bed watching Caro make herself up, backcomb her hair and spray it. Before taking his bath, Dad would come in – in boxer shorts – and start on about 'rumpy-pumpy' and 'not having had enough of it recently'. He would fondle her and make grunting noises, while she'd laugh, and mutter 'Ssssh, *mon chéri! Pas devant les enfants!*' She'd pull up the shoulder of her pink bathrobe and curl her neck like a swan so that he could kiss it. And I would pick the thread from the quilting and concentrate my gaze so fiercely as to imagine myself subsumed by its leaf-green circles.

In relation to his marriage I was confused. They appeared to love each other passionately in the mornings, a little bit less at lunch-time, and hardly at all by the evenings. More confusing for me than any of that, was that in some scenarios I was my dad's confidante against Caro, and in others, not only was I ignored, but humiliated.

The relationship he had with animals, on the other hand,

was his solace, and he enjoyed a connection with them unlike any he had with any human being. Rounding the corner of the stable yard I'd hear big smacking kisses and he'd be there, astride his horse, bent forward along its back, with his arms around its neck as if he was part of it. He was Steward of the Race Course on the island for a time, and he accepted the job as personal defender of horses. If a jockey fell during a race Dad would march to and fro on the side-lines, growling 'Bloody fool! Rein was too damn short! Poor, dear horse! Only trying her best.' Similarly, when he feared the local authority would ban dogs from public places on account of their appeal for pooper scooping, he retaliated in their defence, switching the attack onto humans, as was always his wont. 'What about the tourists who foul our town? Chewing gum is small beer compared to the human vomit and urine that smear our streets, particularly on Monday mornings. It's them you should be picking on, not the nice dogs.'

His animals pardoned his mood swings and loved him, no matter what. Always faithful. Always there. Always looking out for him. It was the love of a pet that my Dad sought in me.

I was just six when I first remember recognising what was required of me. His head dropped onto my lap, and his tears wet the skirt of my smocked dress. I stroked them away, leaving muddy streaks round his eyes, and thrust my legs upwards to rock the swinging seat. I scratched at the dried bird poop stuck on the green stripes.

I'd been in the flower border a little while before,

watching fairies, when I had heard his footsteps on the gravel the other side of the gate.

Just as elephants sense danger from miles away, I sensed my dad's state of mind long before I caught sight of him. It was as if his steady flow of feeling saturated me through some invisible current, and I found it hard to know where I ended and he began. I was like a circle with no perimeter; a person with no skin; a house without a door. It had always been like that. What he felt, I felt. How he saw, I saw. I carried him inside me, fusing with him, or him with me. I never had the mental dexterity to construct a border between us and as such, I mopped up his moods as my own. Due to their potency, I prioritised them until I was oblivious to my own feelings, or the fact that I even had any. My antennae, tuned to pick up his every wobble, had the prescience to anticipate any external stimulus that might provoke it, and when I wasn't able to thwart that, I learned to absorb the resulting chaos. I would suck it up to scoop *him* up.

My propensity to empathise to the point of losing myself was applied to everyone, to greater or lesser degrees, depending on their importance to me. I always had the sensation that I was wide open, tuning into the woes of mankind, as if electromagnetic waves rolled out from my heart. So, in family situations I found myself switching from one person to the other, each of their hurts becoming mine, whilst my own were lost in the chaos of theirs.

As the garden gate creaked open, the melancholia seeping from him zipped a thread of tension down my spine. It was late afternoon, which seemed always to be his most maudlin hour. I ran to him, forced a smile, and hugged his leg. His tears were not far away; I knew that they would spill over any minute.

I had to divert them. I had to distract him from himself, to turn his attention to cheerful things.

'Daddy, come see my fairies!' His straight back began to crumple like a paper bag. 'No. Dad. Come on! No crying! They're so pretty! They've got foxglove skirts and poppy petal capes – come, they'll cheer you up!'

But it was of no use. His dam quickly burst. He pulled me down with him onto the swinging seat. Tears poured down his face and he cupped my head, his hands trembling.

'Why did your mother leave me? All alone? Why, my baby? Why did she do that? Why? Why?'

Oh, Dad. Did you feel that each successive echo would release the torment stitched into your words?

His breathing became less inhibited, more childlike, so that he found it hard to catch his breath. I stroked away his tears and scrunched my eyes tight to cloud my hearing against what was to follow.

'Off she went. Just like that.' He waved his hand. 'Was left with nothing. Nothing. My only ally was… yes… was the barrel of my shotgun. Oh, baby – all I could do was look down its end day after day, night after night.'

I kissed the creases of his tanned temples.

'I'll look after you my Daddy. It's ok. No matter what, I'll look after you. Forever and ever. Don't worry.'

And before it's too late, I thought.

I prayed that talk of the gun might finally blow away.

The wretched moment of him being left by Mum was also indelibly printed on my mind, although if what I remember was his version or the original, I don't now know. From the back seat of the Land Rover, I turned around to see his khaki-clad figure at the gate, gun slung over his shoulder and Boo, our Doberman, at his side. Mum drove fast so that clouds of red African dirt blew up around them in angry gusts. As it settled, I caught a glimpse of his twisted features, wet with tears. Boo licked his hand and they moved off towards the stables just as we drove behind the burnt rocky clusters of the kopje. It was like a prehistoric giant slumbering on the plain, and its enormous bulk blocked my last view of home.

The swinging seat rocked a bit. My fingers interlocked with his. I closed my eyes against the glint of the late afternoon sun as it dipped below the awning. His face was slack on my lap.

'My best baby,' I heard him whisper. 'You'd go to the far corners of the earth for me, I know that. My little soldier.'

I watched the evening shadows elongate across the lawn through the boughs of the cherry tree and wondered what sort of bird it was cheeping noisily like that.

Caro was pregnant, in wafting smock dresses, some months away from giving birth.

'Dad, think how exciting it will be when Caro has the little baby. Come on, I will give you three guesses what it will be. Boy? Girl? You never know Dada, it might even be a pixie! Dad? Come on... smile!

Chapter 14

'Love conquers all' were the vicar's words. His stern eyes bore down on me as if I were guilty of something. Mum collaborated with him by digging me in the spine, and hissed from the corner of her mouth 'Stop fidgeting!' So I tried to tune in to his sermon, but it sounded like magic spells – Hubble... bubble... hubble... bubble. I imagined steam like a mushroom cloud bursting from the pulpit, and just as his arms swung upwards a clap of thunder, and a frog or two. I caught sight of the patchy bristles on the underside of his chin before he gazed at me again and drummed his fingers on the embroidered crucifix of his robe. Silence hung in the air. Minutes passed, I shuffled my feet, twirled my hair, and my attention strayed to his eyebrows. They were long-haired, and fell onto his eyelids even when arched, and I wondered why on earth he didn't cut them. I hoped mine wouldn't get like that. I already had visions of them growing into one, like a fat caterpillar across my eyes.

'Love conquers all,' he pronounced a second time, with

long pauses between each word, as if he was passing a decree. He accentuated the 'all' as if it were an ultimatum.

That time round, the words seemed to jump out of the cauldron and hit me like a thunderbolt. 'Love conquers all.' It echoed around my head, filling it, and I felt something of significance happen inside me – an understanding, or a knowing that my world suddenly made sense. Had he delivered my battle cry? Would it spur me into combat, and act as an anchor to return to time and time again?

Spreading his hands in a gesture of supplication, he nodded his head as he stated: 'By this we know love that he laid down his life for us...'

Mum nodded in unison.

'Put others before yourself, Nix! No matter what,' she always told me. She was famous for doing so. Friends and relations always referred to her as 'a saint', often with teary eyes, to demonstrate how much her selflessness touched them. She was a good Christian, my mum: altruistic, generous, humble. She was admired for it, adored even. In my eyes she was an angel; a hard act to follow. She came from a culture where the ego was silenced. 'Me Me Me' was considered showy-offy, vulgar, 'not done'. She clung to values, virtue, grace – spelled out early on in nursery rhymes like, 'Patience is a virtue, virtue is a grace, and Grace is a little girl who wouldn't wash her face'. Being anything less than virtuous I took as being bad. Terrible in fact.

I was the heir to her heritage. I made another vow with myself: I would put Dad before myself, no matter what. My love for him would conquer all his fears.

The Big Bad Wolf

1976

Chapter 15

In the summer of 1976 I left prep school. I was twelve. Before the term had finished, a record-breaking drought was affecting the whole country and would last until the end of August. The sun shone and shone, drying up rivers and cracking the earth. Tinder-dry fields burned, fanned by strong winds. Water supplies petered out and restriction notices were put up everywhere. We placed bricks in our loos to reduce the flush, and our lawn, which turned a weak tea colour, felt prickly underfoot. Sometimes Mum would take me to Cromer where the North Sea breeze and wide beach rescued us from the sweltering inland heat and oven of her car. There were rock pools, crab nets, fishing boats, the amusement arcade on the pier, and elderly men in string vests and knotted handkerchiefs on their heads. I dived through the cool grey water and afterwards ate fish and chips wrapped in newspaper, and Mr Whippy ice creams with chocolate flakes.

It was too hot to do anything except play Swing Ball in

the darkest patch of our walled garden, which was shaded by the generous beech tree growing in the cemetery next door. I sucked tangy orange ice cubes made from Rise & Shine powder and hit the ball for hours until my hand was too sweaty to grip the bat, and the metal ring of the ball was red-hot.

My interest in being a poet and painstakingly hitting the keys of a typewriter, had waned somewhat, and my rug and candle making kits had been replaced by David Niven's book *The Moon's a Balloon*. I read and re-read the naughty bits in it, and to stop it falling open at those pages if Mum were to pick it up I weighted the book down with my flower press. A poster of Donny Osmond, my previous pin-up, was used now as a dartboard in my playroom, and Paul Michael Glaser took his place above my bed. On my record player I played singles over and over again. Brotherhood of Man's 'Save Your Kisses for Me', 'Don't go breaking my heart' by Elton John and Kiki Dee, and Dr Hook's 'A Little Bit More'. The world they sang about was unknown to me then, but the music and lyrics seemed to reach into my heart, kindling mysterious yearnings.

In front of the mirror I yanked my hair, hoping to lengthen it. It was chestnut, so the hair-cutter had told me, and streaked by the sun. 'Beach hair,' she'd added, and showed me pictures of Californian girls with blonde streaks. But to *my* eyes, there was no comparison. Mine looked like streaky bacon. I'd glanced over at the row of ladies under the hooded hair dryers, some of whom were having blue rinses, and I knew I'd rather mine be bacon-coloured than blue. I tried on Mum's bikini with the pointed bra cups, and her corduroy flares with flower-print wide-collared shirts, worn unbuttoned as low as she dared. She was so pretty she could have been one of Charlie's Angels. I wondered if I could ever get close to looking like them. I stood on tiptoe in my denim clogs, stuffed socks down my t-shirt and strips of white paper over the gap in my teeth. I painted my lips with gloss from Woolworths and tried to smile like Jaclyn Smith. I tried shimmery eye shadow around my dark eyes and then mascara. 'Spider eyes' they were called by the girls at school, because of their double layer of lashes. 'Eeugh! Look how they grow, even in the corners!' they would say as they breathed in my face. I rubbed foundation all over my face with an extra thick layer between my eyebrows to conceal the growth there, but it made me look like a corpse. So I 'rouged' my cheeks and wrapped a long yellow scarf around my forehead. I posed like a model, my right hip out, my left knee forward. I tilted my head to the side and swivelled my gaze towards the mirror. I imagined a photographer in the corner saying 'Look over here! Smile! Yeah… beautiful! Now give me coquettish, darling! Give it to me… Yes!' Flash! went his bulb.

But no… I just looked silly. I sank back onto my bed and squeezed my old teddy bear. I was never going to make the grade. Never. With my hand towel I scraped off the make-up, streaking it apricot-pink, and pulled off the scarf. I wasn't pretty enough, tall enough, slim enough, feminine enough. My dad was right. I was 'a funny-looking little thing.' Yes, that's what I was.

A hunger to be part of my culture and to have a social life did, however, begin to eclipse my feelings of inadequacy. The magnetic draw of music enticed me out of my shell. Made me want to be part of the world. Its conveying of the human condition seemed to be like a universal language and through it mankind drew together like a tribe, whose gods were its celebrities and stars.

Showaddywaddy's 'Under the Moon of Love' was playing from the barn when my Mum dropped me at my first disco. She wound down her window as I hesitated outside the car and whispered, 'Nix. There'll be sex'n'drugs in there. Are you sure you want to go? Remember what I've told you, won't you? Be careful. Ok?'

She waited until I'd struggled across the muddy field in the dark, and when I turned around to wave, she called out, 'You can come back home with me if you want. You don't have to go in…'

'Mum shush' I hissed, and waved her away.

I was wearing a brown floral maxi skirt and white cheesecloth shirt. I searched for a face I might know and tried to get my mouth to open to let a word out, smile even. Come on, I said to myself. I must have things to talk about. Surely? I wracked my brain but there was nothing but blackness in there. Come on. Come on. God. How could I be so useless?

A fuzzy feeling of shame descended on me and pricked my eyes. I felt hot and trapped.

Then out of nowhere a flash of inspiration shot through my mind like a comet. I had just been to the Wimbledon final. That was something to talk about, wasn't it? Borg, my hero, had won against Connors. Everyone loved Borg. Well, that must be a good enough opening shot for a conversation, I thought.

But even with the words lined up and ready, I still couldn't open my mouth to release them.

Girls and boys with glasses of punch bounced up and down to songs like 'Tiger Feet' and 'I Love to Boogie', then to 'Hotel California' they huddled up close like a flock of sheep. I loved that song. In fact, I loved everything Californian. It made me dream of flowers in my hair, drive-ins and Clint Eastwood. Names like San Jose, Napa Valley, Venice Beach conjured up sunshine, golden tans and free love.

I sat on a hay bale in the corner where there was least light and tried to forget myself in the music. A blade of straw pricked the cotton of my skirt and felt like a thorn. I pretended to look unbothered to be alone, and when feeling someone's eyes on me I fiddled with my hem or picked my fingernails. After a few tracks the DJ's voice rose above the Bee Gees' with the surprise announcement of a beauty competition. Immediately boys rushed amongst the crowd, eyeing up girls and making them pirouette to check out their backsides. They jumped up and down with their arms in the air when they'd found a likely one, calling 'Here, here! Here's one! She'll do!' and slapped her bottom. I shifted mine further into the shadows to avoid scrutiny.

But from behind me a boy said, 'Hey, Guy wants to see you.' He yanked my elbow and pulled me off the hay bale.

Guy?

God.

He looked scary, grown-up almost.

I thought immediately of my mum. I wanted her.

The boy led me to the back of the barn, through a curtain into a darkened cubicle. Outlines of bodies writhed on the floor, leaving no space for my feet. I turned to leave but his hand on my back pushed me forward. Stumbling over some legs, my hands landed on moving body parts that felt like slithering snakes. I tried to get up but the legs kicked at me, and an irritated groan came from the top end. I was pulled back up, swivelled round, then shoved back down again. Guy was slumped in the corner, propped up on a beanbag, his floral shirt shredded and his eyes dazed. He was nursing a bleeding shoulder – 'Motorbike crash,' he slurred – and his stale smoky breath hit my face.

'Sex'n'drugs, sex'n'drugs' rang in my ears.

I held my breath.

If I didn't breathe, this wasn't happening.

'What the hell!… How old are you, for God's sake?' Guy erupted, looking down my shirt in disbelief.

The DJ's voice next door dropped suggestively. 'Now for some smooching, boys and girls… here's David Soul… come on now… 'Don't give up on us baby'…'

'S-sixteen,' I lied.

He shoved his tongue into my mouth and his hand over my chest.

Hold your breath! I told myself.

I pictured my bedroom – its dark wood panelling, my basin behind the secret door.

Hold your breath!

I heard the tap running as Mum brushed her teeth, then the click of her light.

Hold your breath!

I felt her hair on my face as she kissed me goodnight.

Hold your breath!

She cleared her throat. Two little coughs.

Hold your breath!

But then I couldn't any longer.

I had to breathe.

God. I wished he would stop.

I hated his foul-tasting mouth, the smell of beer on his skin and his sweaty armpits. I hated his hand on my bottom… how he pressed me into his pelvis, which felt so hard. I hated his heavy breath on my face and how he edged my hand onto his crotch. I hated his groans. I hated my tears. I hated the arguments inside my head, and particularly the louder one screaming, 'Stop being pathetic! Come on… If you want to be liked…'

Suddenly I heard a familiar voice the other side of the curtain.

'Bit early, I'm afraid. I've come to collect Nix. Have you seen her?'

My mum!

'Oh! That's my mum outside!' I faked disappointment and struggled to get free.

'Oh bollocks. Your mother? Tsk. What a cock-up!' Guy rolled his eyes and pushed me off him in disgust.

On the way home, I howled like a feral animal.

'What will become of me Mumma? He kissed me!'

I had committed a sin. Tarnished forever. I was a bitter disappointment. To Mum, to God, to myself. *And* to Guy.

'I'm sorry, Mumma. So, so sorry.' I snivelled.

My lost virtue was clearly not as pressing, in comparison to her other concern.

'But drugs, Nix? Did you take drugs?'

Chapter 16

Despite that first defeat, a growing chorus encouraging me to break free from myself bubbled up from the skittish atmosphere of my self-imposed prison, its fizz tempting yet daunting. It was a cry for confidence, for poise, and for outward looking sight. All of a sudden I wanted life. I wanted friends. I wanted to plunge into the world I had shut out, and strip off every adventure and opportunity it had on offer. I wanted to be reeled and tossed and hurled into romance, so that my heart would burst with its pounding heat. I wanted to sing and dance until I keeled over, euphoric with being alive. I wanted to say 'Yes!' when in the past I had said 'No'. I wanted new ideas, new cultures, and new horizons. I wanted to finally feel free. Although the path to get there was still vague, I had an inkling of its direction.

Joan Collins was a big star at the time, and her film *The Stud* had recently been released. She was beautiful, glamorous and seemed to hum with self-assurance. What if, I wondered, I had an on/off switch inside me and its 'on' function was *being* Joan Collins? I could turn her on as I needed illuminating, and off again when I got home. Wouldn't that be nice? Yes. I will be Joan Collins, I thought to myself. I will act her, and act her, and act her. Until I *am* her.

I studied her mannerisms, the way she threw her head back when she laughed, her hair bouncing over her shoulders. I studied how radiant she was. How physical she was. How powerfully feminine she dared to be. How comfortable in her own skin she seemed, whether she was in a strappy-topped dress, nipple baring t-shirt, white trouser suit with plunging neckline, or even naked. I studied how generous with affection she was. Pictures showed her hugging other 'beautiful people' and flashing her glossy, open-mouthed smile and dark, wide-apart eyes. Wow, she really knew how to use her eyes! With a single bat of them she suggested sweetness, coyness, and 'I'm all yours' sexiness. It was an art form.

Yes. I would reinvent myself. As Joan Collins.

I was invited to a party in London and plucked up the courage to go. I insisted that Mum stop blocks away but she wanted to drive me to the door.

'But darling, you're wearing heels. It's dark. What if….'

'No Mum! No! You have to stick to my plan.'

I too had to stick to my plan. I was to arrive alone like a grown-up. I was to concentrate not only on my Joan Collins performance *but*, I had decided, on the other people there. I figured that if my Mum had been right all along, that if everyone was in the same boat – frightened of being different or not being liked, I would concentrate primarily on putting *them* at ease. Getting outside of myself would be, I reckoned, a helpful trick to deflect my attention away from myself. Joan Collins would help me do it. Her largesse would be catching.

Kensington Market was a treasure trove, but a ramshackle, grubby and edgy one. To shop there was a rite of passage. Its subculture was intimidating, and its eclecticism bewildering until your eye was in. Choked with cannabis smoke and incense, the rabbit warren of stalls wound on and on – a melting pot of bohemia, punk, tattoo art, vintage, and fetishism – a melting pot of race and cultures. I had tried on lurex flares, PVC leggings, satin hot-pants and footless tights, jester suits and string vests. In the end I'd opted for a blue silky cat-suit with a strappy top. My stilettos were original fifties, knife pointed toes of gold lace that I had found in Flip on the King's Road.

I pushed open the shiny door in Kensington Square, and *Rat Trap* pounded over the din of chinking glass and chat. My mouth was dry from nerves. I wished that I had used Mum's make-up to create angles in my round cheeks. Other girls wore frosty lipstick, mascara, blue eyeliner. I felt unsophisticated in comparison. Lame.

But I couldn't let myself sink. I had a plan.

My hair wasn't quite long enough, but nevertheless flicked when I tossed it. My lips weren't glossy but could stretch to a big smile. I learned quickly that touching an elbow here and a shoulder there made me likeable and seemed also to put others at ease. Throwing my head back when I laughed gave me the air of confidence. The more I faked it as Joan Collins, the more I freed myself of inhibitions.

Disco strobes flashed across the dance floor at a frenetic pace. Gloria Gaynor pelted out 'I Will Survive'. A boy grabbed my hand and led me to dance. He wore tight pink jeans with an angelic face. His name was Maximilian. Max had gentle features; his blue eyes were framed with long lashes, and he danced with a rhythmic power I hadn't seen before. Beams of light burst through him and over him, and his teeth blazed fluorescent white. The music filled my head, grabbed my soul, and my hips moved instinctively as if I was a part of its beat.

Shouting elementary questions to each other we shrugged and laughed, trying to lip-read. He swung me to him and whirled me round, every one of his muscles it seemed, moving like the instruments themselves. 'Night Fever', 'Do Ya Think I'm Sexy?', 'Heart of Glass'… we danced and danced. We danced the whole night. I neither drank nor ate nor paused to catch breath. I danced as if my life depended on it.

My habit of self-imposed entrapment was undone momentarily. I caught the glimpse I needed to catch. The glimpse of who I might be. Being Joan Collins was the road forward.

'Nights in White Satin' slowed us down. Max pulled me close to him, hesitant and questioning. Against mine, his body felt right. He kissed me shyly on the mouth, his hands around my face, and not until the early hours of the morning did I let him slip his tongue between my lips.

He became my first real boyfriend. I lost my virginity to him and loved him unreservedly. We made love in his parent's bed, high in the trees of Lennox Gardens, and afterwards guzzled bowls of sugary Alpen and double cream. It was delicious but sinful. I was just sixteen. Just legal. However, sex before an engagement or marriage carried the scent of sin in my mother's family. She had missed out on the sixties' seismic love movement by living abroad, and still clung to safe, puritanical views. Although *The Sun's* page three girls were bursting out across British breakfasts, and *The Joy of Sex* nestled proudly on the shelves of the avant-garde, sex before marriage was something that wasn't 'done', and certainly not discussed by Mum in any format. There'd been village rumours of a woman called Betty who had been 'living in sin', and whose entrance into the fish and chip shop had brought deathly silence to the normal bustling atmosphere – like the moment when a director shouts 'Cut!'

The shame of pregnancy was such an odious spectre that after sex I would often practice a medieval old wives' tale of lying in a scalding bath and swigging neat vodka to kill any potentially fertilized egg. The vodka made me gag, but shame squashed any thought of visiting my doctor, and buying condoms was then as uncomfortable as using them. But quitting my burning love for Max and his illicit appeal was out of the question. So we continued our love-making, on a wing and a prayer, and vodka and boiling baths. But the guilt I was feeling about it all dribbled into my consciousness like sweat down my brow, until one afternoon I plucked up the courage to confess it to Mum. I picked at the tapestry thread of a cushion, and tears of disgrace cracked my voice. Over it, Mum's whisper was faint 'You're not pregnant, are you? Tell me you're not?'

Still at boarding school, Max and I wrote letters to each other over the course of a year. We yearned self-consciously for the next time we would meet, but in the end there was too much time between each reunion to sustain us.

Chapter 17

I was twelve when I started at public school. I hated it there
and, with the exception of lacrosse and tennis, found the
teaching numbing. I had a photographic memory, making
it possible for me to visualise reams of history books and re-
write them verbatim. In all wordy exams my results hovered
around the top three, though Maths remained an anathema.
Generally, I was considered a top student. My dad ruffled his
feathers proudly and boasted about my achievements.

'My best baby!' he'd say with a heavy-handed pat and a
soppy expression.

He had two children with Caro by then, Kate and
Dickie. There was seven years between me and Kate, and
ten between me and Dickie. I loved them to bits and the
experience of being a member of a family, even as a part
time player, was still so new that it thrilled me. My title of
half-sister felt prestigious, and although there was always a
nanny on hand, my role as childminder was one of which I
was eminently proud.

Then Kate fell on some rocks I was leading her across and cut her head so badly that Caro rushed her off to hospital. I fled to the other end of the beach, with Caro's anguish echoing in my ears. '*Ah mon coeur! Mon coeur! Ça va, ça va. Tout va bien!*'

I hoped to be spirited away by the tide, the gulls, the sea urchins, or even another family so that I wouldn't have to face the sharp stab of blame twisting in my gut, and I hid in the hollow of a stack of rocks, praying repeatedly to God to make her better. Time passed without me noticing until the air was cool, the sun was hovering above the horizon, and the tide was fast approaching. I ran back, past a couple of stragglers shaking out towels and pulling on terry towelling tops. And when I got to our picnic spot, it was deserted, everything cleared away.

This is it. Really it. This time, they've gone for good. But, I am twelve now. I can manage. All is well.

I scanned the sand, the rocks, the cliffs above, but there was no one. A movement at the top of the steps caught my eye. I recognised it immediately as the nanny's blue sunhat, and I bounded towards it at lightning speed. Just as I got to the top, one of our cars was pulling away, and the other was still being loaded up.

'Oh, look! It's you, darling!' Dad sounded surprised at my being there, but squeezed my cheek as I opened the back door. 'Thank Heavens, we're off! Got bloody sand everywhere.'

With three children, he got confused with his 'my best baby' accolade. We all did. One minute I had the prize, the next minute Kate had it, and the next Dickie. Whilst one of us was smothered in his embrace and told they were his best, the other two had to pretend that they were fine with that. Not hurt. No. Not hurt at all. In his arms, pressed in the smell of stale smoke and horse, I winced at the discomfort of knowing how it felt for them.

Because his devotion to beauty was inflexible and looking pretty a prerequisite for any woman being loveable, the tribute was given to us girls generally in accordance with our appearance and behaviour, and to Dickie when he had 'stepped up to the plate' to accomplish some onerous duty or achievement. Dad played us off against each other unwittingly, and in the end, I understood that 'the best baby' award was more to do with his own need to be loved by the one he deemed as hero in that instant. A sort of reflected glory for him.

***

My Mum remarried when I was fifteen. I'd first met Tom when I was a bridesmaid at a cousin's wedding, two years earlier. I had worn a Laura Ashley dress and daisies around my neck. During the course of the afternoon I discovered that young teenage bridesmaids were alluring to old men after a few glasses of champagne. I was stuck with one who was promising to call me in five years' time to teach me 'the ways of the world.' He winked at me over the rim of his glass, lifting my hair to kiss my neck, his hand on my bottom, stale breath on my cheek. But his attention was not enough to distract me from Mum's preoccupation with another man. So, when he turned to top up his glass, I threw myself to the floor and wriggled up into the space between them. Mum poked me in the ribs – a sharp prod for me to be charming. My antennae, however, picked up that Tom was a threat. I stuck my back to her front and disrupted their conversation with demands and glowering stares. Not even her palpable disappointment had the power to stop me.

***

Boredom and my new knowledge of intimacy shifted my priorities away from school. Even with the background threat of my dad's displeasure, I felt drawn helplessly towards the bigger picture, like a barge towed by a tugboat into the ocean. I could hardly wait for exeat weekends. I hopped onto the train to Charing Cross, and in the tight space of the loo, a friend and I ripped off our ugly wool uniforms. We pulled on t-shirts held together with safety pins and wriggled into Fiorucci 'spray-on' jeans. We sang songs from The Clash's album *London Calling*, and circled our eyes with kohl. At Sloane Square tube, she forked right towards Eaton Terrace, and I down the King's Road.

The brand-new sense of my own sexuality opened up a virgin world of freedom and excitement, and curiosity about my physical effect on the opposite sex was insatiable. I exploited my power by wearing fewer clothes, and sassily held the gaze of admirers as I wriggled down the street.

Joan Collins flashed her eyes through mine, and though it was a game I played, it wasn't one I took further. I had yet to fill out properly and didn't see myself as a 'woman'. Even with my smug grasp on sex, in my mind I was still a young girl, playing at being one. And although feeling attractive was a dizzying new experience, it was as much about the light-hearted pleasure in playing the game with a girlfriend as it was about flattering eyes. In fact, if I gave it proper thought, being attractive made me unsure of what to do with it; nervous even. Did being attractive mean that I had an obligation to give myself away? The untoward attention from stale breath and wandering hands had led me to assume there was some truth in that. I had heard older brothers of my friends say things like, 'What a waste!' in reference to a pretty girl who didn't want a boyfriend. As if she should, because of her alluring appearance, be passed around and devoured like cake.

To be attractive or not? To be loved or not? It was a perplexing puzzle.

It was Saturday, early afternoon. Bobbies with whistles edged solicitously alongside groups of punks on their way to Boy, as if they were packs of snarling wolverines. Bursts of tartan and slashed Union Jacks, safety pins and razor blades, towering Mohicans and truculent posturing, drove Diana Spencer lookalikes in high-necked frills hurriedly across the road to Peter Jones. Fashionable people spilled out of Picasso's café onto the pavement in a patchwork of PVC and fluorescent spandex, while harlequins and pirates sailed by with neck-ruffs, Captain Hook cuffs, and billowing sleeves, towards the King's Road Theatre where *The Rocky Horror Show* had just finished. Hits from the Motels, Ian Dury, and Jam lured otherworldly creatures into the Great Gear Market, to forage for records, dog collars, hair extensions, footless tights, stripes, polka dots, leather, and lace. Sometimes on the pavement outside there were androgynous-looking boys and girls, in ripped fishnet and blue jean, bleached hair and black lipstick. Fags hung limply from bottom lips, and their skin, as white as snow, was taut over hollowed cheek-bones. Their spacey eyes hinted at horizons far beyond my comprehension.

It seemed heroin use was exploding on every corner.

Chapter 18

Home was a leafy backwater off the King's Road. Left past
Antiquarius, down towards the river. It was Tom's flat. I had
my own bedroom there and in it – the height of luxury – a
television tucked away in a cupboard.

I had spent a year being horrid to Tom. I hadn't liked
myself for it and had tried to stop but hadn't had it in me
to do so. Like the savages in my nightmares, he'd taken
my mum from me, and she'd even changed her name to
his. I tried to rationalise it. For God's sake, it was normal.
Everyone did it when they got married. Yet for me it still
counted as a sickening betrayal. We were a partnership, she
and I. Joined by a name. Our name. My name. Replacing
it for his was as good as deserting me. My mum was still
my lifeblood, and I was frightened of losing her, irrational
though that thought was. I swung backwards and forwards,
with both sides of the argument staking their claim in my
mental chaos.

Why could I not just be nice? Smile at him. Chat with

him. Stop thinking of myself. Accept his kindness, and his willingness to look after me. Accept him as part of our lives. Just. Be. Nice.

A moment came when we were walking down the wide stone steps of a cousin's flat in Cadogan Square. I don't remember what I said to her but no doubt it was spiteful, and Mum turned on me. She'd never before done that.

'You're ruining every chance of happiness I may ever have. Do you hear that? Nix?' She was properly upset, her face blotchy.

An elderly couple appeared on the other side of the street, framed by an arch of Ceanothus in blue blossom. They were walking unsteadily through the gate of the square's gardens. Hearing our raised voices they looked startled, and the man steadied himself with his cane. Mum continued to cry, louder and louder. I looked round to see if anyone else had noticed, then fixed my eyes on the couple, hoping to look apologetic. The man urged his wife on, and they lowered their heads, as if in shame. The clang of the gate startled Mum. She wiped her nose with a handkerchief, pulled her shoulders back, ran her fingers through her hair, and started walking as if nothing had happened.

'Come along,' she called to me. 'I'm late for work.' She was running Blake's, a flower shop just off Sloane Square, whose jungle of foliage and heady scents swept its customers straight into the tropics. I followed a few paces behind, deep in thought about how to move forward.

Tom had had an American upbringing and the fridge now stocked Tab (an early diet coke), along with exotic snacks like Boursin and Taramasalata. There were Arctic Roll and choc ices in the freezer, and Baileys in the drinks cupboard.

Mum's full fridge was symbolic of comfort and love, of home. My route from the front door to it was well-worn and instinctive. If love were a ruling country, I ruminated, then food would surely be one of its satellite states. Certainly, my memories of warmth, tenderness, wellbeing, were all linked to nourishment, and my relationship with food was a greedy one. I devoured cookbooks instead of literature and dreamed of writing my own. I ate with the anticipation of what I would eat next.

I began cooking for Tom. I didn't know how to say sorry, but I could cook. Once I had finished school, Mum decided I should 'do something' with my life instead of 'loafing around dreaming of boys and movie stardom. A cookery course will add a string to your bow,' she said, and found one for me on the border of Notting Hill. The area's reputation was still smarting from past rioting at its carnival, and its underground drugs culture still visible in the litter of needles around Portobello's streets. Every morning I cycled there, humming songs from Fleetwood Mac or Blondie. Punk was on its reluctant way out, The Sex Pistols had broken up, and Sid Vicious had died of a heroin overdose. Diehard punks still paraded up the King's Road, but movements like The New Romantics were stealing their show. You could be whoever you wanted to be then, and still be seen as stylish. I was touching on a military look, and everything had to be vintage – army shorts rolled up, string vests defiantly worn without a bra, fifties stilettos, sparkly earrings, and deep purple lipstick. I arrived at the cooking school usually soaked from the rain with streaks of filthy puddle water up the back of my legs. A starched apron and chef's hat were briskly handed to me on entry, accompanied by a disapproving glance. Once class began, I learned old-fashioned recipes and techniques for chopping, peeling, shredding. The discipline was strict, but it proved to be a successful bridge building exercise with Tom, for every dish I made I took home for supper. His reaction was favourable.

I was so buoyed up at us finally coming together I continued 'nourishing' him long after I finished the course. We went shopping together in Safeway. I made meatloaf, cheese soufflés, chicken Kiev. I grilled cheddar cheese on apple slices and added them to Waldorf salad. I chopped up ginger nut biscuits and smashed them into vanilla ice cream in bowls of stem ginger syrup. I melted Mars Bars and poured the sticky sauce over strawberries or baked bananas. Touched by his magnanimity, I perched on the table, eager for applause, and watched him wade through mountainous meals. When making my shopping list one morning, he raised his arms in defeat and said, 'Stop! Stop my darling! I can't close my jacket anymore!'

***

'No one will want you,' my dad had said, at a family picnic on the beach a little while before, 'with those big thighs and big bottom. Don't want to be chunky darling. Yuk! Men like women to be women.' The others giggled when Dad slapped my bottom and the wine from his plastic glass slopped over the edge. I wrapped a sarong around my waist and dropped my half-eaten pork pie into the rubbish bag.

The walls of Dad's drinks cupboard – in fact, it was a small room – were pinned with posters of half-naked girls, and among them Cheryl Tiegs stood out conspicuously for wearing a full bikini. They and his Playboy magazines, hidden under Country Life in the downstairs loo, shaped my education, or at least the way I thought I should be: be slender and delicately curvaceous, be soft and fluffy, be feminine. To flout the doctrine was asking to be rejected.

His visible distaste for fat ladies was no secret. When he caught sight of any fat lady – on the streets, the beach, or even at family get-togethers – his mouth would turn down at the corners and he'd frown with open distaste.

'You've lost your way, dear girl – the zoo is in the other direction!'

As a child I had reacted with nervous giggles, shocked by his impertinence, but in awe of his humour. 'Daaaddy! Shush!' He had laughed with me, a laugh that soon transformed into 'tee hee hees'. He had held my hand so tight that I'd almost lost feeling, then thumped it against his leg with childlike pleasure. I couldn't permit myself to turn around and check if the fat lady had heard. Of course she had. Dad's voice travelled far.

He was slim, my dad. He raced his horses, doing mainly point-to-points, and as a jockey, needed to keep his weight down. He ate meagrely, forever watchful of getting fatter. His habit of pinching his stomach monitored his diet, while his disciplined timetable and impeccable turnout became his framework for self-respect. He knew who he was within that, and no matter how far he went to shake its cage, its rules always stuck.

***

As Tom filled out with my cooking, my own shape did too. Lying on the beach when I was younger, I would drum my hands on my tight tummy muscles, tapping out an African rhythm, and the sound then had been hollow. Now it was muffled.

I wasn't sure what to make of my new curves, or the nicknames given by male friends in reference to my backside. As a child I had never been anything other than thin and muscular, even with the towering portions of food that I had tucked into. In my mind, therefore I was still that way, so I found myself chronically startled to see that I wasn't. Parts of me I still thought were ok. My collarbone and shoulders, for instance. And arms. I liked my arms. I quite liked my bosom too. Other parts, namely my bottom half, I would have liked to have lopped off, shaved down, replaced. I dressed according to the bits I wanted to hide or expose, in high-waisted baggy trousers and bright-coloured boob tubes or vests.

With Dad, particularly in the evenings, I was conscious of a new feeling of suspense in my interaction with him, which coloured the way I behaved. His glazed eyes followed me around, and his lips curled as if there was a bad smell under his nose. I wondered if I was imagining it and made efforts to distract him with extraneous things. But every time I turned to look, his gaze was on me, moving as I moved, like a gun trained on a prisoner. After dinner he would slump in his chair, a burning cigarette between his fingers, and unless I sat quickly, I felt his fixed stare bore into me and detected the first mutterings of distaste. To an outsider they would have been just audible, but barely comprehensible. But to me, the familiarity of his dialogue was imbued in my cells. It didn't matter that the words either lacked consonants, were all strung together, or that onomatopoeic noises replaced them. His language was well known to me, nuanced by his exaggerated facial tics. 'Tsk, rather gone off the boil.' 'Losing her looks.' 'Great big bottom.' 'Too much flesh.' 'Eeugh.' I watched the glowing embers move down the cigarette while round segments of ash broke cleanly away, dropping onto the arm of the chair, and disintegrating. 'Dad, your ash! Careful!' And his arm jerked stiffly to the side, like an oar moving through water.

Invariably on tenterhooks, I would position myself behind sofas or tables in order to hide my lower half, even in his sober and seemingly ambivalent presence, threatened as I was by either the prickly discomfort of scrutiny or his possible change of heart. Furthermore, I never dared be certain which dad was the real one. Whilst I wholly believed I knew the sober man inside and out – my gentle, anxious, and mischievous dad – my own self-doubts made me wonder if it was the drunken one that spoke the truth. *In vino veritas?* Wasn't a loose tongue an honest one? I kept asking myself. Due to my abiding sense of disappointing him, which seemed to be upheld within this new layer of my growing up, I tended towards believing that. My body, it seemed, was doing its own thing without any input from me. Like a car with no brakes, it was speeding towards its crash.

I distanced myself. I stopped meeting him in London for dinners. I stopped going to stay with him. I declined invitations to family gatherings, impressing on him, when he complained, that my life was busy, and no, of course it was nothing to do with him. It was easier to run from failure than to face it.

During my short-lived escape, I thought I would find peace from his sharp judgement and mercurial mood. But I found that the sting had already matched my own shaky perception of myself and blended into the soundtrack of my mind. So, whether I turned inside or out – north, south, east, or west – it still lingered, like a monster in the shadows, waiting to get me.

Chapter 19

I never returned to boarding school once I'd opened my O Level results. I dropped all contact with everyone associated with it; even my best friend. Not wanting to encounter my shame in their faces, I had to divorce them.

Every subject that I had previously shone in, I had failed. Failed.

My luck had finally run out. My achievements? Puh! As suspected, I'd never even been the agent of them. Like a parasite, I'd fed off the flukes awarded to me. I'd ridden the wave, nervous all the time of the big one that would catch me out. Now it finally had. I'd been exposed. All that striving for perfection... delusional of me! What was I thinking? I was, in truth, good for nothing. Not my sporting and academic accolades, not my popularity, nor the pride of my dad. I was worthy of nothing. Except ridicule. I had been right all along.

My headmistress sent me a consolation letter. She included the exam board's response to her query about my results. 'She produced high quality work,' they wrote 'but failed to accurately answer the questions'.

High quality? So what. I didn't care anymore. I had fallen from the best to the worst in the opening of an envelope. I couldn't bring myself to make the call to Dad or see him. I shot straight back into the shell of the defective child hiding from the world, with the roar of hopelessness resounding in my head.

Inside that commotion, a voice from long-ago resurfaced. It rang as clear and true as the church bell next door that had summoned me to seek Sunday pardon.

It was the story of Little Red Riding Hood.

My room was dark except for the dim light from the landing outside, and Dad, on the edge of my bed, tossed his hands into the air like claws just as an owl hooted outside. Their huge shadows danced menacingly across my sloped ceiling, and his sinister whisper as he told the story lilted with the same tempo. 'All the better to see you with my dear... Tee hee hee hee...' and the shadows got closer to my pillow, blocking the reflection of the passage light, until they were on me – smothering my face... eating me up... and I hurled the blanket over my eyes.

His laugh was muffled, but he dug me in the ribs. 'Oh really! It's just a story. Come on! Dada loves you. Didn't I do that rather well? Come on!' He kissed me through the bedding.

As with the vital piece of jigsaw without which the picture makes no sense, I saw that since then, the myth of the Big Bad Wolf slotted perfectly into my psychological portrait. Like a brick in the wall of its construction, it coloured every other one laid on top – influencing the pattern of the build and impacting its strength.

Does the collective education of fairy-tales shape our minds? I wondered. Yes, of course it does! Look at Cinderella for goodness' sake! She messed us all up! Torn forever we are, between our prince and independence.

And Little Red Riding Hood?

For me, yes. Like a branding iron, it stamped its message on my vulnerable psyche and pinned its figures onto the pivotal characters of my own story. It echoed every expectation and judgement, and the catastrophe predicted by both my mum and dad.

'Now be a good girl! Do as I say! Take this basket of remedies and go straight to your grandmother's house! Don't stray from the path or dawdle along the way! And remember! *Never* talk to strangers – the woods are dangerous!' Such were the mother's instructions given to Little Red Riding Hood as she set off to visit her grandmother. But she was distracted and wandered off, thereby disobeying them. With that, a stranger emerged from the trees with a sinister voice affecting friendliness. He asked her where she was going, and suggested she stop a while to pick flowers. While doing that, he ran ahead, ate up her grandmother, and then, disguised in her clothing, lay in wait for *her*. She gasped at her grandmother's appearance.

'But Grandma, what a deep voice you have!'

To which he replied, 'All the better to greet you with my dear!'

'What big eyes you have!' she said.

'All the better to see you with my dear!'

'What big hands you have!' she said as the Big Bad Wolf lunged forwards.

'All the better to grab you with my dear!'

The shadows of Dad's claws loomed above me, swinging hither and thither before swooping down to my face.

'But Daddy what big teeth you have!'

'All the better to eat you with my dear! Tee hee hee hee hee!'

As it was Dad who I took care of, I substituted him for the grandmother. Me not being a good girl resulted in my loss of him, eaten as he was by the wolf who had tricked me into wandering even further off course of my mother's orders. Once the wolf disguised himself as Dad, the two had merged in my mind: the wolf with his insight that I wouldn't pass muster, and Dad's judgement and absence its endorsement. Answerable for that first catastrophe of him leaving me, there was no doubt in my mind that I would be answerable for every future one.

Unless, of course, I could be perfect.

Fear of not being so and its inevitable drama were inexorably linked. The guise of the wolf came in all shapes, and in a slippery, shady fashion he shifted from one thing to another in my mind: the lion under my bed; the man on the train; Mum's predators; Father Christmas; the hospital staff; my dad; my failings; catastrophe; fear in general.

In and out he went, hiding behind an ever-expanding assortment of masks.

Chapter 20

Dad's propensity for the extreme meant that his range of affection was wide and vacillating. He'd push me into his chest while he kissed the top of my head. Patting my back with his heavy hand he would bring his face to mine and pinch my cheek, muttering 'So lost I am without you.' There was a clinging desperation behind his warmth, an un-negotiable contract of reciprocation, and a covenant therein never to exploit his vulnerability.

But I cherished those moments before they were withdrawn. I buried my nose in his chest, into the traces of stable yard engrained in the well-worn cotton of his shirts, and wrapped my arms around his lean, muscular frame.

His humour too, I treasured; it was bawdy and scurrilous, and with his stories, he wielded the power of a magician over his captivated audience. There were tales of 'a great hairy backside in the bed of so and so's wife', and the 'jig-a-jig-jig that brought down the ceiling in one fell swoop'. Whether it was the risqué content or his premature giggles that infected them, his audience would laugh so hard he'd have to repeat his story over and over again before they caught the punch line. When I was little, a friend would inevitably dig him in the ribs and, with a faux scowl and tut-tut, say 'Oh love, honestly! You are awful! *Pas devant les enfants*, surely?'

He'd reclaim my hand and bang it against his thigh, hooting with laughter with his head thrown back.

'My little African baby? Shockable? Puh! There's nothing that'll shock her. She's a chip of the old block, she is!'

Laughter was the potent drug amidst the tears. Nuggets of gold for the miner.

Maybe because of his child-like nature, his sense of empathy was razor-sharp. When Caro, a natural party-goer, got me invitations to fancy dress dos, without knowing of my anxiety nor the hours I spent at them loitering around the loo, he protested for me, having picked up on my jitters in the blink of an eye.

'Do let her off the hook, darling,' he'd say to Caro. 'No reason whatsoever that she has to go to the godforsaken party.' And as I waved him goodbye from the backseat of the car, his eyes filled with tears, his facial tics undisguised. 'Poor little mite' he'd mutter, over and over again.

But as he grew older, his behaviour grew less predictable – or rather, it became more predictable that he would misbehave. Dinner with him was always harrowing, as the 'eggshell walk' was more tenuous in the evening. I knew how to take things carefully, with docility, looking pretty, and pretence. Once Kate and Dickie were old enough to stay up past seven o'clock they ate with us, and I felt an even stronger impulse to hide his difficult side. They were only little and needed protection. So, no matter how fiery the atmosphere, I had to make believe, keep the peace, fake it to make it.

At eight o'clock, Dad's heavy footfall on the stairs prompted in me immediate suspense, like the crack of a starting pistol. Get set... Go! A thread of tension zipped up my spine again. The race had started to shoot down the chaos. Or better still, nip it in the bud! If that failed, I would smooth it over! Make believe! Happy! Happy! Happy! The pressure and pattern of his descent varied from evening to evening. To measure it, my antennae were as attuned as a heart monitor and picked up the first intimations of trouble long before he walked through the door. My heart sank. His footstep promised another arduous evening.

To the outside world Dad's life had all the trappings of happiness. So how had I failed to make him cooperate with all his advantages?

I must try harder.

The door of the kitchen squeaked. I braced myself.

He'd shaved and dressed for dinner in blue open-necked shirt and crisp pink trousers. His eyes were heavy-lidded and stony, speech already slurred.

'Hi, my Dad,' I said breezily. 'You look nice.'

He grunted and moved unsteadily to his chair, scowling at Caro, who was stirring a buttery sauce on the Aga. He muttered under his breath, his gaze unfocused, his head low.

When he sat down, I patted his hand. A 'there, there' sort

of touch. And once we were all at the table, I picked up my knife and fork and scraped them around my plate, filling in the tension with its grating noise. I threw sidelong glances at him to weigh up every nuance of his behaviour, so that I could intervene before it inflamed the atmosphere, as quickly as fire on petrol. I directed my conversation to Caro and the children, sticking to routine subjects. We may as well have been actors on stage, performing the same lines night after night. The weather. The horses. Her cooking.

'Prawns are delicious, Caro. What's the spice? Don't you think they're yummy, Kate? And the lettuce – is it from the garden?'

But I had picked it earlier, so I knew it was.

I scraped my knife and fork a bit more. My voice was too loud, too brave, too much, but for a while it felt like I held our fatuous chat together. I prayed that we could eke it out until the end of dinner. And so long as Caro didn't speak to Dad, we had a chance. Please, God, keep her attention on me. When I saw her wanting to respond, I sent beseeching glances when his head was slumped. Keep quiet Caro. Please. I was hot with nervousness. My cheeks burned. To no avail. She reacted to Dad's mood with dizzying speed, and her counter-reaction was always combative.

I knew what would ensue. Every time was the same. I ducked my head and closed my eyes. Stinging vituperation was his favourite weapon.

'Who the hell do you think you are – talking to me like that?' it would start. 'How dare you? You, of all people!' He sneered.

It was hard to look at him after that for fear that I would

become the next target for his contempt. There was always further poison ready to be dispersed.

There were rows. Big screaming ones. I darted between them: pleading, placating and throwing myself at their waists. Caro with her tearful French expletives, and my Dad with his arrows.

'It's ok, Caro. Don't cry. He loves you, I promise. Don't take it like that.'

'Dad, calm down, she didn't mean it. Come on. Dad. Be nice. Please.'

Though the shouting and threats were routine, the breaking glass of one occasion was as dramatic to me as any life or death situation. I had to make it better, make peace between them. Or else. I had to stop his menace before things went too far. The fear of going too far was like a drum roll in my heart, like film music that warns you something horrid is about to happen. That was my signal. Once I got that, I reacted. Amidst the clatter of dishes and a break in his diatribe, I grabbed his hand and pinched it, in order to draw his attention away from her.

He turned on me then. 'What the bloody hell! What are you doing, you little brat…? Look at you, eergh.' The look in his eyes – one of revulsion – was worse than his words.

'Dad. Please. It's me. Look at me. Me? Ok? Come on Daddy. Let's calm down. Eat your dinner. Look, you haven't even touched it. Let's try and have a nice time, hmmm?'

He played with his food while I kept my hand on his and gauged his mood, exerting pressure accordingly. His head got so heavy it would drop close to his plate and I'd push it back up again. Up, down, up, down. His belligerence quietened and became less coherent so long as Caro kept quiet.

Often, I would push and pull him upstairs, my muscles trembling with the brunt of his weight. On the flat of the landing I directed him to the right down the corridor that led to his bedroom, but occasionally he would veer towards mine mumbling something about ''s ok darling – 'm ok – 's late – your bedtime, my baby –'ll be over-wrought tomorrow if you don't sleep now – 'll tuck you up.' But the words were all strung together, like molten glass, with no real consonant sound to break the words.

His dark silhouette against the light from the door swayed while his hand groped clumsily for the wall. With a brisk, matronly tone I announced that it was time for sleep. 'Ok my Dad? You must get to bed too. You're tired.' I stood stiffly with my calves pressed against the mattress. 'You want help getting there?' The tick-tock of my bedside clock was loud. The glow from the kitchen light downstairs cut a gold vertical line where the curtains met, and then suddenly it went black. There was the chink of a lock turning, and Caro's brisk footsteps on the cork floor as she headed to the sitting room.

'Yep. Yep. Yep,' he repeated and lurched to hug me. He tripped, and his dead weight was suddenly crushing me.

'Dad, come on' I wriggled free of him.

The space between the wall and his bulk was skinny, and his body cool like a stone. A snuffly snore sound broke through his slow heavy breathing.

'You're not crying are you Dad? It's ok. Come on! You're

tired. You need to get to bed.' I tried to push him away, fearing he would fall asleep.

He made a hoarse grunting noise in response and moved even closer. And something suddenly felt 'off' to me. I sensed, in that brief moment, that in his mind I had switched from being his daughter to being 'a female'. Yet I fought off that notion. Me being silly. Imagining things. But the length of him was pushed against me, and from his trousers there was a sudden hardness as his hands fumbled around my chest. It was so quick and so fleeting before I shoved him off that I wasn't sure if it had happened at all. He hit the floor with a double thud and a jumble of shocked expletives, but he didn't seem to have hurt himself.

Once I had him upright, my mind cleared. I had felt so unsettled by the transition from Dad to stranger that I hadn't articulated the unfolding sequence of his behaviour. I led him to his room, and he stumbled up the few steps to his and Caro's wing. He tried to steady himself by thrusting his hand out onto the door, and a loose cufflink rapped the glass making a little brittle clack.

'Ah! Loud' he said, pronouncing the word so it rhymed with 'plough'. 'Where am I darling?'

'You're going to bed. You're tired, Dad.'

'Why? Whasatime? Is'ni' dinner time? Mus'n' keep Caro waiting. No.' He made grunting noises. 'She'll breathe down my neck again – Out to gemme... *dans la merde... dans la merde...*'

Oh Dad. My poor dad. How on earth did we get to this?

It wasn't *so* long ago, was it, that you had a grip on yourself? Or was that just my naive perception?

The last forty minutes ran through my mind, minute by minute, but the crossing of wires in his brain got crossed with mine in the thinking. I had never had a drink, but I felt how he went from fuzzy, slow-motion, white-out when he couldn't recall why he was in my bedroom, yet *knowing* that he couldn't recall why, to a state of groggy dizziness, and the room spun and his legs and arms wouldn't move, and it felt as if he was resisting an anaesthetic. He lost his balance and it was black behind his eyes, with a beating pulse-like pressure around his head. His reality hummed with a staticky crackle and peeled away from him, with his mind no longer steering his physical body. A bit like watching a prisoner escape. And it was here, at this point, that he lost connection between right and wrong, and accordingly the *knowing* of losing it.

Seized by that demon! Again. Drink. Drink. Drink. When will he understand its poison? When will he see how horrid he is when he's like this? Does he not sense that his code of behaviour, once so upright and decent, has slipped from its pedestal, and that his head, once so clear and sharp was now woolly and disoriented? Has he no inkling of how bad he has got? Maybe he does, and loathes himself? In one way I hope for his ignorance. Being aware of his descent, *could* mean a return to his gun.

But in any case, I reasoned, it hadn't been that bad, had it? Nothing much had actually happened. Or even, I asked myself, had anything really happened at all?

I had the wherewithal to disassociate Dad's unseemly behaviour from other men's; not just because of his alcoholic
transformation from good man to horrid, but because of
the sympathy that tinted my love for him. After all, I was
attuned to his thin-skin and emotional see-saw and used to
progressing with him incrementally inside the reels of his
mind. Compassion outweighed everything else, and it was
hard not to forgive him.

All is well Daddy. All is well.

Notwithstanding that, when I was more grown-up my
moral code struggled to find sympathy, especially on the
odd occasion that he turned lascivious eyes onto Kate or
her friends. Instead, I saw him through the eyes of an outsider, and I felt horror. My face burned, my scalp prick-
led, my heart pounded. A sense of guilt for not having
restrained him clashed inside my consciousness. Yet in
those moments I could find no right way to act. I didn't
want to ruin Kate's birthday dinner by having to temper
his belligerence. There would be no meek compliance, after all. Yet I couldn't allow things to deteriorate to a point
when she or her friend was also filled with shame. I saw it
all coming long before it came, in his leaden eyelids, slack
mouth, and barely intelligible muttering, and dreaded the
lecherous winking and fumbling attempt to grasp a knee,
arm or hand. So as his body slipped sideways, pulled by the
settling of his gaze on their blonde hair and youthful limbs,
I wanted to shout.

Why was no-one else reacting? Did they not even notice
what was happening? Dinner at the other end of the table

was rolling on with giggly stories about terrible teachers at boarding school. All that while Dad's conduct was losing all semblance of control! Was I imagining it all? No! There was nothing imaginary about this stark truth of degeneration. Nothing! It was so shocking that association with him felt like violation. Yet all I could think of was how to get him out of there, casually, as if everything were just fine. Pretend, pretend, pretend! Hold onto that dignity, no matter what! I kicked him in the ankles, tugging at his elbow so that his position was at least upright.

Caro and I made an attempt to play Snap once, after one of those terrible evenings, but it got no further than her shuffling. She was crying still and talking about leaving him. 'But,' she sniffed 'those poor children… *mes petits coeurs*. Can't make them suffer any more.' Poor Caro. She was so good at holding it all together. Putting my arms around her shoulders, I watched the faded, dog-eared cards slot rhythmically in and out of themselves, and prayed for the King of Hearts to be dealt to me.

The King of Hearts reminded me of Dad. On one side, he was resplendently dressed and a symbol of love and seduction; on the other a blurred, blackened pattern of lines. Like the wires of his brain, I thought. I hoped to cast a spell on it, turning the black lines into a duplicate of the glorious king. Like that, there would be no 'bad Dad' – no mess or blurred morality – and morning and evening he would reign.

I had seen girls at school make a drawing of a classmate, and then stick pins in the cartoon's leg. In netball later that week, the classmate fell and fractured her knee. I was simultaneously unnerved and in awe, and from thereon in made sure to give them a wide berth. But the idea stuck with me. I figured that a wish, a spell, a prayer, must be able to work positively too.

I had viewed his drinking, until then, with a shrugged acceptance. It was normal. And normal wasn't questioned. My brain hadn't incorporated the possibility that there was another way to be, and I concentrated only on trying to fix the effects of it, rather than stop them. I had vaguely heard grown-ups talking about 'alcoholism', in reference to other people. They referred to it as 'a bit of a problem', either whispered quickly so that the children couldn't hear, or in a teasing way and described as 'a fondness for the bottle', their smug tones implying that they were impervious to such weakness.

Chapter 21

Once I got my driving licence, I visited rehabilitation clinics all over the country. I had many meetings with senior counsellors, all of whom furnished me with glossy brochures picturing group walks, cookery classes, and communal singing. Smiles. Hugs. Camaraderie.

I knew it would be considered 'a step down' by Dad to do such a thing. Even the hurdle of admitting he was flawed would be too shameful. And an alcoholic? No. He wasn't an alcoholic, as far as he was concerned. He just liked the odd glass of jungle juice. Everybody did. Nothing wrong with it at all. It would require a reserve of bravery, I realised, that he might not be able to access. And even if he could, to open the shutters onto his true self, to peer inside, observe the chaos and accept that it belonged to him, might, I feared, defeat him. But it was worth the risk. One never knew.

I boarded the plane armed with the brochures and a positive vibe. But watching the clouds, pondering his life, rehearsing my speech, I felt the talons of doubt puncture my hopefulness. What was I thinking? Had I persuaded myself of another fantasy? That, hurrah, he would lie down, roll over, accept defeat and be cured? He'd already lived half his life! Most of it with the belief that he was the seductive King of Hearts. Why, I asked myself, would he abdicate to acknowledge the fearful child and messy wiring within? Why? Absurd of me!

Yet, I reasoned, the King was no longer performing with the dazzling sharpness of his youthful days. Dad's alcohol levels didn't drop anymore, which meant that with less physical resistance, his broken core bled into his regal persona, quickly overwhelming it until all that remained of the old heartbreaker was Dad's unshakable fantasy of him.

On that note, I felt compelled to follow through with my conviction.

'For fuck's sake! You honestly think I'd go spend a week with a bunch of characters like this? You must be mad!' He stabbed the image of the cookery class with his index finger.

'No Dad. I'm not thinking a week. No. I am thinking weeks, months – however long it takes.'

He knocked back the contents of his glass and swiped the brochures of the table.

'I'm perfectly alright! You are *not* going to coax me into hugging a band of happy-clappy bread makers and to… to 'tooooork', damn it! I don't give a tinker's wank what you think I should do. I won't! Do you hear?' The long hammy vowel sound of his 'tooork' was accompanied by an elaborate mime of earnest do-goodery: arched eyebrows, round eyes, round mouth, shaking head. He crashed the glass down onto his desk. 'God forbid! Aaah – yuk!'

His bottom lip quivered, his head dropped, and he sagged back in his chair like a burst paper bag. I wrapped my arms around his head and a clammy wet patch on my t-shirt grew as his tears spilled.

'Oh darling. Am I that bad? The Grim Reaper isn't at the door yet. Is he? I'm alright, aren't I? Tell me I'm alright… Tell me…'

Tenderly, I kissed his head and breathed in the smell of hair oil. You're fine my Dad. You're fine. Don't cry. It will all be alright. Come on, breathe! All is well.'

Chapter 22

With the spectre of the Big Bad Wolf, I had never landed in the safety net of feeling 'the best', even in the relief of success at school. There were just brief moments of reprieve, in which I thought to myself, 'Phew! Got away with that again' – which forthwith soured into heart-thumping panic over not being able to repeat the triumph. I thought of my success as only fleeting, like sand slipping through fingers.

But my O Level fiasco had been a slap in the face, a blatant endorsement of its ephemeral nature, and of all my self-doubts.

The decision not to eat crept in incrementally. There was no conscious 'I want to be thin' decision or 'I'll stop eating.' There was no conscious desire to deprive myself. No. It was broader than that. And deeper. My inner chaos was out of control. I was tired. Defeated. Like a whipped dog. The build-up of struggling to please and struggling to fix, but failing, failing, failing had now, with its external affirmation, broken me.

I turned inwards. I disengaged. I retired from life as I had known it. I wanted out. I drew down my defences, determined never again to allow myself to be vulnerable. Facing life meant facing that Big Bad Wolf on every corner. Shutting it out was safe. Yes. Safe. Like a padded cell.

I'd had a place at a school behind Sloane Square that they then revoked on receipt of my results. Not good enough. Well, they didn't say so exactly but the message was clear. In fact, there was no place available at any school in London. While I spent a week at the beginning of term shut up in my room, Tom fought for me in the headmistress' office. He waved his hand at her and said, 'You take her in and I guarantee she'll make you proud. Now let's get to work and make this happen. No ifs or buts. Ok?'

Remaining at school was not what I wanted.

I'd had enough of being tested. Had enough of testing myself, pushing myself, in the vain hope of an award.

Tom and Mum insisted I finish my education.

'It'll serve you well, darling. We have every faith in you. Come now. Stick that smile on your face even if you don't feel it.'

I shuffled into assembly late. Fade into the background, I told myself. Fade. Judging from the ensuing whispers that travelled along the bench, I could only imagine that stuck to my forehead was a neon sign that flashed *Failure!*

The A level course had begun and its exams, shadowed by my anticipatory doom, loomed on my horizon.

I made a pact with myself to succeed. *Really* succeed.

Pride in achievement would iron out the creases inside.

It would cleanse me of shame and self-contempt. I had to do it. After all, my life would be a washout if I failed again.

I threw myself into the cause. Like a horse in blinkers, I focused single-mindedly on my studies, blind to distractions. I locked myself away, surrounded by books, and purged my life of everything else from one day to the next. Family. Food. Social life. Fun. None of them had a place in my crusade towards self-vindication.

I remained in the library during lunch, and until it closed, returning home later and later. Avoiding food was not pre-meditated. The will to do so evolved once I recognised the spark of control I suddenly felt. It was just a small spark initially. A fizz. A glint. A flash. But it was the hint of redemption I needed.

I was hungry for it, even secretly so. I didn't need fanfare. On the contrary, I wanted no attention at all. My task was solitary and covert, its motives unrecognised even by myself. I did sometimes suspect that what I was up to might be damaging, but tended to brush this away, as if it was of no concern. Recently aware of how much I tried to reign in my dad's bursting emotions, I saw myself as strong, and the carrier of other people's woes. I was straight-forward in comparison. I had no confidence of course, no faith in myself, but that was normal. Wasn't it? I didn't have 'issues' though – it was Dad with the issues, wasn't it, not me? Despite my self-assumed strength, I still identified the hit I got from that spark. It felt like a pat on the back. I wanted more. I wanted a string of sparks knotted together to combat those taunting tentacles of fear and worthlessness.

I made continual excuses to Mum. I felt sick, had already eaten, got work to do, didn't like pasta any more. But thanks. Conscious of her vigilance, I pushed salad and potatoes round the plate when she was watching.

But soon I was rejecting all meals, and there was nothing anyone could say that would shift my stance. Nothing. As if my brain were a machine, I locked it. Even a crack in its door threatened my survival.

How I had slipped into that tyranny without conscious thought I didn't know. Didn't understand. I sometimes wondered if I'd been possessed, so startled was I by my transformation. But my trajectory was set. Nothing could re-route it. I was caught in the snare of my own black-and-white thinking. Rigidly in control, keeping at bay my emotions, and, of course, thin: or out of control, swinging from 'best' to 'worst', and of course, fat. Huge. Ginormous. There was no room for middle ground in my thinking. I was perfect or worthless, loveable or un-loveable, acceptable or unacceptable. There was nothing in between.

***

For months and months, I ate just an apple a day. Chopped up small. Sometimes a few raisins and a spoonful of yogurt. Sometimes not. My 'allowance' was merit-dependent, and my merits contingent on the quality of my revision and discipline. Preparation of my daily food was slow, ritualistic, reclusive. I made a point of making it pretty, and played with the contrasting colours of apple skin, dark raisins and sweeps of creamy white yogurt. The nuggets of apple I shaped into a flat-topped cone, sometimes building them up one by one as if they were miniature bricks. Then I let the velvety yogurt slip from the spoon and fall like icing on top of them. It tended to run down the tapering sides, and before it thinned, I dropped the raisins onto it so that they would stick. If my meditative preparations needed to go further, I sliced skinny, curly strings from the apple skin to decorate the top.

Nothing else except tap water passed my lips. Nothing. Not a crumb or a sip or a lick. I ate slowly, silently, mindfully, and savoured taste and texture. I ate alone. No prying eyes. No worried frowns.

I was beginning to feel normal again. Though normal for me was, I realised, an alternative normal. *My* normal was a state of self-obliteration, not the sought-after 'normal' I saw in other people. *My* 'normal' was when the tangled knots and corrugation of my mind evened out, as it focused on something else, and bit by bit a sense of calm, verging on numbness, soothed my internal warfare. Numbness felt good. It felt orderly. And ordinary. And blank. Blank like an untouched canvas. Blank like a new diary. Blank like the eyes of a corpse. And blank like a blank slate from which to start again. It was, I thought, a similar state to my not breathing trick which absented me from feeling. Was that what I was doing in another sort of way?

I was definitely absenting myself from self-analysis. Feeling blank was such a relief after the chaos, that all thoughts of self, I shied from. The Big Bad Wolf was quiet, and the only languages I allowed to trespass across the blankness were French, Art, and History of Art.

Just occasionally I allowed a few questions to blot it. If fat was bad, and thin good, was thinnest best? And what *was* fat, thin or thinnest? Would I be fat if I gained seven pounds? Or would I be fat only if I was obese? Dad's version of fat was a slim bar above thin, but for somebody else that might seem still pretty skinny. I didn't want to be considered thin. Or at least ill-thin. And I definitely didn't want to be put into the thinnest category. Thinnest, I knew, was scary looking. A girl with hollowed cheeks and knife-edge bones walked alone to Sloane Square in an empty circle of space. Pedestrians gave her a wide berth or crossed the road. Was it because that skeletal frame was an unwelcome reminder of their own mortality, or was it pure revulsion that turned their heads away?

Looking at myself, inside and out, felt like overload in my head. Keep the slate blank! I would say. To erase my image, I draped sarongs of red and yellow African prints over my bathroom mirror, and on my return from school, dumped bags of books in front of the hall one. But like my shadow, I couldn't shake it off, pinned as it was to my ankles. Shop windows and car windows hijacked me, and shirking my reflection felt like an obstacle race. If I wasn't mindful of where I was looking, down roads with parking on both sides, my reflection shimmied next to me in a long unending line. In and out, in and out, in and out of view, tormenting me like a Hitchcock film. But in Flood Street, where that happened, if I fixed my sight on the bookie's yellow sign at the bottom of the road, I was safe until I swung right, towards home.

When I did look at myself, it was not with a specific 'I am fat' verdict, but with a generalised scathing one. No matter what my shape or how I looked, I was never going to be 'right', or good enough.

What was 'good enough'? I would challenge myself, trying to untangle my escaping thoughts.

Good enough equalled perfection.

And perfection?

Ah!

Who knew?

Was perfection a bar I'd set myself – far out of reach – so that I could actually cling to the defective label I'd adopted as a child, and which had moulded my perspective?

Did I purposely set my standards so high that self-denigration was the only alternative? Was self-contempt my addiction? And was that a propensity of addicts, or of everyone?

Paradoxically I was ashamed of what I was up to. Ashamed of the weakness I was displaying. What was the matter with me? I was strong, wasn't I? 'As strong as an ox,' Mum always said of me. What was I doing then, with this pitiful behaviour? I badly wanted to shake it from me but didn't know how.

Chapter 23

The word anorexia, like alcoholism, wasn't bandied around in 1980. It was spoken hurriedly in hushed voices, and, like alcoholism, referred to only as 'a problem'. You had to be brave to say it. It was ugly. Dirty. Embarrassing. Taboo. And its association smeared a family's shine and isolated them. A hint of Schadenfreude was spotted in the raised eyebrows and nodding heads. 'A problem' was a fall from grace. And you were given a wide berth.

As if the walls had ears, Mum whispered into the handset while talking to our family doctor. The day after, I walked to his surgery through Kensington Gardens. On the way there, buses rushed past, sporting posters of a young Brooke Shields in her Calvin Klein jeans. Her lean colt-like shape made me think I wasn't so thin, and what a fuss my mum was making. I hadn't wanted an appointment and felt betrayed by her for making one. Shall I not show up? I wondered. Lie, tell her that I went, and that there was nothing wrong with me? But I knew that wouldn't work.

She would telephone him herself and get all the details out of him with the efficacy of a private detective.

The façade of Dr Granger's surgery was clouded with wisteria which dropped its pendulous blooms over the porch. While weighing me and making notes he chatted about the sunshine, asked how Mum was, and without looking up said 'Now Nix. Remove all your layers. Yes, all of them. How many trousers are you wearing for goodness sake? And all those big sweatshirts? Gosh you must be hot. Come on. Let's try again, shall we?' While I stood on the scales for a second time, he handed me a jokey prescription. 'EAT!' It read in big letters. Checking his watch, and patting my shoulders, he walked me to the door. Afterwards he relayed to Mum the widespread assumption that anorexics are terrified of losing their childhood and maturing into women, so she quizzed me surreptitiously, while opening the fridge to show me the tarte aux fraises she'd bought for me from Partridges.

Leaving a few crumbs and a custardy smear in the box satisfied her that I'd eaten it, but for me, knowing that I'd thrown it down the waste disposal was chastening. However, the repressed sorrow and worry in her eyes were too heart-rending for me to address, and I ducked from her caressing hands and timid knocks on my door. I couldn't stand the misery I felt in her, and I couldn't stand myself for being responsible, so I pretended it wasn't happening. I did what I had always done. I closed my eyes and held my breath – if I didn't breathe, I didn't exist – and for a few moments I found respite by disassociation. On days such as this, I would let nothing pass my lips.

Contrary to opinion, thinness was a symptom of my addiction, but not the cause. Its roots grew from my dread of disorder, and my instinct to cut back and repress its pervasive growth. I still had no key to deactivate my mind's lock mode, even if a corner of me longed for a biscuity-custardy-strawberry-ish mouthful, or even lunch in Blushes. No. The idea of unlocking it still provoked heart palpitations and dark thoughts. I couldn't make that step, however much I wanted to. I would spin out of control. And then what? I'd be a mess again. Splattered. I'd be back to square one with that kaleidoscope of self-contempt rattling before my eyes.

Physically, my energy soared, and I cycled to school as if I had wings, as if at any minute I would take off. Late for a lecture at the Tate, I ran there. My body, as if blown by a tailwind, flew. Up, up, up – higher and higher – as light as a feather, and strong – while my feet barely touched the ground. I was a bird, a rocket, a butterfly. I was pure energy. There was enough of it in my veins to fly me round the globe and keep London alight. The faceless white stucco of Alderney Street streaked past me, and the roar of traffic from Millbank swallowed me up. Then there, in the middle of the rush, was the strong, sleek bronze of Henry Moore's 'Locking Piece', on which I was writing an essay. I didn't see the clenched fist that he'd seen, but rather muscles, in a trial of strength against each other. Behind it, the Thames was low, and the wet claggy riverbed exposed – its rocks and shingles strewn with bottles, their necks buried in the mud. Dark grey tide-water lapped over them, edged in frilly white lines.

I slept little. Just two or three hours a night, and with exams approaching I revised every waking moment. I was skin and bone, and fine downy fur covered my neck and shoulders. My door was ajar when Mum came in with a mug of sweet tea for me. She stroked the base of my neck.

'Insulation against heat loss.' she stated factually. 'My poor Nix. I read that in the library today. Here, drink this. It's very comforting.' I think she knew her drinks were wasted, but she faithfully brought a variety to me every day for tea.

It was early summer, but the temperature outside didn't alter mine. I wore layers of clothes and revised from my bedroom, sitting on a padded chair to relieve the discomfort of my bony spine and tailbone.

From my terrace I could see our new neighbours busy in their kitchen on the ground floor. They were a couple in their mid-thirties. She was fresh-faced with long, glossy, dark hair, her figure slim and toned, in pastel coloured leggings, leg warmers and baggy Pineapple sweatshirts. He, with his mass of curls and skin the colour of Caramac, was bouncy, smiley and handsome. The soundtrack of Fame escaped from their tall open window and her voice floated musically above it while she cooked. On the windowsill swayed the long feathery leaves of a potted fern. Mum had seen a waterbed being delivered to their door, and, from a Christies van, armfuls of paintings. Above the bar where they perched on stools, a colourful Pop-Art-y picture hung. Carmel, who cleaned for us, had discovered their names from Mr Petit, the concierge: Bruno and Rachel. Rachel and Bruno. Their glamour had lit up the street with curiosity, shaking the foundations of our fusty old chintz, clutter, frills, and duck-egg blue. They swept away our traditions of pleated lampshades, and silver framed photos on grand pianos with their cool, white walls, jewel coloured chairs, American bars, and Feng Shui crystals. They bounded to the park in aerobics clothes, past husky-clad neighbours reluctantly pulled by a Labrador or two.

And oh, to be a fly on the wall in that kitchen! They seemed always to be eating. But what, I wanted to know? The whirring of a Magimix gave me clues, and a salad spinner on the windowsill. Healthy food. Fruit and vegetables. Fibre. The F-Plan diet, perhaps?

Wow. There was a lot to take in. They were so new and fresh that observing them felt like waking up to spring after a winter of hibernation. And they were so perfect. Yes. Perfect. It was their all-rounded health that was edifying to me. They looked happy and healthy, and their environment echoed that.

This must be what a normal life and normal, functioning brains looked like.

Normal was a word I used a lot inside my head. I longed to be that sort of normal. Eat normally. Fit in, be a part of life again. Meet friends at BJ's for shredded beef sandwiches and frozen yogurt. Dance all night at Café des Artistes. Share hotdogs at the ABC, and Pina Coladas at Wedgies. I missed the towering BLTs and iced coffee in the new American bar on the top floor of Harvey Nichols – the mayonnaise that seeped out between the layers of white toast and the hot salty bacon grease flavouring it. Mum made a reservation there every week. Weekly she cancelled it. Why could I not break through the self-imposed barrier and just be normal? I was ashamed of myself. Ashamed that I had slipped so easily and comfortably back into the role of odd-man-out. What was the matter with me? Why was I stuck in this endless over-analysis of myself, food, and the consequences of action?

It was in the days leading up to my first exam that something woke me at 3.30 one morning. Unable to go back to sleep, I lay in bed, looking up at the fluorescent butterflies on my ceiling. The dark was opaque and still, but I felt a fresh idea riffle through my mind, despite the stringent regulations I'd imposed. It fluttered like a breeze through the bars of the cage, slackening them, and undermining their strength and tenacity.

Could I, I wondered, just try being normal? Being free? Being part of things again? Could I? Could I?

If everyone else could, I thought... if Rachel could... well, maybe I could too?

I imagined starting my day in Rachel's skin. I would prepare coffee, fruit, and muesli with sunlight pouring through the window. I would tie my hair back in a pony-tail, Bruno would join me at the breakfast bar, and we would chat and laugh. When he left for work, I would work out to a Jane Fonda video, followed by a quick shower before walking up the road to the interiors shop to find fabric for our bedroom curtains. I would buy a few things from Safeway and return home to make lunch for myself. Bruno and I would have steak that evening, so I would bake eggs with spinach now. Maybe I'd have some coleslaw... and granary bread, toasted.

What did I think about that? Could I do it without feeling like the ground was opening up beneath me, or that sand was running through my fingers? Did I have it in me to let go and start over with a different script for life?

The birds began their dawn chorus. Their tone was so pure and simple I envied them.

Yes. I was tempted to try.

Where *had* that little breeze come from? I wondered.

Chapter 24

My exams were done and dusted in under ten days. I tried
to block out my uncertainty over how I'd fared, although
during French I'd passed out, and hadn't had time to get
to all the questions. I had clattered to the floor, disturb-
ing the other students, and had hurriedly been ushered
out. Too little food had made me dizzy. Quietly confident
about Art and History of Art, I walked home after my last
one feeling as if I had been holding my breath for the last
two years. As if I had been detached from the world, and
my body separated from my senses. I hadn't seen anything
outside of myself for so long that when I looked up at the
full green canopy of Plane trees it was as if I was seeing
it for the first time. I noticed how white the houses of St.
Leonard's Terrace were, and the ornate decoration of their
balconies and awnings. I put my nose through the gate of
Burton Court and inhaled the smell of cut grass. The cricket ground looked dense, like cotton velvet. At the bottom
of Smith Street, I stopped and looked up towards the King's

Road. Outside the Phoenix milled a group of fashionable people with pints and cigarettes. I noticed a girl in candy-stripe pedal-pushers and remembered that somewhere in my cupboard was an identical pair. I should wear them again. It seemed like a lifetime ago since I'd thought of dressing up. The idea of doing so felt fresh and exciting. The girl's hair was cropped high on her head like Sheena Easton's, and her lips were post-box red. Maybe it was time I too went to the hairdresser...

I closed the door of home behind me. The sitting room windows were wide open and birdsong from the garden breezed in. From the kitchen downstairs I heard Tom's voice calling up to me.

'Here she is, our girl. Hello darling!'

The chintz sofa cushions were crumpled and still warm to the touch. Mum's mug of tea, now cold, stood on the mantelpiece next to a small ormolu clock. An invitation to a dance was propped up against it, and on the floor a stamped envelope, its RSVP address scrawled in her loopy writing. Two curly edged photographs of me as a child were on the floor, blown down like discarded patches of fabric – too small, they seemed, to cover up my current holes. The television was still on, the volume low. It was a discussion about the upcoming royal wedding between Prince Charles and Lady Diana Spencer, against the bleak backdrop of south London's rioting, high unemployment and deaths of hunger strikers. Discontent was rife. I watched it for a few moments, realising that I'd been so cut off that I'd not grasped the grim socio-economic reality of the times. How lucky I was, I thought. How damned lucky I was to not be living those hardships, and how damned pitiful it was of me to have created my own. I went over to the television set and turned it off. From its top, I picked up a scrunched-up cinema ticket from the ABC. I opened it up and saw it was for *Tess*, Polanski's film with Nastassia Kinski, and I remembered I'd gone to see it, alone. Under it was a Wimbledon Tennis Club brochure and a ticket for the women's finals. That was Mum's. She'd just been. Chris Evert had won. That much I knew. I put them in my pocket to chuck them out, and with my cotton sleeve wiped off the dust from the television top. I gathered up everything from the floor, puffed up the sofa cushions, and picked up Mum's cup to wash it. The smell of chicken stew wafted up to the sitting room. I recognised that supper; one of my old favourites. Chicken and vegetables all in one, in a steaming broth. I used to like crumbling oatcakes into it.

Mum and Tom were laying the table. The charcoal portrait of her at the end of it hung skew-whiff, and the open door of the plate cupboard displayed higgledy-piggledy piles. I went to shut the door and straighten the picture, but Mum got to me first. Her kiss on my cheek was warm and tender, and sparked an unexpected outburst of emotion. Tears poured down my face and she pulled me into her arms, holding me as if my life depended on it. With a napkin from a place setting she rubbed my face, and brushed my hair back. Then she settled me on a chair, padded with cushions, and patted my shoulders, stabilising me, making sure that her breakable egg wouldn't topple over and smash, as if I were Humpty Dumpty. I gently tugged the corner of the table-cloth, and with my flattened palm ironed out the bunched-up creases.

It was the first time in many months that I had sat at the table with them. And the first time that I'd eaten a proper meal. I ate so much and so fast that I was almost drunk from eating. The taste was so overwhelmingly delicious and new that there was no space available in my mind for any other emotion. That came afterwards. The familiar punishing sound track.

Chapter 25

Although at the onset of the eighties, IRA attacks continued and recession and racial tension tainted the atmosphere like thunderclouds, London's corner-shops still maintained the community spirit of my childhood: there were butchers, grocers, and bakeries displaying doughnuts and iced buns on Formica tops. There were eclectic boutiques reflecting the rebellious street fashion; long-established, scruffy cafés where you bought buttered toast and cappuccino; and restaurants steeped still in sixties nostalgia, papered with stills of Christine Keeler, Michael Caine, George Best, and Diana Rigg. A record shop then was a bit like a post office – the hub of the community. It drew you in with The Stranglers, Eddy Grant, Soft Cell, Adam Ant, weed and therapeutic chat. On Saturdays, you formed lively queues that yawed down trash-strewn pavements around Portobello to claim the newest or most esoteric LP. You shared your passions and your grievances, analysing them through the prism of music. It didn't matter who you were.

Music levelled you. You shared your stuff with punks, posh types, and guys with crazy eyes. You knew their craziness was down to drugs. Bad ones. Scary ones. You averted your gaze, and decided to head back to Our Price on the King's Road, for a less edgy experience. On Sundays, the city was quiet, with no trade and few cars. The only sounds were the pealing of church-bells and birdsong from magnolia and cherry trees. The spirit of *my* London was still village-like. Chummy, trusting and – crucially – a bit down at heel, it felt like my own backyard, shared by friends and everyone I'd known then. Yet although we thought of it as *our* turf, we were just the new pretenders, for the old Chelsea streets had once hosted luminaries such as Henry VIII and Thomas More, Turner and Whistler, Oscar Wilde, David Bowie, and Mick Jagger. We had pride in our inheritance.

Mum had decided that when school finished I would do the Season, traditionally the period of debutante balls, dinner parties and charity events. 'Not to find you a husband, for goodness sake, but to broaden your social circle,' she said when I protested. It was un-cool to be posh then, and I was embarrassed by all upper-class associations. She herself had been one of the last debs to be presented at court, and being a traditionalist at heart, she liked the continuity.

Kicking off with the Berkley Dress Show, the Season began with a torrent of invitations from people I'd never met to dances and balls in stately homes, or ballrooms of grand London hotels. Debutantes in frothy taffeta swept across parquet floors with fresh-faced old Etonians under sparkling chandeliers or disco lights. We dined in private houses beforehand, and were instructed by our hostesses on the protocols of curtseying, were we to meet a Royal. Not being a drinker, my nerves didn't have the advantage of being dulled, as had those of my other companions – more so, as evenings wore on with champagne flowing as if it were ancient Rome. Sit-down breakfasts of kedgeree were served to restore the wired exhaustion of having danced and drank and pretended that you'd had a ball. And maybe you had; but I, in my second-hand silk that I'd artfully gathered or tucked with hidden safety pins or glue, felt, even with the help of Joan Collins's confidence, ruefully ill-equipped to be anything other than an observer. My commitment was short-lived, and completely over once I tripped home past some elderly women, homeless but for their cardboard shelters, in the forecourt of the Markham Arms. A searing sense of shame about my life pricked my conscience, and I averted my eyes. Desertion of my social life wasn't, however, entirely militant. I continued to go to the odd party unrelated to the Season, and still got a buzz from dancing all night. Word reached me that my fifties stiletto heels were denting old parquet floors – so when I was invited to Windsor Castle a few years later, for a ball given by the Queen to celebrate the twenty-first birthdays of Prince Edward and his cousins, I made sure to buy a new pair of contemporary ones. But in spite of my efforts to conform, I still managed to foul up a spectacular evening by making an arse of myself. With pounding heart, and mental fog obscuring the memorised protocol of addressing each member of the Royal family, I reached the top of a red-carpeted staircase where a footman announced my name, to the long line of them in front of me. But what happened next is only half-remembered. I know I stepped off the red carpet, and onto a glossy parquet floor. I know I was heading for the Queen, with the image of my curtsey printed clearly in the front of my mind. Lower your head! Hold out your dress! Your right foot goes behind your left, remember! Bend your knees! And gracefully! Bang, bang went my heart! Then, before I knew it, my feet slipped from underneath me, and I shot past her and Prince Philip, with my dress bunched up and knickers showing. It happened fast, and was remedied fast, but in my head the motion was as slow as a snail's, leaving in its wake a sticky trail of shame. How I got through the rest of the evening my memory doesn't tell, and laughter about it came only in retrospect. I learned two things: first, that the Big Bad Wolf's forewarning of failure was spot-on, and second, to always scratch the soles of new shoes.

I was having much more fun at the time, improvising ways to make money, by working in a clothes shop, and selling home-made sandwiches from my bicycle basket, to office workers in time for lunch. For that, no social anxiety was required. I opened an account with NatWest to store my savings and occasionally met with the bank manager there. All high street banks still had bank managers. We drank tea from cups and saucers, with two Digestive biscuits each, and teasingly he opened a drawer to reveal magazine clippings of me at a wedding or dance. The staff at my local launderette ran a tab for me and asked for payment only when they remembered. I knew them all by name. On my daily sandwich rounds, I donated lunch for them in return for their leniency. Traffic was less frenetic, so with the exception of Hyde Park Corner, bicycling everywhere was unchallenging. Popular cars were generally modest – Austin Metros and Ford Sierras – with rare sightings of a Porsche 911 or a Rolls Corniche. Occasionally on sunny days, vintage cars filed along Knightsbridge on their way to rallies in Hyde Park, beeping jovially when stalled by a Harrods van stopping to make a delivery. Buses were open at the back, and you could hang from the platform pole, waiting to jump off at traffic lights. They had conductors with ticket machines who told you off for doing so. There were still milk floats, newspaper boys, letter writing, telephone landlines as the only means of contact, telegrams announcing births, deaths and marriages, and fewer rules. We smoked in cinemas, pubs and clubs, and on public transport, and jobs were easier to come by without the need for impressive CVs, as the population was considerably smaller.

***

Later that Summer the royal wedding took place at St. Paul's Cathedral. For weeks the media had built it up into a fairy-tale, and up and down the country street parties were being choreographed and roads sealed off in preparation. A contagious rejoicing for what was to be the greatest extravaganza of our generation filled London.

It would be unmissable, I told myself. I couldn't *not* join in. I had known Lady Diana, though only fleetingly because of a three-year age gap, at the schools we'd both attended, and our time at them had briefly overlapped. She seemed, because of that, not so very far away from me – our lives had touched, and shared some of the same moments. I genuinely wanted, therefore, to be a part of her celebration, and to feel as if I could rejoice with her.

I would push myself out from my little cell – out into the revelling throngs – and into the rush of excitement. On the eve of the wedding the centre of London was transformed into a giant party. Streets and parks spilled over with droves of well-wishers, and along the procession route, snaked a river of red, white and blue Union Jacks. Street entertainers and vendors hawking drinks, candy-floss and ice cream weaved in and out of them, accompanied by thousands of mounted policemen.

Looking back, I don't remember who I was with that night. I remember only the skyrockets and bursting gold fireworks in the sky above Hyde Park, the giant Catherine Wheel that shot hundreds of feet above our heads and tossed out rainbow-coloured light like a revolving sun. I remember that Prince Charles lit a bonfire, followed by roars of applause that seemed to fill the world, and the euphoric intoxication on people's faces flashed wildly in and out of the lights. Dancing broke out and bodies were thrown against each other – crushed but laughing – and music competed with the overhead drill of helicopter's engines. Anything could happen, I felt. Anything and everything was possible. Drunken youths climbed on top of each other, waving wine bottles and beer cans, their squiffy eyes ablaze, like those of feasting hyena caught in a helicopter's searchlight. A sense of feral lawlessness surged through the crowds. Broken glass mingled with Union-Jack hats, bunting, and streamers, strewn all over the grass. Bare feet were cut but nobody cared.

The next day I watched the wedding on television, in a friend's high-ceilinged drawing room close to the procession route. The windows were open and the noise from the crowds lining the route joined those on the screen, as Diana, in miles of ivory taffeta, was driven to St. Paul's Cathedral, in her horse-drawn pumpkin. Magical images of trumpeters and choirs, pomp and pageantry, feverish goodwill, her fawn-like eyes, her dress, their kiss – were nothing less than hypnotising.

And I, I went away thinking that fairy-tales happened after all, and that in the end Cinderella always got her prince.

Beside Myself

1988

Chapter 26

A few princes sashayed through my heart before I got together with Will, but we were young still, and attentions easily turned. A few were all-night partiers, smashed on something most of the time, and others more serious, with whom I shared chunks of life. With them, I explored a far-flung place or two, attended concerts, The Grand Prix, The Grand National, Wimbledon, and Royal Ascot.

Yet my life with Will could not have been more different. Until now. I think of our time in St. Tropez where we had come together, and where, I remember, I'd begun my unspoken instruction in drug addiction, and then of Val d'Isère where we'd stayed with Emma and Paul a few weeks ago.

From the restaurant's terrace there I watched him shaping graceful curves down the mountain and then come to a flamboyant stop, spraying snow all over me and laughing infectiously. We'd come so far, I thought in that moment. I dared even believe that the chain of addiction was finally broken.

He had tried to get clean before, but never without methadone. He had battled against his demons in a repetitive cycle of fighting, conceding, fighting, conceding. He had made lists, hundreds of them. Lists of his defects and how they negatively affected his life. 'Things to change by X date'. He had left them by his bed as reminders on waking, and as he smoked he would flick through them, and make new ones, adjusting their order of importance in neat columns. Most damaging. Middling damaging. Least damaging.

I imagined a graph measuring his last ten years. The troughs would have been long and low, broken by a sporadic climbing ridge – breakthrough moments when he'd held onto the light at the end of the tunnel.

Heroin had got hold of him quickly. 'The first high was amazing,' he'd said, 'and in a way I never stopped chasing it. I remember how it filled me, and nothing else mattered, least of all my fuck-ups – pain, shame, self-consciousness – you know the kinds of things – they just dimmed. It made me feel invincible, or at least protected. 'Course, you never get that high the same way again. And it was only about three weeks in when I realised I was hooked. God. Was sick without it. More than anything then, more than any high, I needed to score, just to feel normal. It's been like that for all these years. On and on. Until now.' His smile, like a ray of sun, chased the clouds from his face.

We took a table outside. The wind blew at our backs and the ice in the air pricked our cheeks like pins. We lifted our faces to the sun, up towards the ring of mountains in front of us. Criss-cross trails cut across the snow. I looked over at

Will, lying back in his chair, his legs askew, and I thought about those lists by his bed. It seemed that they could be ticked off now, as *faits accomplis*. Instead of spending two hundred pounds a week on drugs he now went to restaurants, the theatre, exhibitions. Tick. Took holidays. Tick. He'd gained hair, weight and muscle. Tick. His shoulders had broadened, the size of his hands had returned to normal and his scars were fading. Tick. His sight had improved, and he'd finally stopped his compulsion to exercise his eyes with test cards. Tick. He renewed friendships. Tick. His – or our – social life took off with dinner parties and weekends in the country. Tick. His fear of 'being found out' by others was lifted. Tick. No more game playing, no more deceit. Tick. No more awkward schedules to accommodate his three hits a day, no more having to leave work early, take long lunches or dash to the loo and pray no one suspects him. Tick. No more self-loathing. Tick. No more sense of under achievement. He'd recently sat and passed his stock exchange exams and was holding down a job with a big bank. No mean achievement. Tick. He was being a grown-up, and the man whose skin he had wanted to fill since his father had died and left him as heir. Tick. He was, for the first time in his adult life, tasting success, self-worth, liberation, health, fun, and love. Tick. He was, for the first time, leading a normal life. Normal had been his dream. Tick.

His affection for me knew no bounds. 'You're the best my Billy and you're mine,' he flirted, sticking ski sticks between my legs or attempting sex in swinging bubble cars. Like a celebrating bear, he threw his arms around me every time I made it up a button lift or down a slope, and every time I didn't. I teased him. I mimicked his buckling knees and swinging hips when he skied. I mimicked his laugh and the way he bit his bottom lip in concentration or anticipation of food. When he laughed, he clasped his tummy as if it hurt.

On the train with Emma, en route for Geneva, she and I had chatted about Will. 'What keeps you with him Nix? You keep giving and giving to him but get nothing in return. And your life literally spins around him. I mean I love him to bits, but...'

'I must give him my all Em, before it's too late.' Unbidden, the reply had slipped out without me understanding its origin. It unnerved me as well as her.

'What does that mean, for God's sake?' She asked.

I had to think hard. It was true, I did have the impression that I was racing against time. But why though? My logical explanation, based on my age-old fear, was that he would leave me for one of those blondes. Or... and here my stomach flipped... he would start using again.

I chased the thought away. Probably just my customary expectation of disaster. It always got in the way, that, and spoiled things. All is well! Think positive!

Two weeks after my conversation with Emma, Will and I sat naked and cross-legged in front of the fire. He was in a reflective mood. I watched the light flickering on his skin and asked him to share his thoughts. He shot me a resigned glance before looking into the flames and saying, 'Lady Luck has finally deserted me, Billy.'

Lady Luck was his guardian angel. He believed that she'd watched over him all his life, and protected him from 'going too far'.

'I've come to the end of the road, darling. This is it. I really feel it this time.'

He said this with such a hopeless air I asked him to shed light on what he meant. He didn't know. It was just a feeling, he said. As I listened, I was aware of my own strength of will beginning to seep away – slowly, surely, at the faltering pace of soldiers' footsteps in retreat.

'I'm scared, Billy. I'm really scared. What if I'm right?'

'No Will, no, you're feeling vulnerable – that's all. You'll be alright. It's ok. It's ok. I love you.'

We clung to each other. We cocooned ourselves against this unknown fear that had all of a sudden seeped between us. The soundtrack to *Bilitis* played on the stereo in the bedroom and we got into bed. We remained there for forty-eight hours. Stitched together. Holding on for dear life. There wasn't a patch of his skin I didn't touch or gaze at. I took snapshots with my eyes of every hair, mole, bone shape, and blood vessel. Of every shade of green and grey hidden in the depths of his eyes. I folded the tips of his fingers over mine. I willed him to merge with me, to stay with me forever so that I would never, ever forget. We talked and talked. About the choices we'd made, what we'd have done differently, and what we would do in the future. We talked about marriage. Our marriage. Where we would live. How many babies we'd have, who they would look like, what we would call them. We talked about death and about the spirit world.

'What do you think Billy? You believe in the spirit? You think our souls carry on?'

'Yup. I do. I think they're everywhere, spirits – like my fairies, remember? Maybe there's one here with us now – you never know. Of course, I believe in them!'

'Oh Billy! Tsk! Why did I even ask?!' We were nose to nose, and he was grinning playfully. 'You and your magical world...'

I started to protest but he sat up and reached over to the bedside table for his pack of cigarettes. He lit one and the faint crackle from the burning tobacco mixed with his deep intake of breath. When Will smoked he made it look delicious. Made me think I was missing out on something. I leant towards him saying 'Here. Give me a drag.'

He propped himself up against the headboard, with his legs stretched out.

'You know that Mum went to mediums after my father died? Have I told you that before? She said that when they were good, she could actually talk to him through them. Like... properly talk.' He shrugged and said 'Wonder what they talked about? After all, they hadn't been having such a great time together, what with his drinking habits...' He looked away, and stacked his packet of cigarettes, notebooks, pens and lighters in two neat piles on his bedside table, centralising each object perfectly. The ashtray he put in the middle. He was turning back to me, when he noticed that the corner of a notebook was slightly askew, and he straightened it until the symmetry was exact.

'Anyway... Billy, Billy...' His eyes were misty. 'Now. What

we were saying? Oh yes. Tell me something.' He dragged deeply on his cigarette and squinted through the smoke. 'In all honesty, do you really think that if, say, I died tomorrow, you would be able to see me – or my ghost?' He raised his eyebrow with a sceptical and teasing look. 'Billy?... Is that what you think? Yes? That *is* what you think, isn't it? My funny little Billy Goat.' With his free hand he rubbed my head.

But no words came to me. Just thoughts crowding my mind. Die? You're not going to die. No. I won't let you. I can't let you. Not till we're old and grey will I let you die. Then we'll go together. Holding hands. Yes. That's what will happen. I will not let you die. No. No. No.

'Billy. Talk to me. Say if I am right? Say if Lady Luck really has gone...?' He didn't finish his sentence, but rolled into my arms again, and curled himself into as tight a foetal position as he could.

'I'm scared, Billy.'

'Sssh. It's ok. I'll look after you, Will. My beautiful Will. Maybe I can be your Lady Luck. All is well.'

Tears trickled from my eyes with no let-up, yet neither of us could understand why. There was nothing to cry about. Nothing had happened. We were just scared. He kissed them away and attempted to tease me again. But the more his body sank into my arms the more I sensed his resignation. Seeing the light in his eyes fading, I willed him to salvage belief in his luck, but with waning enthusiasm – for I too felt that our power had gone.

Chapter 27

He had known more than I. Without conscious thought he had verbalised his instinct.

Twelve mornings later I am getting ready for his funeral. Wanting him to be proud of me, I can't decide what to wear. It is warm outside, but I am cold. My teeth chatter and I yawn all the time, which sends shivers across my flesh. I have thick black tights on, to cover up the wounds on my shins, but I have no hat, and I'm worrying that I will be conspicuous for it. I spin around his bedroom. Hot, cold and sweaty, my heart skips beats. How on earth have I forgotten to think about clothes? I never forget anything. I am efficient. Always have been. It's one thing I'm proud of. Mum, whose forgetfulness is legendary, is in awe of my competence. God, how could I have messed up at a moment like this? How stupid of me.

Now. Be calm. Take a deep breath. Concentrate. It doesn't really matter what I wear, surely? I'll look at what I have. Skirt – jacket – shoes. Which are the most appropriate?

What colour can I wear – does it have to be black? Black is for widows. Black is for mourning. Neither status do I want to accept. I want colour. Head to foot colour. I want to flip the foreign implication of a funeral on its head.

But courage fails me.

I choose a black skirt and cream coloured jacket that Will likes on me. It's an Yves St Laurent hand-me-down from a friend, with big gold buttons and puffed shoulders which look like the young growth of an angel's wings.

I feel sick. I have no knowledge of funerals. I have no knowledge of death. Why should I have? No one ever talked to me about death. But why hadn't they? Why didn't my education teach me, or us, what to expect from it? Death is integral to life, so it seems absurd that it's rarely addressed. Even the word is avoided as if it were dirty or embarrassing. Why had I not been warned about the madness and grief that swallows you whole, how to master it, how to survive it, how to follow the steps one to ten of practical formalities?

Tears stream down my face and, surveying the chaos of strewn clothes, my heart races. I think I'm having a panic attack. I gasp for air. My breathing is so shallow my throat feels restricted, as if there's something stuck in there.

I want to stay here. Be alone. Feel safe. Put on his t-shirt. Get back into bed.

A horror of breaking down in front of people stirs up waves of nausea. I run to the bathroom and throw my head over the basin. Tears slide down the white porcelain and circle the plughole before disappearing. Down they go into the dark, dank drain, to join all the other bits of discarded life that clog its sides. I think of the parts of me that are in there already, clinging to a glob of something else – parts of Will too – not wanting to be washed away into the bowels of hell. Get away from it! I say to myself. It'll suck you in, wash you down! Down, down you'll go, crashing against the sides.

I reel backwards, and onto the bed, stuffing the duvet into my ears to stifle the ghostly echoes. But still I hear them. Clang! Drip, drip… glug, glug… Clang!

A burst of emotion shoots though me from a place I've not connected to before. It's a rasping holler of fury, and it takes me by surprise. Here I am, screaming at God, pointing my finger at Him, blaming him for this hell. He – the Almighty, the All Great – how could he have allowed my pack of cards to tumble? He could have prevented it. Yet he didn't. Why not? After all my hard work, my energy, my love for Will? Damn him! Damn him! Damn him! I beat the mattress, choked with rage, yet through it all I keep thinking I must get moving. Get up. Get going. Can't be late. No. Not today. Get up. Get going. Can't be late….

My head hurts. My eyes are sore. On opening them, I get a shock. It's Will! He's there! On the edge of the bed! My Will! In front of me! Tapping his wrist, I think. In that first second he is so clear but quickly begins to fade. I reach out to him. Don't go! Please! But before my eyes his shape dissolves, and then bleaches into a colourless outline. Will! Stay with me! Will …! His smile lingers on in the air between us, and I fancy catching it before it too disappears.

Driving to church with Flora and Louise, our previous

chats about marriage bounce through my bemused mind with the rhythm of ping-pong balls. Beside me, Louise lists everyone who's coming to lunch with us afterwards. It's a day of sunshine and blue skies. The blossom on the trees looks like puffs of fleeting hopefulness, and in my head I picnic in bluebell woods with Will and our babies.

Adjacent to my dream plays another recording: me going down the stairs to the chapel in the morgue, a day or two ago. My mouth is dry. My heart pounds. Inside my head its threatening thud sounds like the echo of a prehistoric footstep. I start to giggle. Giggle? What's got into me? God. I cover my face with my bag to muffle it. But I can't stop. It's because of the dim lighting and Jesus on the cross – it's all so reverential that it's ridiculous. Will would hate it. And the silence is so complete I wonder if the walls are sound-proofed like those of a recording studio. The staccato of my laugh sounds so sharp and booming I feel swallowed by it. Who on earth's going to be making a din down here? I keep thinking.

It's the size of the coffin that strikes me first. It's too short, I think. Much too short. Not impressive enough to hold the magnitude of my prince. I take little steps towards it. His hands are next to come into view, being the highest point of him, positioned just under the lid once it closes. They're folded, as if in prayer – and so at odds with Will's light-hearted personality, that in that instant, my rein of etiquette slackens completely, and I fall on him with a wail. I try to unravel his stiff fingers, while taking in his swollen blue face, and in the corners of his mouth is something I recognise. It looks like saliva. Saliva? What? God. Is he still alive? Has it all just been a terrible mistake?

I kiss him. Searchingly. Alas, when I run my tongue across his lips it is only the soft dryness of cotton wool that I kiss. My warm breath bounces back at me, as if it stings him, but it's because his skin is so cold. To the touch he is like a stone statue, cool and hard, and my instinct is to cup his face to try to warm him. I trace the contours of his head and neck and arms, willing his DNA to blend with mine. I fill the hollows of his eyes with tears, and place his lucky dice and a love letter from me under his hands.

'See you soon, darling. See you soon.'

The car pulls up under a tree behind the rush of traffic on the Brompton Road. I follow Louise and Flora through the throng moving into the church. My legs buckle. Someone pulls me up and whispers in my ear. Emma is in the doorway and I catch her eye. She gives me a wan smile, presses her chest and mouths 'Be strong'. I bite back tears. I can't let myself go. Make a scene. Not now. It would be awful. I look around at everyone there, so that I can tell Will who's come to say goodbye to him. He'd be chuffed to see so many. There are the oldies looking expensive and elegant in lace and suits, our friends with painted nails and dancing hair, and pockets of chain smokers with trembling hands, loose jackets, thin ties, and skinny legs.

Sunlight pours through the stained glass and the scent of lilies hangs sweetly in the air around his coffin. There are twenty-six of them. One for every year of his life. My parents are there. It's the first time I've seen them together since I was little. Regret that it's for his funeral and not our wedding stabs at me. Mum pats my father's hand. His facial tics seem exaggerated. They sit close to where I am sitting with Will's Mum and sister. The three of us, I realize when my Mum mouths something to me, are masked in blank stillness, absorbed in our own conversation with the lonely box in front of us. The flinching tension of our interlocked hands is the only giveaway to our stress.

I feel strangely comforted with Will lying so close and knowing how he looks, dressed in the blue jeans and sloppy sweater that I provided, with his dice and my letter under his hands.

The service begins. Above the muffled thunk of the organ peddle the front door creaks, followed by a click clack of heels on the stone floor. There are whispers of apology as the latecomer shuffles past people in a pew at the back. The vicar stands to address us, and his voice fades in and out of my ears. It's Will that I seek conversation with. Only five feet from me, he is as close as he'll ever be now. There's an intimacy in our propinquity, and my mental reality shifts into the bubble between us and away from the exterior goings on. I lose myself in our world, but kneel, stand and sing in unison with the congregation. It feels as if I am beside myself. Watching me, watching us.

How, I ask, have we got to be here – you in a box and me in unbroken stinging solitude? How, Will? Talk to me. Make sense of this mess, so that I can understand.

My mind drifts effortlessly. The centuries of the human soul settled in the fabric of the church, shape a womb of comfort around my doubts. Our twilight existence – lurching from one upheaval to the next – floods my thoughts, while questions that have been haunting me appear like ghosts waiting in line at the post office, holding packets of answers.

So how *have* we got to be here? Hmmm?

I go back to the beginning.

Did I know when secrecy first crept covertly between us, or the point when we went from balanced equilibrium to oscillating – like a see-saw – and my inner alert button switched suddenly to *on*? Was I aware that from there on in my focus pivoted around him, to the exclusion of everything else – work, friends, family? No, I don't think I did.

Was I too blind and too ignorant at the time to see how my role morphed from adored puppy to vigilant guard-dog, or was I just too frightened of the consequences to admit what the change between us meant? Were my own fears of not being good enough the blanket that suffocated the truth? Or was my inbuilt programming to make believe – bring order to disorder – the reason for my inaction? When his sexual desire failed, did I feel responsible, and was that a good enough reason for me being pushed away? When drunkenness got the better of him and he hit me in the face, did I turn it into my fault? Did I reproach myself for lighting his fuse, and for allowing him to order that bottle? When his spaced-out inertia left me feeling discarded and worthless, did I feel accountable? Was I failing him in some way? Was I not doing enough, or being enough?

Yes. Yes. Yes. Yes. I answered to every question.

What did I feel through those long nights waiting for him to come home, until sometimes he had only enough time to shower before rushing off back to work? Or when, even from under the duvet – with my skilled ear trained on the tone of desperation in his howls – I'd long for his sigh of relief when finally he hit a vein? Was I frightened and lonely when he spent the rest of the night with his head on the kitchen floor? Or was I not even conscious of how I felt? Was I stupid enough to be reassured by his conventional suit and tie and his breezy 'See you later darling', as he left for work? And what about the blood that looked like brash paintwork all over the kitchen units every morning? Was it so easy for me to normalise my daily routine of wiping it away before I'd even drunk my coffee? Why did I think it normal to live with sickening dread from the moment I woke up, then spend the rest of the day intercepting its possible effects? What about driving him to score at night? Did I think that a regular thing to do, when I knew that my friends were in restaurants or cinemas or making suppers at home? Did I not compare myself to them as I sat for hours in unlit streets outside buildings with boarded-up windows, their broken glass left as warnings?

Oh Will. I can see you now, in the passenger seat. Hellbent on scoring, keyed up, swivelling your head from side to side, checking for cops, and issuing monosyllabic directions. It was always Notting Hill, and the same deserted streets clustered off Westbourne Park Road, where the heavy bass of Motorhead from a boarded-up window was the only sign of life.

'Ok. Here. Pull over. Just pull over.' And you opened the door while the car was still moving, and ran off, into the curtain of rain. Sometimes you'd stop, already drenched, turn back to me, and shout through the open gap of my window.

'Billy – don't get out of the car. Promise me that. Just don't, ok? They're armed. They don't fuck around. Stay where you are. I won't be long...'

Why did I think it my responsibility to save you from falling asleep at the wheel? I was frightened in my car on those forbidding streets, frightened of the armed drug dealers, frightened of what could happen to you. As the hours slipped by, I always thought '*this* time, *this* time, *this* time is it'.... '*This* time something must have gone wrong.' You should be out by now, Will. What's taking you so long? Are you partying in there, or have they killed you? And did I dare go in, to find out? What would they do to me if did?

Did it not occur to me that my focus to save Will had become a risk to myself?

No. It never did.

Saving him was more powerful and all-consuming than saving my own sanity.

***

A friend of the family is giving the address. He laments how Will, having dropped his guard for a moment, lost his life at such a tender age, with so much potential in front of him. He talks of Will's courage in his battle against drugs, reminding us how he never gave up. And for that, he said, he went out winning.

Behind me a girl sniffs and I hear the click of the clasp on her bag. I wonder if Will is listening, if his soul is hovering above us, and watching. I like to think so. I wonder if he is touched by the loving words said about him, the sweet messages on all the flowers. Does he see it all? Does he see our sorrow? Is he regretful? Or is he now just a stream of pure light, free of all negative energy? I look up at the coloured sunlight streaming in through the stained-glass windows and down onto his coffin. Is he up there within those rainbow prisms?

Oh, damn it, Will! Damn it! What the hell did you do? What were you thinking after all we went through? It wasn't meant to be like this, our life. Damn you! We were meant to 'live happily ever after.' Fairy-tales are what I create. Magic. Remember? Not horror shows. Our story wasn't meant to be cut in half like this. Torn and shredded. Ruined. Damn! I am a fixer, for God's sake! *You* know that. Why could you not just have hopped on board my miracle train? Hung around for the ride? Had a life? I wipe away tears and a runny nose with the back of my hand. I have no tissues.

I feel bitter, and my mind turns to the times when I couldn't cope any more. The darkest times, when he needed multiple hits a day and one by one his veins collapsed. He took to injecting into his muscles instead. They were often 'dirty hits', when dirt is pushed into the skin by the puncture of the syringe. We spent most nights of every week in Emergency, waiting to get another pus-filled abscess lanced, some of which swelled his thigh or arm to double their normal size. I was embarrassed and angry that he was taking the time of medical staff, who had emergencies to deal with. Real ones. Not self-inflicted ones.

Thinking about that reminds me of a letter I received before Will died from a cousin who regretted the disrepute I had brought on our family name by dragging it through the mud with drugs. Shameful, she said. Shameful. Attempting to control my outrage, I wrote back explaining that there should be no shame attached to a troubled mind, only sympathy and compassion. I wanted to say it was shameful of her to regard it so harshly. I remind myself now to feel as I preached. Even in memory.

Soon after that, I took off for ten days. Said I needed space. To be alone. I didn't go anywhere. Instead I sat in my flat and dwelled on my options. Could I leave him for good? Was I up to it? Or would it break me to do that?

I thought of the suffering I would endure if I did. The emptiness. The pain. The sickness. Or the jealousy of him with another girl.

I couldn't do it. No. I resolved to find greater resources within myself, to master our relationship – and his drugs.

It was close to my birthday when I next saw him. I went to his flat and he greeted me at the door. The pupils of his heavy-lidded eyes, like tiny black beads, made him look like an alien. He was unable to walk – to stand even – without a stick. His legs, arms, and ankles were wrapped in bandages, as if he had come back from war. He looked emaciated.

We talked. My back was to the door while he leant on his stick and winced.

'What the fuck Will?' I could not conceal the shock I felt. 'How's this happened so quickly? You're like the walking wounded, for God's sake...' I started crying.

'Yup, I'm a mess.' He drew in his bottom lip. 'A fucking mess. And no more fucking veins.' He had even tried to shoot up between his legs, he said. 'I'm desperate, darling.'

I remembered a friend of his who, once all his veins collapsed, jacked up in his eyeballs. I asked Will if he too had reached that moment, though I immediately turned away and put my hands to my ears. I took hold of his fingers, which were discoloured and swollen. I lifted his t-shirt and saw that the tracks that scarred his stomach were red and angry.

I too was angry. Ready to burst with anger. I was disgusted. Disgusted at the energy – no, love – that I had invested, disgusted at myself for being blind and stupid, disgusted at him for his lack of fortitude. Rage woke me up. I decided there and then I'd had enough.

Chapter 28

Father-like, he tends and spares us
Well our feeble frame he knows;
In his hand he gently bears us,
Rescues us from all our foes
Praise him praise him praise him praise him
Widely yet his mercy flows....

The choir's singing is soft and sweet. Mercy. I have it for everyone else, but do I have mercy for myself? I wonder. Can I forgive myself for my ignorance, my blindness? My total failure? Flora squeezes my hand and offers me her handkerchief. Her fingers are the same shape as Will's. I'm momentarily confused by the difference of texture. Hers are soft compared to Will's, and finer. Why isn't it Will's hand around mine? It's his hand I need, his hand – where is it?

Above the hymn and inside my head, I hear past voices on the telephone, telling me I was as sick as Will.

It was love, not sickness, I protested. And love heals!

There's nothing sick about love, for God's sake. Love conquers all.

But every therapist I talked to had the same response.

Their verdict of 'co-dependence' initially incensed me, but after a while I accepted it with a sickening sense of defeat. Co-dependence. What a dour, sterile-sounding label it is. I still struggle with it. It doesn't explain the bottomless well of love I have felt. It doesn't justify the tightrope that I've walked between life and death, nor the web in which I've been caught, rescuing and failing, rescuing and failing; firstly my dad and then Will. It doesn't touch on my willingness to forgive, the limitless endurance I've exercised, or the obliteration of my own feelings – and life – in lieu of theirs. It doesn't hint at the energy I have spent, analysing and circling them, trying to prevent their next crash, or the confusion of pretending that all is well, normal – happy even. It doesn't cover the tenacious sense of culpability I have had for their every drink, fix, or wrongdoing, or my self-punishing soundtrack from failing to stop them. It doesn't give worth to the bleeding sadness that I have carried, watching the disintegration of someone I love, or the weight of preaching morality. It doesn't speak for how those things chipped at my psyche and carved it, before I even learned to read and write, or how the spectre of catastrophe tailed me like a shadow. Nor does it describe the easy prey I was; how the roles of Saviour and Peacemaker were handed to me as routinely as a coat in winter. Or were they just there, like available seats on a train, waiting for me to slip into them?

The vicar talks of love. Of its patience, kindness and endurance. He says that while faith, hope and love abide, the greatest of all is love. He tells us to love one another gathered here today. How love is the power that gets us by, brings light to darkness, gives strength to the weak. Give it freely he says. Give! And we will heal.

Isn't that what I've been doing forever? And did it heal? I shrug. I don't know any more. Doubt and failure have tired me.

Conceding that my sort of love – the warrior, shock absorber and healer – was powerless to conquer everything, I have come to terms with having 'a problem' in the way I love. I also understand that my way is negative. Wrong.

Yet, the way I love is who I am. Seeing it as wrong is like crumpling up my soul and tossing it in the bin. As good as admitting that my knowledge of life is worth zip. So too my history.

Was I born with the addict gene? Or was I a radical convert to a faith whose instruction was as intrinsic as breath is to life? My response to the gift of my dad's broken soul was the innate response of the maternal instinct. I think. There's no escaping the mothering gene. Its natural affinity with its own blood, elicits watchful attention on them and a responsibility to meet their needs. It's unconditional and, regardless of conventional role-playing, its switch is *on* if one is deemed more vulnerable than the other. It was of no matter that I was so young – my instinct was tuned to respond to my dad's demands, as if he were my child. It was tuned to balance his imbalance, like weighing down the other end of a see-saw. To care is to love. It's the 'doing' side of loving. Why the frosty clinical label of co-dependence?

Co-dependence didn't happen overnight. Instead I slipped into its culture over time, without noticing my personal sacrifices, but just doggedly galvanized by Dad's reliance on my devotion to him. A bit like a child, lured by the deepest part of a puddle, who acclimatizes quickly to the discomfort of the muddy water in her boots, compelled as she is by the satisfying effects of her splashing. Sacrifice of her own comforts and needs becomes a habit – second nature, normal life – particularly if the parent's behaviour endorses it.

Dad was my mirror, and his reflection shaped me. I was not yet wise to his needs being all-consuming to him, or that he hadn't the wherewithal to take care of another person – not even his child. I hadn't yet understood that his disregard of my needs and his yo-yo affection was not a personal slur against me, but a flaw in his own make-up, stemming from a broken and thirsty spirit.

Was the forgetting of myself, the point where love crossed the border into the land of co-dependence? And was I a victim? No, I don't think so. Were there not also unconscious contracts written in *my* sacrificial deed? Weren't its underlying messages 'I'll give myself wholly to you, so long as you love me back?' 'I'll lay bare my heart to you, so long as you don't hurt me?' Or 'I'll be the best for you, so long as I matter?'

Once I had understood that my dad depended on me as his ally there was no turning back.

'What would I do without you, my dear little mite? I'd be lost. Don't ever leave your poor old Dad. Promise?'

The contract between us was sealed. And so, I begrudgingly conceded, was our co-dependence.

Chapter 29

I stubbornly clung to a grain of myself and instead of heeding the therapist's advice and checking into a clinic, I enrolled to train as a counsellor so that I could fully understand addiction.

At the same time, I walked away from the man I loved. Oh, Will. You remember that?

Tough love, tough love, tough love was their gospel. I walked away as a demonstration of tough love. It was one of the hardest things I ever did. My heart craved him. My soul craved him. I hurt mentally and physically. But tough love was the only way through to an addict, I learned.

'They have to hit rock bottom before they want to get clean.'

My telephone rang throughout the day and I buried my head under a cushion and left it. When the doorbell buzzed without let-up, I crawled around the flat to keep out of sight of the windows. I gave his flowers away and left his letters unopened. Some I even threw bravely in the bin.

The others I carried with me, and ran my fingers over his handwriting of my name and address. I threw myself into my studies and reconnected with friends who had dropped me because of my 'junkie boyfriend'.

After some time, Will stopped his relentless attempts at communication. Silence fell. It unsettled me. I lay awake at night worrying if he was dead or alive. I worried that I had been substituted for a blonde. I held my churning tummy and thrashed around. What had I done? What an idiot I was. I had nothing now. I loved a man I had turned away and he was gone. What was I left with? Nothing. Nothing. I shrugged. A wavering belief in fate? An instinct to survive? So what.

I fell briefly into the arms of Christopher. His kindness was balm to my damaged self-esteem and he shone light laughter into the dark of my heart.

Two months had passed when the phone rang in the middle of the night.

It was Will.

'Billy, Billy I am clean! Believe me. Please. Come back to me Billy, yes?'

I felt whole again. Alive. I felt love. They were the 'happy days', beginning of my world days.

Feeling, for him, was a new and fresh experience, and filled with wonder. Like being reborn, he said. Pain, joy and love had been dead to him under heroin's anaesthetic; so too had been the empathy for the anguish into which those who loved him had had to dive. Now he threw himself wholeheartedly into life. We went to the theatre and cinema, took a trip here, a trip there, and ate in restaurants. We went skiing and dancing, made endless love, teased each other and laughed. He revelled in his born-again senses and was jubilant with the subsequent physical healing from being clean. With increased blood circulation in new veins, the repair and fading of his scars was apparent.

He rejected my pleas to go to NA meetings. 'Been there, done that' he said.

I nagged more, but not enough, when I noticed that in the evenings a new habit was creeping in incrementally. To begin with it was so mild that I was able to turn a blind eye, to brush away any niggling question marks I had with it. All is well, of course.

A new superstitious belief in numbers was pulling him into an impenetrable trance. He had got it into his head that derivatives of the number four brought him good luck, and all the others bad. This led to him either rolling his four dice until number four showed up on all of them or tapping a doorknob or electrical socket a number of times – until he felt 'safe'. After a while, this practice was swallowing up a couple of hours or more of every evening, and once it had lifted, he seemed surprised that supper was cold, the film was finished, and I was beside myself with anxiety, my head once again under the pillow. It was as if he was taken – hypnotised – into a separate world, and though I longed to shout at him, to 'snap out of it, for God's sake,' I feared that an attempt to do so would have led to an explosion, the consequences of which could have been catastrophic. He would score. And that would be it.

We once drove for over three hours to Wales, but as we approached the hotel his paranoia that he had left the iron on made me turn around and go back. Once home he tapped it – a slow rhythmic tapping – eight thousand, eight hundred and eighty-eight times – with his eyes glazed, his body inert, his bottom lip drawn in, his jaw tight. It was over two hours later that he finally felt 'safe' and skipped over to me with a hug and smile as if nothing unusual had taken place. It was, he said, the only thing keeping him clean. It was 'his safety net'. Without it, 'that would be that'.

Was fear the pumping heart of all addiction? I wondered a thousand times. Was it so familiar that, in its brief absence, another one and another one would be contrived and drawn in, so that the addict could continue to live within its grip? Had Will not known how to be, in silence and peace? Had his distrust of the ceasefire – the longed for 'being clean' – sent him searching for fear again? Was fear too deep a habit that without it he was lost? Was fear his Big Bad Wolf? Was it the menacing voice that followed him, reminding him that he didn't have it in him, he was too weak, and not up to it? Was his resulting obsession with numbers a mechanism to escape from it? A numbing, self-obliterating escape?

The singing around me pulls me back for a second. Its sweetness is soothing.

Drop thy still dews of quietness
Till all our strivings cease;
Take from our souls the strain and stress,

234

And let our ordered lives confess
The beauty of thy peace.

**

Will had passed his stockbroker exam and was working for a big bank when his 'number obsession' intensified. His job in the Old Masters department at the auction house had been interesting, but his ambition to drop the legacy of spoiled little rich kid, and to prove himself a successful breadwinner fired him to change direction. By then, money was king, and his peers were making pots of it in the City. He had no intention of being left behind, and wanted to be as good as them, if not better. Being a stockbroker, though, came with pressures that he'd not anticipated, and a formidable fear of failing in his job eclipsed them.

His early starts made weekday evenings a little calmer, but Friday and Saturdays were manic. Hours and hours were spent in a demented trance. My plans to distract him with weekends away worked only once or twice. And even then, I could feel him only half with me, the other half desperate to get back, to zone out and reach 'safety'.

Soon my state of alarm was as high as it was in his using days. I was gauging his mood – measuring it against the last one – sensing how susceptible he was to any downward swing – blocking the external stimulus – chatting nine to the dozen to distract him.

I telephoned his old dealers, whose spooky houses I'd waited outside a year before. It was reckless of me. I knew that. They were a scary bunch. I gambled with a threatening tone of voice and said I would shop them to the police if they supplied him with drugs.

'Remember. I know your phone number – where you live – your names. So, don't do anything stupid. You know the score… Ok?'

Oh God. What was I thinking? Were they laughing themselves silly, at me and my big threats?

Chapter 30

Once Will began to drink that evening, I knew we'd arrived at the beginning of the end. It had been a year since he stopped taking heroin. A year of being clean.

On that particular day, he chose Valium and Vodka as the prelude to his undoing.

Breathe through the heats of our desire
Thy coolness and thy balm;
Let sense be dumb, let flesh retire;
Speak through the earthquake, wind and fire,
O still small voice of calm!

I hear my own voice sing along with the congregation. 'O, still small voice of calm.'

I think back through that day, minute by minute, with my eyes glued to his coffin. Oh Will. Come to me now. I need you to tell me it's been a bad dream. Tell me. Please. Tell me that I'll wake up and you'll be there. Laughing at me. Pointing mockingly, as if I had been gullible enough to fall for such a trick. Come to me, Will, and tell me.

Slumped in the pew, it feels as if all the stuffing has been removed from me. I no longer have the oomph to stand or kneel with everyone else.

If only I hadn't believed he was 'off to buy cigarettes.' If only he hadn't bought Valium instead. If only he hadn't taken so many. If only he'd come back at lunchtime. If only he hadn't opened the vodka. If only he hadn't reacted to a joke I'd made. If only I'd kept my mouth shut and not made the damn joke. If only I'd been able to keep pace with his speeding car when I chased him from Clapham to – I don't where. If only I'd been able to stop him, calm him down. If only I'd known to which of his dealers he was heading. If only I had got to his flat earlier. If only. If only. If only.

In the early hours of the morning, I dragged my feet up the stairs behind Flora, whom I'd woken to ask for help. I'd had no sleep for twenty-four hours. I'd called Will's telephone all through the night, but he hadn't picked up.

Turning the key, I fought against the impulse to bolt. But the image of his 'please forgive me' smile urged me inside.

When we opened the door, a stench hit us. God. What was it? Similar to acetone, it was like a wall of stagnant acrid air. My heartbeat accelerated immediately, and pounded with such violence I put my hand to my chest to hold it in. A quiver at the back of my throat signalled that I would throw up, and I swallowed hard to stop it.

The corridor was dark and still, the doors of every room closed. I'd never seen it shut up like that. We called out to him, but nothing came out of our mouths. I stopped breathing. His car keys weren't in their usual place on the windowsill, but yesterday's croissant crumbs were still there in the corner on the floor. I forced myself down the passage to check out the sitting room. The comforting regularity of its condition came as a huge relief, as did the weak shadows on the carpet. Next I turned the handle of the kitchen door. Very slowly I opened it. I realised my eyes were closed. Old episodes of what I'd found before anticipated what I might find then – a spray of blood and him comatose on the floor, a tourniquet wrapped around a limb. I was astonished, therefore, when I opened my eyes to find it spotless, and just as I'd left it the day before.

A crack on the wall and a small stain on the carpet grabbed my attention as I reached his bedroom. Why had I not noticed *them* before? My teeth were chattering then, and I was cold. As if the cognitive function in the computer of my brain was down, my hand wouldn't make the movement required to turn the doorknob. The smell was strong and it restricted my breathing, and when finally the door opened, it engulfed me. Bile rose in my throat. My chest tightened. The whisper of his name remained stuck and silent in my passageways. I managed – with effort, as my arm was suddenly heavy – to raise my hand to the light switch. In that split second I noticed an indentation in the duvet at the end of the bed, and my gaze dropped to the floor directly under it.

Next to a pool of blood lay his foot. Contorted and discoloured.

A shrill howl filled my head and ears. I ran to the window, opened it wide and retched. Flora rushed in, pulled Will's t-shirt away from around his neck, and called out orders to me. She had to repeat herself; I couldn't comprehend anything she said. I dared to look at Will. I dared for a brief second and then I couldn't. I retched again. Flora shouted again. I tried to pull myself together. I understood we had to get him to the kitchen.

Will's body had stiffened and was bent out of shape. His skin – a deep blue – was splattered with burgundy-coloured stains. His contorted shape terrified me. Disgusted me. As I grasped his shoulders my stomach heaved and I began to convulse. I was unable to hold him for any amount of time with my body shuddering, so it took time to drag him from the narrow space between the bed and the wall. Why were his limbs so grotesquely misshapen? It was as if he had fallen and his thighbone had twisted from his hip socket, his arm from his shoulder socket, his foot from his ankle joint. Then like a bronze cast he had set like that – rigid and stuck.

He was heavy. Really heavy. Like rocks in a sleeping bag. Dragging him down the corridor took a long time. I walked backwards towards the kitchen with my hands under his arms, and Flora directed me. I tried to still my body, to stop its uncontrollable shakes. I had to find it in myself to be calm, to help bring him round. To help Flora. She looked so brave and pulled together, but the tremor in her voice gave her away. Once we got to the kitchen, I was able to look at Will without retching. His colour and distorted shape no longer filled me with disgust. Instead I longed to warm his frozen corpse, untangle his limbs and wipe away the red and blue stains from his skin. His black tourniquet fell lightly upon my feet as I lay him down, and his head rolled heavily across my forearms. How gentle and serene his eyes were. How shocking that felt to me. Why was there no panic, no 'Help me!' look in them?

One of us telephoned Louise and the ambulance. I lay down next to him and wrapped my arms around his head. While I kissed his face I searched for his smell.

'Will. Darling.' I whispered in his ear, 'It's ok. You're alright. Ambulance is coming. You'll be fine. I'm with you. Hang on in there. Will. Please. You're there, yes? You're listening, right? Will?'

The next time I looked up his mother was standing in the kitchen. She knelt down beside me and put her hands over his eyes to close them. What was she doing that for? He wasn't dead. No. Then she removed his watch and signet ring. The watch she put on Flora's wrist, and the ring she slipped onto my fourth finger. My wedding finger. I was shaking my head. A jam of words was stuck in my vocal chords. A lump in my throat. He's not dead. Not dead. Not dead. No. He's not dead. What are you all doing? We can't give up. No. Not now. We must save him. Come on.

'He's dead, I'm afraid. Passed away, 16th May. I'm sorry for your loss.' It was the paramedic's quiet affirmation. The first thing that came to my mind was that the date must be wrong. 16th May 1988. Four times four equals sixteen and eight plus eight equals sixteen. Sixteen is a derivative of four, is it not? These were his lucky numbers, not unlucky.

'No. No. He's not dead. He can't be.' I was shouting at them as they began to zip him up in a red rubber body bag.

'Four is his lucky number. He's not dead. I know he's not. Please! Listen to me! Pleeease.' I could see my arms and legs lashing out at the paramedics. One of them stood behind me, trying to grab my wrists.

A far away voice demanded I 'get a grip, come on Nix, brace up!' a voice from my childhood – my mother.

Magnified faces with furrowed brows peered closely at me. Policemen's helmets materialised in a blur on the coffee table. Someone pushed me roughly to the floor and as I went down my elbow hit the ledge of the open window. It made a thudding sound, and everyone stopped what they were doing to look round at me.

'You ok over there, miss?' someone called.

I'd felt nothing. I'd heard the thud, knew it was attached to me somehow, but had had no pain. No feeling.

Policemen's radios in the sitting room, where I was, made scratchy noises, but their volume in my ears faded while the paramedics on the street outside amplified. My hearing was tuned to select only where Will was. The grating of aluminium on tarmac and the sharp whoosh of his body being pushed into the ambulance was heightened, as if it came from inside my head.

I collapsed on the floor. My body was convulsing again. My teeth chattered. I covered my head in his t-shirt and draped his tourniquet around my neck.

Chapter 31

'(Love Lifts Us) Up Where We Belong' is our song. We danced to it. Sang to it. Made love to it and cried to it. Over the loudspeakers it resonates around the church, enough to fill everyone's cells. His coffin is carried down the aisle and I follow it behind Louise and Flora. I glance at friends wiping streaked mascara from their cheeks, whispering with heads bowed. Outside I thank them for coming. I feel like a rag doll in a hundred embraces – floppy and without substance. From the corner of my eye I see his coffin being pushed into the back of the hearse. I hear the same sharp whoosh. I hear the engine of the car humming. I panic. I feel torn. Torn between duty and an ache to be with him. The hearse moves away. I can't leave him, to go alone. No. I can't. I kick off my shoes and run. It turns into the crescent and brushes a branch of pink blossom that falls like confetti. My mother's voice calls, 'Darling, darling!' Like a hunter, I keep running. I'm twenty yards from it. I see his coffin amidst the flowers. He can't go alone to be burned. No, it's not right. He mustn't be alone. Just as I think I might catch them, tell them to stop, to let me in, they round the corner and speed away.

I spin around. Now what? What do I do now? I'm like a tracker dog that's lost the scent she's following. It hits me then that I will never ever see his face again. Within an hour he will be burned. Gone.

I run back to the empty church and chancel – the spot where his coffin had sat. I stretch myself out on the cold marble and howl. A torrent floods out of me until there's nothing left to hold me together, no roots, no structure, no plan. It's like a landslide. I blame God. I blame Will. I blame myself. I beat the floor with my fists and allow tears of rage and defeat to run in small pools under my neck.

Footsteps approach me.

'You must let him go now, Nix.' My mother's tender touch wipes away my tears. 'He needs to find peace. Heaven. Please help him do that darling. Help free his soul to find the peace he deserves.'

I roll onto my back as she talks. She strokes the hair from my forehead and tucks it behind my ears. The fan vaulting of the nave lifts my mind towards Heaven. Mum's words come to me like a chink of light in the darkness. They offer me an 'out' – a glimmer of renewed will to live – a hopefulness. Yes. She's right. I must concentrate on his soul now. If I can't encourage life, I can encourage peace.

Our story doesn't need to end after all. That feels good. I feel lighter and purposeful again. There is a continuation of sorts.

Mum slips an envelope onto my lap. We are sitting in the front pew. Inside is Christina Rossetti's poem, and the four-leaf clover she gave me when I first went to boarding school, which she had re-found in an old box of correspondence. 'For luck,' she said, and squeezed her hand around mine.

> Remember me when I am gone away,
> Gone far away into the silent land;
> When you can no more hold me by the hand,
> Nor I half turn to go yet turning stay.
> Remember me when no more day by day
> You tell me of our future that you planned:
> Only remember me; you understand
> It will be late to counsel then or pray.
> Yet if you should forget me for a while
> And afterwards remember, do not
> grieve:
> For if the darkness and corruption leave
> A vestige of the thoughts that once I had,
> Better by far you should forget and smile
> Than that you should remember and be sad.

To the End of Love

1990

Chapter 32

In an ebony wooden chest that belonged to my grandmother I have a secret place. It's a drawer within a drawer,
inlaid with mother-of-pearl. Here I store my writing – an-
ecdotes, poems, and stories dating from childhood to the
present moment. I lay this manuscript in there, with a mind
to revisit it, once I have picked myself up and brushed myself down. It is messy, covered in crossings out, arrows and
asterisks, and held together with staples and paper clips.
There are sketches of Will's mouth and eyes in the margins,
and his name in every font and colour. A bleeding heart
replaces the 'O' in his surname.

I have to learn a new way of life in a new skin now. I have
changed. Trauma now defines me. Like an ink stain, it colours my responses and bleeds outwards into relationships
and everyday challenges. I see, feel and react differently, or
just more so than I ever did before. Its long shadow casts a
solemn analytical depth over my thinking and makes me a
stranger to frivolity. People say to me, 'You can cope with

anything now. All future difficulties will fade in comparison.' But instead I feel like a hunted animal, always ready and alert for the next attack. My childhood fear that the unthinkable could happen has been validated. It has happened. Why would it therefore not happen again?

It defines me also in other people's eyes. 'Oh yes. Her. Isn't she the one whose boyfriend died? Heroin, right?' I am pushed into the category of people to keep at arm's length, avoid eye contact with. Like one's opponents just before an election.

The status feels like prison. Privately, I'm struggling to free myself from the tangled mess of my mind. I work hard at it and am tested every second of the day. It feels as if I am fighting my past to make good my future, fluctuating from glimmers of victory to defeat. Being pigeonholed is lonely. I need people to accept me as one of them. I need their support, patience and understanding of my efforts. I need them to see me as they'd always seen me, but wounded. If I had lost my leg I would be carried until I could stand alone. Scooped up and forced to join them for supper, even whilst I bled. They'd ooh and aaah at the horror, but rush to my aid with bandages. It's odd, isn't it, that we tackle physical damage without a second thought, but feel ill at ease around bereaved hearts?

Someone told me a story once about a group of female French Resistance fighters. Though unrelated by age, background, and provenance, they'd found themselves deported to the same concentration camps. Their bonds had become close and interdependent. Their unity, photos, and dreams of reconciliation with loved ones had conjointly kept them going through their suffering. Yet within a few years of being freed and sent back to their respective villages, many of them had died – some still young. The separation from their comrades had brought a new pain: loneliness. What they'd endured together had been incomprehensible to the families who'd remained at home during the war, and the women, isolated in their psychological disparities, had not been able to slot back into the framework of their previous lives.

I've reached the point of knowing that I can't continue to bang the same drum, on and on about my misery. Everyone else has moved on from the shock of losing Will; their lives have led their minds away from it. I am lonely, and fantasies of death or suicide co-habit with a determination to have a normal life again. I berate myself without excuse – I should be 'better' by now. But I am not. The dark, sticky depression still sucks me in like quicksand, filling every empty space. Even a struggle to heave myself out of it feels like it could drown me.

Will's flat is on the market, so I've moved back to mine. Some days I'm unable to get out of bed because of migraines. The pain pumps with dogged determination around my head – bang, bang it goes like water hammer in pipes – and its ferocity makes me sick. My teeth chatter with cold, and any form of light hurts my eyes. I remain in the dark, my body motionless to stave off nausea, my head raised with several pillows.

His tweed jacket still holds his smell, and I lay it beside

me. My answering machine sits on the bedside table, and without moving my body, I can reach the green play button, to slip inside the throaty timbre of his voice, inside the chortle that lifts up the Y of my name – 'Oh Billy! You're never in. Just checking what time you said. It was 8.30 at Julie's, yes? Not the flat? Hope you're having a nice birthday darling… See you soooooon!'

See you soon, he says. See you soon.

Oh, Will. Wouldn't that be nice?

There is a skinny crack where the curtains meet. I watch the daylight slipping through it, silver at first like a knife blade, then gold like the flame of a candle. I smoke. It worsens my head, but I don't care. The smoke curls upwards in front of the shard of light. Reminds me of November bonfires, toffee apples and sparklers. Leonard Cohen's voice is comforting in the darkness. He sings 'Dance Me to the End of Love' – his haunting surrender to its finality.

My doctor pays me a visit. She comes with her leather doctor's bag, twinset and pearls, strokes my forehead with soft hands, and gives me super-strength pills.

'You'll recover, darling,' she says popping one into my mouth and smoothing my hair. 'It's guilt that holds up the recovery process. But you don't have that. You'll be fine. Just give it time.'

Once she leaves, I lay on my side watching the movement of the clock hands that glow in the dark. I wait for the headache to disperse and subside.

Guilt?

Of course I feel guilt. Clouds of it darken each thought.

The guilt is so overpowering I shy away from contemplating it. Contemplation gives it life and thereby ownership. I concentrate on the glowing green clock hands instead. They remind me of a conductor's batons, and the slow tempo of an Adagio. Second by second and another minute moves solemnly through the score.

The window next-door opens with a squeaky swoosh. A man's voice filters out. He sounds so close I can hear him discussing the portrait he's painting – the distance between the hairline and the forehead, how the light bounces off his sitter's temples. After a light clunk, he is quiet. Then there's the strike of a match. I catch a peppery smell of smoke through my open window, and I reach for my packet of Marlboro.

Guilt? I feel it on every level.

Guilt for not having done enough. Surely I could have prevented him from dying, no?

Guilt for not having been enough. I'd complained to friends of feeling second best, of being 'the stay-at-home wife' while heroin was his mistress. But had I been more of a pull – more of something – who knows? He might still be alive.

Guilt for not having forced him to go to NA meetings. Why had I not bullied him to do so? My shying away from confrontation had stopped me. Yet NA saves so many. It could have saved him.

Ultimately, I feel guilt for having been present. For having come into his life. For having loved him.

People are kind and tell me how blessed he was to have

found happiness and love with me. They tell me how rare it is. How fortunate we were to have had it. I acknowledge that a soulmate is a lucky find. That many people never find theirs. But what if I had never graced his path? What if he'd continued to take heroin as many do, and got clean when he was older? He might have survived.

This last layer of guilt is my torturer. That my mere existence could have been his destroyer plays out in my nightmares.

Chapter 33

'Time heals.' That's the universal platitude I hear from everyone. It is also, I understand, a truth, but one that I can acknowledge only in retrospect. While living through 'time' I find no medicinal power in it, yet with each day that passes I become acclimatized to my wound with incremental steps. Once I've realised that an open wound makes daily life unmanageable, I learn to cover it up, even from myself, in order to survive emotionally. I think about an amputated leg. Tissue grows over the wound, and the fever, bleeding, swelling, and pain die down. You can get to the shops and call the plumber now. You can write your thank you letters and cook dinner for eight. But you're still an amputee. There is no running away from that. Half your leg is still missing.

I feel the same about grief. It doesn't vanish; it hides. I shape myself around it, but its impact is carried in my cells for me to return to time and time again. Nevertheless, I cope. Survive. Get by. Coast.

I don't drink alcohol. Never touched it. The spectre of my Dad's boozing haunts me. Any bottle of alcohol, in my eyes, even the finest, may as well have a skull and cross-bones warning on its label. And other than the odd drag I never used to smoke. Now I coast from cigarette to cigarette – each one a step towards nightfall, the close of another day and the end of time. Sleep eludes me, issuing me with more hours in which to smoke. Dark, cavernous hours of the night spawn a remote loneliness, whose only friends in the silence are a distant siren or a vixen's high-pitched scream.

I am up to three packets a day now. Sixty cigarettes. £4.50 in total. That's a lot. Bad for my wallet, bad for my health.

With time, my coming through the tunnel of grief is contingent on a belief that Will's soul continues in an afterlife. It's a belief I choose for me, not one I presume everyone to share. I choose it, whether it's factual or not, because the alternative – in which he's completely extinguished – worsens my despair. And I am a Romantic.

Ghost is a film I go to see several times. It supports my wish that Will's soul is now un-tethered, part of everything, and everywhere. Not being tangible makes him huger. Omnipresent. And pure. No more demons. No more needles. No more enslavement.

I visit mediums and wonder if he's watching me.

Come to me, Will. Talk to me. Tell me you're here.

I travel to suburban streets in outer London, and other than my Christian name I supply no personal information. Mr Cotterel is the first I see. His room is lined with sixties wallpaper – yellow and brown sunflowers with matching curtains, now threadbare. I sit in an armchair whose springs are broken, whilst his cat purrs loudly from behind my head, kneading the crest with its claws. The tick-tock of a grandfather clock is the only other sound while Mr Cotterel takes a few minutes 'to reach spirit'. The atmosphere is soporific as he begins to detail in a monotone, facts about Will, his death, and his funeral. His eyes are closed but the lids flutter behind his magnifying lenses.

Listening to him, I am blown away. Stunned. How can he have known Will had died on the 16th? How can he have known about the lilies on his coffin? Or his watch that Louise gave to Flora and his ring, which she gave to me? And how can he have known the cause of his death? Or that his eyes were green? That we'd recently been skiing? And that the birthday of a close friend was on the nineteenth? How can he have known all those things if Will wasn't telling him? Tears of relief and gladness overwhelm me on my drive back, and I pull over onto a grey street somewhere in Hendon, lined with Edwardian houses and scruffy cars. I no longer feel quite so alone.

One morning Flora calls me. She sounds hesitant and apologetic. 'I know this is asking a lot Nix, but would you mind parting with Will's signet ring? I just, well... want to keep it in the family, you know? Had a thought that you might marry one day – though of course you can't imagine it now – but if you did, the ring would be lost to me forever. D'you see?' Her words, gentle as they are, shatter my mind like the circular break patterns in glass when it has been struck. Taking his ring off my finger is an unbearable prospect. To do so would be to betray Will. Divorce him. I can't do that. No. I can't let him go. It's unthinkable. It is all that I have left of him in material form. To me, it *is* him. I refuse to give it up. It's to remain on my finger for the rest of my life, I tell Flora. And after that conversation I leave the phone to ring in case she calls back. But it niggles me on a daily basis. It creeps into all other thoughts, imbuing them with a sense of doom. I twist his ring round and round on my finger, praying for guidance. I wrestle with myself. Part of me says that the ring is not rightfully mine and should be returned immediately. The other part rebels; the sickness in my stomach swamping the rational voice.

I make an appointment with another medium, and again provide no information. That day the BBC are filming on the Fulham Road, and finding a place to park takes longer than usual. I am late. When I run up the stairs Mrs Mary is waiting at the top with the door open behind her. She is checking her watch and twisting it round her slender wrist.

'There's an impatient young man with me here.' She gestures inside her flat. She is wearing high heels, a frilled liberty print shirt and frosty lipstick, 'Banging on about a ring, he is. Does that mean anything to you?' She throws her hand into the air, and with it her right eyebrow.

I haven't yet got to the top of the stairs but lift up my ring finger. Keen to catch a glimpse of him, I crane my neck to look past her, willing him to show himself. My eyes take in the hallway – its hessian walls, wicker table and mirror, leafy houseplant and bright Casa Pupo rug – but there's no sign of Will, and I am disappointed.

'Yes, yes, that's it. He says you don't even need to come in. "Give the ring to his sister." That's what he says. Does that make sense? Says it means nothing to him. "Just a ring," he keeps saying. "Give it to her this week." Ok?' She looks at her watch.

'Thank you.' I say to her retreating back-view. 'Thank you.'

'Oh,' she says over her shoulder. 'And why've you stopped playing music? Is it Ry Cooder, or Brian Ferry that he likes? I'm getting the 'ry' syllable loud and clear.' She runs her fingers through her layered hair before closing the door.

I am still half way up the stairs, leaning against the banister.

'Both. He likes them both,' I say, dropping his ring into my wallet.

Chapter 34

Sometime a few months after his death I am in a bad way, late at night, with the Big Bad Wolf's taunts haunting my mind. 'You weren't quite up to scratch, were you?' 'Had you been, he'd still be alive.' 'Wouldn't have got eaten, would he?' 'Never been good enough, good enough, good enough.' My stomach somersaults and dread thumps in my heart like the dense drum and bass of heavy metal. I find myself in front of the mirror, having taken a bath and scraped the skin from my shins. Yet I am still not distracted by the hideous inculpating voice. I don't even have it in me to stanch the bleeding. Blood, the colour of cherries, streaks my hand, and drips in a wiggly line down the side of the basin, and my face, which I have rubbed with it, is marked with red smudges that resemble tribal paint. I think of ancient African scarification rituals.

'Tell me the point of it all,' I whisper to my reflection. 'The point. What. Is. The. Point?' I let my eyes travel slowly across my face and neck. A pulse beats below my ear. I push my index finger into it and imagine extinguishing it. I ponder how long it would take before I crumpled to the floor.

Is this my rite of passage? I wonder. Have I hit rock-bottom?

The next morning I make an appointment with a psychotherapist, based in Kensington. His office walls are covered in dark green fabric, and hanging from them are gilt framed eighteenth-century-style portraits. He is tanned with dark hair and lots of white teeth, and clicks the top of his pen while I sob.

'Change me! Change me! Please change me!' I plead, flopped over my knees. Despair pours out of me like vomit and restricts my breath. 'I've nothing left in here. Nothing!' I jab my heart. 'It's all gone. I don't want to be me anymore. Help me to change! Please!'

He stops his clicking, and the abrupt silence jolts me. I pull a clump of tissues from the Kleenex box on the desk and rub my face with it.

'I'll tell you straight.' He looks at me for the first time. 'I *can't* help you. There's little doubt in my mind that transference will occur.' Seeing how perplexed I look, he continues. 'Not familiar with that term? Well. Put simply... You will fall in love with me. That's patently clear.'

I switch from crying to laughing, thinking he's teasing, but stop quickly when he slides his invoice across the desk.

The confusion in my brain is thick, as compliantly I shuffle out, concurring with his statement. I am still nodding my head as I walk down the cobbled mews. A car horn from a shiny red car rouses me. I jump out of the way and the realisation of what just happened sinks in. I am dumbfounded.

God! Was that personal rejection or professional care? I am outraged. 'What conceit! What egotism! And how dare he?' But in its wake is a sense of hopelessness. Without protest, I yield to dashed hopes for a different future. I am a joke. I can't even get a *shrink* to help me, due to the way I love. When I get home, I slam the door so hard that a long strip of paint falls onto the door-mat.

Is it even worth trying to change myself? I wonder as I light a cigarette and switch on the kettle. To change the way I relate, not just to myself but to others too? Maybe it's just not possible? I need to re-write my script. Can I do that? And can I accept responsibility for, not just my choices but also the outcomes? Besides, even if there is no 'cure' for addiction, I hope to goodness, that one day I can achieve balance between both ends of my love, between the lack of self-love and the all-consuming one for someone else. I long to do that.

As I grew up, it never occurred to me that how I learned to love was different from how other people learned. I had presumed that how I felt was universal, that love meant the same for everyone. The same 'give your all, for the sake of the other', be it a slog or an uphill struggle, because at its end, there'd be the 'happy ever after'. To be told that that is an addiction renders every one of my thoughts questionable and unresolved, especially since the shrink's sanctioning of its liability to us both. So what is addiction? Is it a dis-ease, or a symptom of it? Are genes to blame, or is it a state of mind – an 'all or nothing', 'win or lose', 'live or die' thinking? Is it a habit left unchecked, stemmed from a distorted reality? Is it the act of self-obliteration, its roots in self-contempt – and the escape from the Big Bad Wolf? Tom's equivalent of the Wolf is what he calls 'failure-itis', which sounds to me like a skin disease – befitting, I think, of its character. Failure-itis. Yes, it does itch. It itches, and prickles and stings and no amount of balm can really cure its soreness, though you still try – with drugs, alcohol, love. The reward system. Is that what it is, addiction? Or is it all of these things, mysteriously rolled into one? Is it a bond of self-indulgence? A curse of the privileged West? I can't help thinking that if your primary concern is to provide for your family's survival, your views probably focus outwards instead of inwards. Or is the hunter-gatherer-cattle herder also at war against 'failure-itis' and the Wolf?

I think of Mark, a Masaii man, with whom I once spent a few hours. I wonder what his answer would be. I remember the walk we took and our conversation then, which I realise has solutions to my predicament now.

The dirt track, unbroken and infinite, had sliced through the shimmering horizon like the shaft of an arrow, and the blurred forms of shepherds and goats appeared like mirages in front of us. We had stopped to chat to them, their goats in the shade of thorn trees. Gossip was swapped; so too was news of the drought from far-off corners of the bush. There was banter and laughter, and they playfully poked Mark with their sticks.

That evening he and I talked about the differences between our cultures. 'In the West', he said, 'your family structure has fallen apart. You make your lives in isolation, meet your partners in isolation, then suffer in isolation. Here we have our elders to guide us, and the community as our family. We look out for each other and the children belong to all of us. They are the branches of our collective tree. We're not alone here. Aloneness is an issue of your society, and I dare say, the most dominant cause of many of its mental problems.'

It made sense. If you're wired to connect with others, being alone inside your head where doubt and fear run free, conflicts, does it not, with your inherent needs?

Isn't it the broken core whose cracks are split by fear, which cries out for care? Isn't it from there that the rot grows, in the forms of addiction, depression, and phobias? If the soil and roots of a tree with tree rot are tended to, the thinning canopy and wilted leaves improve. It must be the same for people. I have a fantasy that I am an onion whose skin and layers of learned rules, vows and language I can peel off all the way to its inner core. Who is the core I wonder? Who would I be now, had I had a different emotional environment, or lived in another country? Would my perceptions have been different, my pursuit of love the same, and would I again have been its captive?

As is everyone's fate, like a sponge I soaked up the emotional language and perspectives of my parents, in addition to the culture of society. Any harm done from the rule that female objectification was permissible, or at least unquestioned, I noticed more in retrospect, when its insidious ripple effect in the way I perceived myself, was clearer to me. I definitely had a feeling that 'a woman's place was in the kitchen', but what stuck with me most was my sense of being passed over as just a pretty face. Years later even, when I wanted to express an opinion, I tended to persuade a boyfriend to do it on my behalf, knowing he would, as a man, give more credence to it. Coupled with being born into a privileged background, Mum held the quiet assumption that I would marry a man who would support me financially whilst I ran his estate and took care of our family. The word 'career' was never mentioned as I grew up, which, looking back now, seems peculiar since money was so short; but it meant that the role of caretaker was a time-honoured and acceptable one to take, slotting neatly as it did into Mum's motto of 'Putting others before yourself.'

My sense of worth was also demeaned by being groped or the brunt of sexual innuendos, which were par for the course in the male-female dynamic then and taken for granted, notwithstanding my (and every other woman's) frustration at its coercion. By the same token, I *was* complicit of engaging in it; unconsciously or consciously, I played the game, and recognition of the power of sexuality undoubtedly encouraged me to dress accordingly and use my feminine charms. In hindsight, I could have chosen to fight against that role, but the thought never occurred to me. Weren't we, or aren't we – at all times – all of us – men *and* women, victims of our culture?

Chapter 35

Women Who Love Too Much by Robin Norwood has recently been published. It is an avant-garde illumination of the different kinds of love relationships: rewarding and destructive. It encourages ownership of perceptions and responses, and the undertaking of self-understanding and self-reform. I find it in the bookstore in South Ken which stocks a new and burgeoning section of self-help books that have yet to become mainstream. Apart from me, it is deserted. That I am considering buying a book from there, is a signal to others that I have 'a problem'. I skim titles, with furtive sideways glances to check who's watching me, and as customers catch my eye, they look away, embarrassed.

With piles of reading matter and self-observation I set off on the psychological quest to strip away my history. Off to peel the onion! And to scrape away the accumulated dirt, irrelevant to the real me. I work like a detective, removing layer after layer to get to the bottom of it. I imagine my brain as a library, each row a year of my life, each book a reference to my relationships, responses and needs. I wake in the middle of the night, too restless to sleep, so I drive. Night time and Sundays in London are quiet and lonely. My windows are open as I drive down the Embankment. The air is cold and blows my hair. The smell of the river is brackish, and fog clings to the water, obscuring the barges. Albert Bridge emerges like a ghostly schooner, with its masts soaring through the mist. A horn from a boat cuts through the air, and from a tollbooth a gull takes flight over my car, the arrow of its black-tipped wing flashing in the gloom.

Dawn reveals bottled milk on tiled doorsteps. With the accuracy of a darts player, a newspaper boy hurls bundles of papers down next to them. The clean white facades of Oakley Gardens come to life mid-morning. Labradors are tied to the black railings and children in wellingtons catch rusty coloured leaves, waiting for nanny to take them to the park. I count the blue plaques linking artists of the past to the houses they lived in. In the enclosed capsule of my car Tanita Tikaram plays loudly. *Twist In My Sobriety* is on repeat. Her dark torch-singer's voice takes me down into a reflective melancholia so conducive to unveiling myself, that the ritual becomes a form of prayer. I start each trip where I left off the time before, travelling back through each marker of my life, measuring them by homes, relationships, and the loss of them. With ruthless dissection I observe my position and actions. What was I seeking when I let that happen, and was it my duty to do that? Did I think I could change him? Had I lost myself in him, or had I never even known myself? Did I mould myself to suit his requirements, adopting the roles of mother, puppet, shock absorber? Were my actions the conscious means to be loved or heard, or was I instinctive, like a dog following the scent of her needs?

Next, I learn the language of courage – courage to say 'no' when I strain to say 'yes'; the courage to re-write my mental script and, braver still, to act it.

Contact with my dad is the practice I need. But before that, I must identify how his behaviour makes me feel, and weigh up at what point to stake out the new border between us, so that losing myself in his side of mayhem will be a thing of the past. How comfortable am I, I ask myself, with his see-saw formula of love, and bouncing up and down between confidante and scapegoat? Or with blocking his march to the drinks cupboard to minimize tears and mud-slinging? How comfortable am I pulling him up from the floor, or rescuing him from his gun, his enemies, and imminent disgrace, and pretending that life is happy for dignity's sake, when dignity is long-gone? How comfortable am I grooming myself according to his requirements, and knowing my own don't matter – at least in a proactive sense? And where, oh where do I draw the line?

My head is scissored by conflict – between prioritising his needs yet living according to my new rules. Knowing how to, but doing it, seem unconnected. It's a new language; uncomfortable on my lips and one that *he* has never learned. I try out its Americanised vocabulary. He is perched on the edge of his chair, which has seen better days. The blue herringbone is well-worn on the arm, at the spot that his wrist sits, whisky in hand.

'Boundaries are what's missing.'

'No more distorted boundaries, Dad.'

'No more collusion against the big bad world.'

'No more deceit, or pretence that our life is perfect. No more hypocrisy!'

'No more mythologizing that your problem will just fade away.'

'No more denial!'

'No more of your helpless victim role or my caretaking protective one.'

'From now on I'll assert my needs.'

'I'll no longer be available for your daily tears. Or responsible for your chaos.'

My poor Dad. He flops backwards as if he's been hit. Ice cubes chink as he swipes the air peevishly with his hand.

'What?!! What are you on about?!' He yelps, flummoxed, pushing his hair off his forehead.

'Boundaries? Victim? Collusion? What? It's not a fucking war darling! Have you lost your mind? Sound dotty, you do. Do sit. Come!' He pats the chair next to him.

'Are you alright? Do look a bit pale…Here, have a sip. Go on!' He winks and leans forward to nudge me 'Tsk … it's six o'clock somewhere in the world, you know! Go oorn….!'

He throws his head back and laughs. When he opens his eyes again they're filled with tears. He covers my hand with his. I cover it with my other one, and he puts his glass down and covers that with *his* other one. Stacked up, intertwined. My daddy and me. A game we played when I was little.

'Now... being assertive... hmmm.... not terribly fem-in-ine, you know. Come on my baby, be nice to your poor old Dad. Why are you so brittle with him?'

Like a burst paper bag, I yield. My hot air ebbs away, and with it months and months of self-analysis. It is blindingly clear in that moment that I lack the necessary courage and strength for such an overhaul. And why, anyway, should I expect him to understand, with his upbringing and his perspective on life, what I am trying to say, when I can barely get the hang of it myself? Stupid of me. Stupid Stupid. Stupid. The pattern between us is set in stone. I should have known that. I surrender completely to it, and I am aware of the tension falling away from my muscles. My heart, so strong a minute before, wobbles like jelly.

He is my maker. My puppeteer. My child. He is part of me, and me him. How I learned to love him was as inherent as breathing.

But the craving to re-programme myself with regard to the rest of my life, returns. Like an infection, it blisters ordinary thoughts, reminding me sharply and repetitively to get on with it. I walk along the towpath in Battersea Park, early in the mornings, passing the same dog-walkers and runners. In the stretches of solitude, I scream at the Big Bad Wolf to leave me alone. I am hating him. Hating me. Hating the discomfort of living inside my skin. Hating my fate. Is this really my lot in life? This terrible self-paralysis? Do I really have to bear it forever?

My most recent psychotherapist says virtually nothing in my sessions with him, other than a monosyllabic prompt from time to time. So instead of me spouting a stream of confused emotion and him clarifying it, like the host of a dinner party I rack my brain for something to say, to fill in the uncomfortable silences. He is not cheap, and after a few weeks I decide that I can – and might even prefer to – talk to a wall, for free.

I see a hypnotherapist too, who promises to re-jig how I respond to relationships, starting with the one with my-self. Now that's what I want! I want an overhaul, preferably without having to work at it. I see her several times. I lie on a long, curvy, chrome-and-leather seat off Harley Street, and do my best to 'lose myself' in her soft commands. My eyes are closed, but from time to time I squint through my lashes to see where she is, and whilst I am meant to be drifting back into a distant corner of my past, I am con-scious that I am faking it, in order not to disappoint her.

I make the decision instead to see Ruth, a Spiritualist, with the hope that I will embrace a clean way of thinking, and find the wherewithal to clear the curse of self-pun-ishment, grief, and a foggy mind. Every Friday I drive to the countryside to visit her, and quickly, she becomes my mentor.

Ruth's garden is her healing place. She has a luxuriant bed of roses in it, but as she encourages awareness of the earth's energy, I sit on the part that is lawn, next to a border of Lupins, their rainbow coloured flowers filled with forag-ing bees. Her monk-like acceptance of herself and others rubs off on me, and I articulate her instruction into a sort of a prayer for myself.

In this life I am here as me, to learn as me. The mistakes I make are my lessons. If this life is a college of higher education, I accept the trajectory on which my soul takes me. I accept that I am responsible for my actions and the part I play in every situation and relationship. I bear no blame for anything or anyone outside of myself. Without my culture, my parentage, experiences, and quests, there are no lessons to learn. I let go of all expectations towards others, and allow mercy and compassion to succeed them. I am my teacher and student. To learn *me*, I must listen and observe myself. I must identify my habits and all that I subconsciously seek externally. I must be governed by the necessity for health – in mind, body, and environment.

We talk about the mind. I say that I think of it as the software that operates the brain, whose data is gathered from the information and constructs it learned from others. From reading and writing, to emotions and identities and everything in between. Ruth calls that the ego-mind.

She brings into the garden a bowl of suds and a wand through which she blows bubbles. Iridescent spheres float in the air towards the mulberry tree, changing colour as the light shines on them.

'Watch them, my dear! See how unconnected they are and how aimlessly they float? Yes?'

I nod, confused at what she is getting at.

'In your head, pick one! Done? Ok. Now. Imagine that bubble as your mind! Observe how it drifts around, all on its tod. Poor little chap! Now *that* is your ego-mind.' She walks to the roses with secateurs in her hands and calls over her shoulder. 'It's not you, you know, your ego-mind. It's only what you've learned to be in this life. Your spirit-mind is who you really are. That's your truth, and the centre of your soul. Your spirit-mind lives in connection with *every*thing and *every*one.' She jabs the air with the secateurs as she emphasises the prefix. 'And never alone, you see. But the poor old ego-mind is, and if you live in *him*, you'll be stuck in those self-serving fear-based beliefs.' She shakes herself and sighs. 'Manipulated by greed and insecurity. Pouf! Come, let's think about tea! Victoria sponge! My favourite.'

A blob of creamy jam squishes out from the middle when she cuts the cake. She reads my thoughts, scrapes it off, and offers it to me from the knife.

She quotes Nietzsche: 'one must still have chaos in oneself to be able to give birth to a dancing star.'

'Are you dancing yet?' she asks every Friday.

I start to answer with a rush of self-judgement, but she shakes her head. 'Nope. Not interested in your Wolf, my dear. You created him, so you let him go. I'll come back in forty minutes,' she says, leaving me by her Lupins.

I lie down and focus my breath.

In-out, in-out. Breathe in the light. Blow out the dark.

Let go of the Wolf. Be still. Quiet. Grounded.

Be. Just be.

Breathe in, and *listen*…

I do.

Birds cheep. Leaves rustle. Bees buzz. A window slams. There's Radio 1 and Noel Edmonds. The water from a sprinkler pitter-patters against a fence. A cup and saucer chink. A drain gurgles.

Breathe in, and *look*...

In the clouds, a fluffy rabbit's face moves into a bird, its ears the wings, its nose the beak. A shard of sunshine bursts its body. A fly circles my face, and leaves flutter in and out of the foreground.

Breathe in, and *feel*...

The grass pricks through my cotton clothes and tickles the palm of my hand. A warm breeze blows up my shirt and pummels my tummy like a soft massage.

As if in neutral I float. Up, up, up. Not thinking, just being. Being part of all, being part of nothing. Conscious and unconscious. Tiny and huge. I am oxygen, nitrogen, phosphorus. I am chlorophyll, mineral, vapour. I am the now, the past, the future. Connected to my true self and to all life. I am no longer alone.

'Are you dancing, my dear?' Ruth calls, swooshing open her sliding door.

Chapter 36

I have a new job, working for a fashion designer as retail manager. Tears still bubble close to the surface of my eyes, but being useful and immersing myself in the superficial world of pretty things is therapeutic. Choosing the fashion industry was a conscious decision, to counterbalance my increasing reclusiveness and entanglement in the spirit world. In order to commune with Will, every day I have been going to the church where his funeral was, and if for whatever reason I have been unable to get there, I have spun in a ball of anxiety. The world of fashion I hope, will redress this dependence.

My home, down the road from the shop, is an old artist's studio with a wide window overlooking the Royal Hospital. It is the one place in which I feel emotionally safe. But recently someone is threatening that. I know his name is Rashid because of the name-tag on his brown overalls. It is the uniform of the Europa food store on the corner of my street. He hasn't tried talking to me, but instead follows me backwards and forwards to work, leaving his trail in the form of letters, whose tiny squished writing is so illegible, I couldn't decipher who the sender was until I caught him posting one through my door. I sensed someone close for a long time; it was a sense of bubbling unease, sometimes boiling, sometimes simmering. But I brushed it away, berating myself for my over-dramatisation. I see him every day now, his head down, lurking on the opposite side of the road, either pretending to count coins in his pocket, or tying his shoelaces. A dark shape swishes past the boutique once I open up in the mornings, or past the window as I ring up the prices on the till. When I dare to look out of my flat window, he is there, in the shade of a car, and his face turns quickly away as he sees me. He's always present. And his paper trail is slotted through the post-boxes of my house and shop doors, folded into small squares, and crumpled, as if they've been squeezed between his palms for hours.

I go to the police station off Chelsea Green. They take down details of descriptions and I leave them the letters. 'Sorry love.' They shrug. 'Not until he hurts you can we do anything about it. That's the law.'

The letters become more frequent. And at the same time another man follows me from the post office, and takes up a daily pursuit. He wears a long wool coat with a belt that's slipping from its loops, but as with Rashid, I don't want to look more closely than that. I hurry my steps, as a ritual to and from work, and glance over my shoulder all the time, my heart pounding, my breath held. There they both are, like dark shadows, Rashid and the new stalker, unrelated I think, one in front of the other, sometimes quick sometimes slow, behind a tree, or brazen on the pavement. The scenario feels like my childhood nightmares. Or the Big Bad Wolf times two! And I keep thinking that, if only it weren't happening to me, I would be able to see the comedy in it. But one morning I go to my car to find it's been broken into, and there on the back seat, is a paperback book and several folded squares. They are grubby and dog-eared and when I open the letters I see the handwriting is big and bold, and the content, though in terrible English, sexual. In them he tells me that his gift of the book I must treasure forever, for inside are the results of his masturbatory activities.

On my request, a couple of friends – burly chaps – march into Europa, string Rashid up against the wall and threaten him. Or so they say. I wait outside nervously and out of view, and ducking behind a car in front of me I suddenly spot the other stalker. Fury charges unexpectedly through my veins and propels me towards him. He turns and runs. I run after him. I roar like a lion, and tear down the street with surprising speed, waving my arms so that my bag is flung onto the road along with my earrings. The tail of his long coat disappears round the corner and I stop to catch my breath. It's the last I see of him, but walking to work the following morning I pass his belt, strung on a railing. It makes me shiver to see it there, so I knock it off and kick it into a basement where there are some bins. I wait a week or two before I brave returning to Europa, and when I do, Rashid no longer works there.

'Tut, tut,tut...' Says Ruth when I see her that week. 'You are walking around open and vulnerable to every baddie in town. Got to get you stronger, my dear. Let's see what we can do about sewing you up, hmmm?'

***

Ever since I'd played Good King Wenceslas's page in the school nativity play, being an actress had been my ultimate goal, though a semi-secret one. On leaving school I had voiced my dream to Mum, but her response had been, 'Oh Nix darling! You don't want to do that. You'll never get anywhere. Competition's too great. Pointless even trying.' Cognizant that rejection would wear me down, I had caved into my fears and not tried, but now, with Ruth's support, and after all that I have gone through, I decide to give it a bash. I get roles in fringe productions, an agent, and following that, auditions for television. But as I walk out of another one, for a part to which I'm not suited, I accept that I am not up to its stings.

'Not right at all.' 'Too posh.' 'Too small.' 'Too tall.' 'Too thin.' 'Too fat.' 'Too this... too that.'

I go to an audition where the sole request is to 'turn round, bend over and put your arse up.' My instant thought of 'Oh God no! It's too big, I can't do that!' is replaced with appropriate anger, but not before I find myself with my bottom in the air. I rush from the room, past the line of girls waiting outside, down the well-worn stairs. I stop at the door, and it occurs to me that I should run straight back up again and tell them all to 'Leave! Get out! Don't even think of bothering with that jerk!' How dare he, after all? Damn him! But I am angry with myself too. Because what the hell was I doing – bending over? What was I thinking? What an idiot, I am. God. To hell with acting! I am out of here...

As an extension of what Ruth teaches me, I embark next on a quest to find my real purpose, or indeed, to find *me*. I have spent so long helping others to find themselves I don't know who the hell I am. I study Buddhism, astrology, reflexology, aromatherapy, counselling, hypnotherapy, neuro-linguistic-programming, and I seek guidance from many different healers. It is a compulsive search, but an oblique question from a shaman highlights the obvious to me.

Even cross-legged in a stone circle, in her Hampstead living room, there is nothing hippy-ish about the way she looks, with her tan, dark nails, and glossy hair. Through the smoky wafts of burning sage, I glance round the room whilst her eyes are still closed. On the pine dresser are crystals, rattles, drums and ceremonial arm-bands, arranged decoratively amongst coloured glass and Postman Pat videos.

'Think of every decade,' she suddenly says. Her voice has dropped an octave. 'Think what consistently occupied you throughout each: zero to ten, ten to twenty, twenty to thirty, and so on'. She flicks a feathery fan impatiently. 'Don't dwell on it – just tell me what comes to mind! Come on! Quick!'

It comes surprisingly easily. Vivid pictures of my younger self appear in my mind's eye. 'Well, I drew pictures. I wrote stories and poems, and sort of took care of everyone. You know – tried to fix them. Protect them. And… well, I guess that was about it!' I shrug, embarrassed by my under-achievements. Lighting another bundle of sage, she responds in less than a beat.

'So? Why are you not practising as a healer? An artist? *And* writer? Professionally I mean. They're linked, you know. I can feel that you're already healing through words, as well as through touch, but giving it no credit. Does that make sense? What *are* you writing?'

'I'm working on a portrait of addiction. Been at it for years, off and on. It's *my* story actually.' I smile inwardly. 'Gosh, it'd be nice if it was helpful to others. I'd love that.'

'And it will be. You will see that in time. Yes. You'll see. Anyway – you knew this already. You didn't need me to tell you. Keep looking inside yourself. You'll see who you are and what your purpose is. Be patient and keep writing. It will be healing.'

Her words resonate with me. Do what's natural to you. If you're trying too hard at something and still getting nowhere, then stop. Stop bashing your head against a brick wall. Choose what feels instinctively right.

Makes sense.

I continue to write. I write and write, even if I scrap it at the end of the day. At the same time, I train in different forms of healing, and from each I take what feels most relevant and natural. I am drawn to ancient wisdoms, spiritual teachings and the energetic web that weaves between us – drawn as ever to healing what the eye doesn't see – to what is there, under the surface, but which is little recognised – the blurred patterns of the mind, the broken core from where the rot grows. Most compelling to me is that all the trainings that I follow articulate a basic faith that love conquers all. Of course, for me healing was a childhood instinct to repair my dad, which then developed into co-dependence and weakened my conviction. Returning to it is like returning home, and its power reiterated when I see that, with just the simple laying on of my hands, through which I channel love, the results are often miraculous – even for physical complaints, so often rooted in a damaged psyche.

Looking back at my history as if it were a book, I see no story, just a numberless chapter of lists – unchecked and repetitive, starting with Fix Dad! Save Mum! Fix Will! Like waveforms on a heart monitor there is the up and down of melodrama; Lines and lines of it; highlighted in fluorescent yellow like photoluminescent safety signs warning me of the danger. The pages may as well have been blank, so circular was my theme, so addictive its nature. Was I not able to step away from the fluctuating wave of my life to seek the flat-line, or did I regard its lack of activity a starvation of the high I got from loving? My 'happy ever after' of inner peace was dependent, it seemed, only on the other being fixed. Alas, I hadn't realised then that that was beyond my control. It is only now I understand the simple truth about healing, most crucial to its efficacy, which is that it can only function once the recipient is ready to receive it. Without their willingness, the energy remains outside of the patient, looking for a way in. This lesson finally convinces me of the futility of co-dependence: that the fixing of another person with no will to be fixed leads only to failure and prolonged suffering.

Chapter 37

A stray thought weaves in and out of the dream I have to change my life. Might the countryside cushion my edges? Might its slower speed be more in sync with my present direction? I am tiring of London. It has changed. Or at least my London has. I feel a stranger to it now, and too fragile somehow for its new harshness.

As the decade has swept forwards the country has divided, its issues oscillating like a metronome. Over the dark undertow of the miners' strikes, Aids virus, peaking divorce rates, anti-apartheid activism and Bob Geldof's Live Aid, the hedonists' hunger for conspicuous consumption flourishes, as do their shoulder pads. The yuppie is born, millionaires are made overnight, and it feels like the boom is here to stay. More people stream into London looking for opportunities, and climb aboard the pleasure cruiser, to quaff Champagne and snort cocaine. Women have big hair, big bags, big shoulders, and bold gold accessories. Money reigns.

My London, it seems, has swapped its soft holey jumper

for a sharp-edged suit, and has turned its back on the social conscience and community spirit it had once had. I am leaning away from this new world *and* my social life, which has morphed into tedious hours of coke-taking, turning my kind, funny friends into arrogant bores. Other friends have opted out altogether, to enter the murky world of heroin. As more and more fall into it and die, it feels as if a plague is striking our generation.

I have reached a dead-end in the aftermath of Will's death. I am worn out. He has been dead four years. Depression has fastened itself around my throat, and it chokes my resolve. It is the bitter taste of failure. It is always there, distracting me, and sickening me. It feels like a fever that I can't shake off. Some days when I am able to get up, I perform. That's how it feels. A performance. All is well. Happy. Happy. Happy. I fake it to make it. And when I go to bed at night I can at least tick one box of achievement – 'performance'. Other days I get up and remain hidden and locked away. Those days are terrible. I rue the day I was even born. Life inside my head is a wash-out. No point to it. I long to not exist and wish I never had. Fantasising about suicide takes up a lot of my time. But then that feels like self-indulgence, and I deplore myself for that too. I don't know which is worse. But its element of solution keeps absorbing my attention. In my fantasy I say goodbye to my mum and dad, and close my eyes. Peacefully. They are sad, but understanding, and present at the ending of my life as they were at the beginning of it. They are at least spared my jumping from a window, a gruesome hanging, or slitting of my wrist. It shouldn't be violent like that. Even the word *suicide* bothers me. It sounds poisonous with its phonic closeness to cyanide. Murderous. *Voluntary death* is preferable. Gentler and more natural. And why shouldn't we be able to choose when to go?

The enduring battle with myself has made such a mess of my mind I have lost the wires that connect me to reality outside of myself. Life is seen only through the dull grey prism of my impotence. I feel like a dog turning in its basket before settling for the night. Round and round I am going, searching for something that will feed the gaps made by grief. I try another relationship, but he is a wild card, and a life of volatile uncertainty will do nothing to close the wound.

France might do it, I think. A new life. A new page. Countryside with sunshine.

Might be medicinal.

Do we, I wonder, leave parts of our souls embedded in the places and people to whom we've given them? 'I've lost myself, I don't know who I am anymore' is a common response when trauma swamps us. Instead of a 'broken heart' is it really our soul that is splintered? And does the part of the soul that has merged with another tarry long after the pairing has come to an end? Might I therefore retrieve the pieces left by Will and me in France were I to plant my soul in its landscape? Walking through an olive grove with him once and feeling that my steps had belonged in that poor stony soil, I had looked back through the silver leaves and touched a twisted trunk. 'God's trees.' I'd said to him.

'Don't you think that the collective step of mankind may have sprung from their shade?' He had shaken his head, and muttered fondly about my magical thinking, while he had cupped his hand around his lighter to guard it against the wind.

I meet Charlie at a photographic exhibition of monochrome images of the naked female form and its most intimate parts, blown-up and close-up. I notice the tall, stooping figure scrutinising every inch of flesh, his nose pressed up to the photos, as studious as if he were an art restorer debating his task. Well, well, well, I think, his shamelessness takes some beating! I myself am too shy to stare at them for too long, in case my interest is misinterpreted as salacious.

He has a wild mop of grey hair that he brushes back in a sweeping gesture, strong black eyebrows, a square jaw, and clear blue eyes. A dark grey loose-fitting suit hangs elegantly from his tall frame, giving him the air of nonchalance. The fabric has a sheen to it, and when he lunges up some steps in my direction, I notice how attractive his long, fine legs look draped in it. He catches me looking at him, stops, and reaches inside his jacket for a silver flask, from which he takes a quick pull. With that, he grins and makes his way to me.

Oh no, I think. Another addict! A drunk! God. How can it be that in a room of two hundred people, the one drunk in it always heads for me?

He is effusive. He is charming, funny, audacious. *And* presumptuous of our imminent familiarity. With an insistent hand up my skirt, he drives me to the restaurant where the party continues; then, sitting opposite me at dinner, he stretches his leg to reach between both of mine until his chin is on the table. He doesn't listen to the women either side of him until one of them ticks him off for being a dirty old man.

He isn't a drunk; just Scottish, with a penchant for whisky. I feel a powerful and loving connection to him, notwithstanding falling asleep during our first few dates. I snore loudly throughout *The Double Life of Veronique*, despite his shaking me, and the audience shuffling from their seats to others, out of earshot. Our next date, he makes me supper, and while he entertains me with Kodak shots of his latest garden project, pointing excitedly at the digger tractor's carving of soil, my eyes close and my head slumps.

Charlie is sixteen years my senior. His big hands around mine feel healing. My physical body responds to that with sleep, and over the next few weeks, my fever finally comes down.

'You have put a spell on me,' I tell him.

It is leap year. We spend the entire month of February laced together, face to face, eye to eye, and as the old Irish legend has it, leap year is the one time in every four that women can propose. I surprise myself by doing just that on Valentine's Day. He is still married to someone else, but separated, and ours is to be his third wedding. 'I've been married for years and years and years' he laughs, 'not, however, to the same wife.'

His landscape-design business is taking a hit from the recession. I broach my idea of moving to France, of starting afresh, he with a new business and I with a new life in a place where no one knows my troubled history, and nor does it matter. I am excited. I can leave addiction behind me, together with depression, sadness and failure. Like an old cloak I can leave *me* behind. I can wear new clothes. Simple ones, for a simple country life.

In the intervening few years since I was there with Will, the French coast has radically changed. It has lost its simplicity, and money has given it a new face. The old peeling patina has been swapped with new licks of paint the colour of cheap make-up, and the roads are now plumped out with more cars, more houses, more crowds.

I go inland in search of the magic that had originally seduced me.

Unkempt vines and cherry groves encircle the old farmhouse, and on the terrace an almond tree crowned with candyfloss blossom looks like a sunset cloud against the blue sky. The house sits on a gentle slope, framed by two medieval villages and the patchwork valley between them, and embraced by hills whose shadows shape hearts in their folds.

On the brow of the hill, admiring the pretty lines of the roof, I remember how, when I was little, derelict houses had been a common sight, and as if they were stranded, starving orphans Mum would stop her Riley Elf sighing 'Poor little house.' She'd wrap her cardigan around her, the tail of her silk headscarf fluttering in the wind. In knee-high grass she'd open up doors torn from hinges, pull ivy from weakened brickwork, and with dock leaves brush cobwebs away from broken windowpanes.

'Just needs to be loved,' she'd murmur, starting the car again.

When I first see the house, it isn't its ruinous state that I notice, but what it could become once I nurse it back to health, once I fix its sad disintegration and breathe new life into it. In my mind's eye I see bread on the kitchen counter, pots of cherry jam, goat cheese, saucisson, and olive oil. I see friends around the old stone table under the almond tree, and villagers with glasses of Pastis in their hands. I see me harvesting tomatoes, radishes, peas – a dog by my side, a baby in a pram and a husband mowing grass. My fairy-tale world. That's what I see.

A few days later I stand in a phone box in the village square next to the Mairie. Two elderly women are sitting on fold-up chairs outside their front doors, terracotta pots around their feet, laundry hanging from open windows, and a cat curled up on a sill. The air is sleepy and warm. An early lizard darts out from a stone wall. A radio interrupts the stillness and the village bell chimes twice. A tanned lady in overalls opens the shutters of her bric-a-brac shop, sparsely stocked with painted furniture and 50's prints of St Tropez. Seduced by the heat, her scruffy-haired mongrel flops down across the quiet cobbled road.

Pushing franc coins into the slot I gesture to Charlie that I need more, but he shakes his head and pulls out his pockets. The women's brazen curiosity burns into my back and I turn to smile at them, holding the mouthpiece close to my ear. My mum's voice in London is faint, the connection weak.

'I've just bought a house Mum!' I screech excitedly, and then, out of credit the line goes dead. 'Mum?! Did you hear me?'

Chapter 38

We marry on Valentine's Day, a year after my proposal, in the registry office in Chelsea with a blessing in the church around the corner. Fog hangs low and the air is icy. A frosty glaze coats the old Beauford I am driven in, and the grass in the forecourt sparkles in its headlights. Charlie has backlit the stained-glass window of the chancel with spotlights from outside, so that its jewel-like beams draw you into the glowing rainbow of an enchanted house and up the candlelit aisle. I wear dark red velvet and gold lace – a copy of a dress from the early nineteenth century – and Charlie a long black velvet coat.

On the eve of my wedding Mum and Tom give a small party which my Dad and Caro were meant to attend. Instead, Dad telephones to say that fog has prevented them flying and 'Sorry my baby, you'll have to do without your poor, old dad tomorrow.'

I retaliate. It's the first time ever that I do. Inside me, rage conflicts with stunned disbelief while I shout and demand he get the morning flight. And somewhere else in the mire is the perplexed anxiety of the peace-maker. 'What are you up to?' 'Brace up! Swallow your hurt!' Circling the periphery is Mum, making shushing gestures and pointing to the other guests. 'Don't make a fuss,' she mouths, 'it's embarrassing.' Her eyes try to elicit silence from me. 'Be a good little girl. Do as you're told,' they say. But still my voice rises militantly, as if it doesn't belong to me.

'Oh, darling, don't boo-hoo,' he says at the other end, 'it's not my fault. S and P aren't bothering to try tomorrow. They've decided to abort the whole shebang. Too much of a good thing.' S and P are my uncle and aunt.

'Shebang? Is that what my fucking wedding is to you all? A shebang? God!' Mum quickly closes the door between me and her guests. 'You just don't get it, do you? For once in your life, Dad – just *once*, for fuck's sake – couldn't you just be there for *me*?'

I hang up, my own worthlessness spot-lit by the neon glare of his rejection. Echoes of his former praise for me make it even harder to bear. 'You'd go to the far corners of the earth for me, you would, my dear little soldier.' Yet he, my dad, can't be bothered to make every effort to do what it takes to attend my wedding.

Miraculously, he and Caro ring my doorbell, an hour before the service is due to begin. He is impeccably dressed, but shaking and puce in the face. 'I've watched him like a hawk, *mon petit chou*,' Caro whispers, 'not a drop as yet. But that's why his hands are shaking.' She pulls a face signifying nervousness over how the afternoon could pan out.

I grip his arm as he reels up the aisle, tugging it upwards

in anticipation of him stumbling. 'Nearly there, Daddy, nearly there.' I whisper. Candlelight flickers over our guests' watchful faces, and there ahead of me is Charlie, sweeping back his hair and sharing relaxed jokes with his best man. With his height, width, long grey hair and dark wild eyebrows, I see him in that frazzled moment, as romantic and rescuing, just in from his windswept Highland moors. To the side of him is the pew towards which I am steering Dad. I have to get him there without him toppling into a candle. His forehead is sweating and his voice carries up the aisle and over the music, as if caught up in a draught.

'Strewth! Can't see an effing thing in here, darling… no bloody lights on.'

'Sssh Dad, everyone can hear you.' I tug his arm higher.

We move hesitantly. He puts one foot in front of the other as if he is feeling for steps, and briefly lurches forwards, when he loses his balance. An image of flames whipping his morning coat flares across my mind, and my erstwhile nerves of messing up my vows are dispelled.

'What? What d'you say?' he asks tetchily. 'Got that ringing in my ears again.' On reflex his other hand swings up towards his ear, and accidently knocks an order of service from someone's grasp. I grip him tighter.

'Two more pews to go, Dad.' I whisper.

'Feel awfully sick darling. Do you think there's a loo at the back?'

From my left, I hear a sudden burst of throaty laughter so familiar I don't even need to turn. I know who it is. It is Will! My Will! He is there, the other side of me, holding my hand.

Chapter 39

As the years pass my Dad becomes lonely and sad. His moral compass slips into the shadows and a taste for prostitutes becomes the final stroke in the ticking time-bomb of his marriage. Much of his money is drained by them, and Caro finally divorces him. He ends up alone in a little apartment looking out to sea. His remaining companions are the two barmen from the local pub who think him 'a hell of a good chap', but his other friends are left unsure of how to have him in their lives. He has a series of girlfriends, considerably younger than me, one or two found from ads in the back of a magazine. He starts each relationship as bouncy as the buoys in his harbour view, but he quickly descends into psychotic paranoia over their sincerity. His daily phone calls to me often swallow up entire mornings, whilst I cajole his tears to stop so that I can at least comprehend his explanations. 'She's lying to me, darling. I'm sure she's still sleeping with Rob... Jim... Jason, or... I don't remember their effing names... little tart she is...' Other mornings the stories are wilder. 'I've been robbed! It was Natalie. I know it was. Saw her dark hair against the curtain. Ransacked my flat! Curtains ripped! Pulled down! Drawers… cupboards… everything everywhere! What? Yes, I'm ok. No – no blood. Wait! Yes! You're right. There is blood. My head is cut.'

A growing obsession with his will starts to eat into his days. He visits his solicitor with increasing frequency, sometimes within a few weeks of each other. He scratches out the last beneficiary, replacing her with another according to the ups and downs of his love life. He accumulates a series of wills, which read like a diary of sorts. Looking behind the legal terminology you see a documentation of his emotions, and who is in or out of his favour.

Although his mischievous humour still ambushes me, his bursts of laughter transform always to tears now. His once fine features become blurred and puffy, his nose red and bulbous. His shirtsleeves still crisply folded like a soldier's, now display soup stains that are ignored or unnoticed.

Then comes his prison sentence. He is stopped by the police while driving in a state of extreme intoxication. A devastating blow. The shock winds me – I feel it physically. The image of him in a cell, behind bars, all alone, scared, slams a forceful whack into my solar plexus. His befuddled shame and horror are mine, and they bubble through my veins, disrupting my mind and daily agenda. My Dad. My beloved Dad. In prison? No! I have to get him out. I have to. There's some mistake. He won't survive it. Can't they see that?

He's allowed a phone call or two. His voice melts like

an incoherent stream, no body left to it – just a gibberish torrent of fear.

He wants me to visit him.

'Oh Dada, I can't, I am in France. I'll come when I'm back in England. Hang on in there. Breathe. Come on Dad, breathe! You'll be alright. I love you darling Daddy.'

I live each day inside his skin. Inside his muddled head, shattered heart and shaking hands. I lose my house keys. An antique vase slips from my fingers and breaks. I leave my paid-for groceries behind in the shop, not once but twice. I open the car door just as a bicyclist collides with it and sails through the air. He ends up in hospital, severely winded. I visit daily, but when he's awake he utters obscenities. 'So so sorry,' I keep saying, patting his clenched fist. I want him to absolve me from guilt. It's punishing enough reliving my initial thought that I'd killed him. The day before Dad's follow-up call, I walk straight into a bollard and fracture my little finger when I fall.

His voice when we speak again is surprisingly chirpy. He has an adored and long-standing 'proper' girlfriend by then, who has visited him in prison, and 'looking rather saucy and dolled up, smuggled in under her sizeable bosom, a bottle of Jungle Juice. Little angel, she is. Saved my bacon.' His former whimper of 'I should slit my wrists now. Give up. The Grim Reaper can have me. Fuck it....' is replaced by chummy stories of cordial respect between him and his guards.

He is released early for being 'a model prisoner'. Sucking up to his guards no doubt, or blubbing. They realise finally that prison isn't the most effective punishment for a dear old alcoholic; the removal of his licence is.

Thereon in he surrenders to his demons and no amount of intelligence can deter him. He never thinks of his deterioration as a slow suicide, but I do. Empty whisky bottles gather up under his bed so that straightening his bedcover jostles broken glass. He is drunk even before breakfast; his tolerance so low he has just to top up the existing levels to be 'out of it' once more.

He is alternately in and out of Intensive Care. In a frighteningly short space of time his visits there become longer, with less time between each. He knocks himself out, fractures bones, has suspected heart attacks and blood poisoning. At least three times I receive calls from Kate and the doctors to 'come now if you want to see him before he goes...' When conscious, he's still chuffed that he's again outwitted the Grim Reaper, but is displeased by the invasion of the men in white coats.

'But I'm not complaining about the nice nurses,' he adds quickly, nervous they'll be removed. Again, that ribald wink, before his eyelids flicker and he sinks back into sleep.

***

I've lost the dad who dazzled with irreverent wit and beauty. I've lost the expansive sweep of his arm to raise his cap in greeting, the unrestrained strength of his hug, expressive blue eyes, raucous laugh and tender loving heart. It's all gone.

It seems I've pedalled uphill forever to keep the 'good Dad' in place, to deter the 'bad one'. I thought it was simple once. He had only to stop drinking, after all. As a small child I couldn't have known that there was no 'simple' way not to drink. That being dependent on it was complicated and dark and impenetrable to anyone who didn't share the same addiction. That no one, not even a daughter, could change an alcoholic's course against his will, or be responsible for his choices.

What I did know about, was the damage underneath his handsome shell. I knew about his broken core, the place from where the rot grew. He had taken me there, to help me understand him, and it was so familiar to me, I mistook it for my own.

The good Dad is a decent and gentle man. An endearing human being with idiosyncratic humour, a sharp eye for the absurd, and a heart quick to melt. Although his pride in duty is firm, he is ill-equipped to always see it through, for he is a casualty of his own war against infinite doubt and fear.

It is his fear, settled like bad bacteria into the well of his broken core, which feeds his sensitivity, the silver lining of which heightens his compassion for animals and those in need; yet its flip side renders him shaky and susceptible to the ruinous escape from it. In the otherwise innocuous act of pouring a glass and drinking its contents, my good, glorious dad is transformed into the unrecognisable, horrid one. Ultimately, he is hostage to his broken core: seemingly caught, like a fly, in the web of escapism.

The waste. How I deplore the waste.

With my bottomless love and magical thinking, I thought I could repair his broken-ness, make him whole, happy and fearless. Make him better.

But I failed.

Shakespeare's *Seven Ages of Man* come to mind and particularly the 'Infant, mewling and puking in the nurse's arms. Then the whining school–boy, with his satchel and shining face, creeping like snail unwillingly to school.' Had my dad, I wondered, got stuck at that stage? Had the trauma of being bullied and losing his nanny halted his emotional development? And were the lover, soldier, justice and pantaloon parts he merely played at, in his 'strange eventful history'?

He told me a story once. Well, he told me the one story, but many times because he enjoyed it so. When he was an aide-de-camp to the Governor of Nigeria he had a parrot – Edward, an African Grey – who was inseparable from him. A talkative bird with a fine ear for Dad's chatter, the bird perched nobly on his shoulder whilst he went about his duties. Dad wanted a promotion and hoped to make a good impression during a royal visit to Government House. He stood in line with the other officers, Edward on his shoulder while the princess took Dad's hand. Enthralled by his pet bird, she asked what was 'the name of the beautiful parrot?'

'Edward, Ma'am.' He said, with his mischievous smile. 'As in King Edward. Abdicating Edward,' and he bowed. As he did so, Edward came face to face with the princess. He looked her squarely in the eye, stretched himself tall and, ruffling his feathers, squawked: 'Fuuuck ooorff'!

Now, as I rest my mouth on his lifeless eye, I think of Edward. Abdicating Edward. I slip my fingers under his frozen hand, and there I place a playing card – The King of Hearts. Folded around it is a drawing I did for him when I was a child, of *Mungu*, his God, with outstretched arms and a big smile, floating in a bubble of light.

Oh Dad. Beloved Dad. You relinquished your crown, at last. You must have been awfully tired to finally let go.

Like a tracker dog I sniff him, searching for the warm whisky breath and hint of hair pomade. But there is no smell.

The morgue is underground, soundproofed and dark. It feels as if we are buried together, with compacted earth around and above us. He is here, dimly lit, in his box beside me. My cheek lies on his stone-like chest and my hands around his shoulders. We are together. Together. But I have never felt so alone.

The Grim Reaper has come and taken my dad.

What on earth will I do now?

Who am I without him?

After a lifetime of entanglement in his tidal wave, I am, like an empty shell, washed suddenly up onto the shore.

Chapter 40

Charlie and I moved into our French house in September. In January a friend calls me after we'd had lunch together and says 'You're pregnant, aren't you? You've got that shine.'

'Course not.' I laugh 'Not something I can do, remember?'

My doctor had told me I couldn't have children. What with anorexia and the stress of Will's death, I had stopped working 'down there.'

The delight of the diagnosis is followed by a hard pregnancy and seeking medical advice in a foreign language makes it doubly so. I am filled with apprehension. I throw up for weeks, losing so much weight that I look like a child with malnutrition, and because I bleed a lot I am confined to bed.

Theodore means 'Gift from God'. That's what we call him. He takes twenty three hours to arrive, a hesitant stopping and starting, unsure how willing he is to disengage from me. For hours he hides in the left side of my pelvis. The midwife on duty is young, with a sleek blonde chignon and lips the same scarlet as her nails. She seems keen to leave for the night – it is late after all – but continues to tap my arm with a bored rhythm. '*Poussez! Allez! Poussez!*' She repeats, echoing the beat.

Bobble, our Labrador, comes with us to the hospital in Avignon, and with her in the car, I send Charlie out to check on her hourly. When the prospect of a Caesarean is broached, another nurse thankfully replaces the blonde. Square-shouldered and big-breasted, she holds me in a strong embrace while my body convulses. On impulse, I close my eyes and stop breathing to leave the pain behind, even if only for a second or two, and I am transported immediately to my childhood bed. My mosquito net moves with the breeze from the fan, a bat takes flight from behind a picture, and the clatter of pots and pans ring in my ears. I am happy. As my muscles tighten like pieces of rock, a searing spasm cuts into my fantasy, yet my mind seeks stubbornly to get back into it. '*Respirez bien,*' the nurse shouts. She's right. Breathing helps. I slump into her arms. I am so tired. So tired. Relax! I tell myself. Relax and breathe! Between the pain and shuddering, the contractions get longer, with less time between each. I focus on her sturdy arms and hands. They look like baker's hands. I visualise her kneading dough – the heel of her floured palm pressing it forward, punching it, rotating it, folding it, pressing it forward, punching it, rotating it, folding it, and on and on… I'm sure it's great bread that she makes. I should ask her. She shouts above my moans: '*Tranquille chérie! Restez tranquille!*'

Theo is the only baby in my wing who doesn't sleep. Worn-out, I wander around during those first nights, singing to him. An eerie glow from the premature ward lights the length of the corridors, a monitor whirrs and beeps, and an alarm breaks its rhythm.

'*Oh, comme il est pénible!*' a nurse mutters as he she shuffles past.

I sing louder. Bloody woman! He isn't being tiresome. He is being scared.

They scold me. There is a right and wrong way to be a mother, apparently. He should learn to sleep alone and separate from me. I should let him cry. He'll soon stop once he learns who is boss.

Let him cry. Let him cry. Isn't that the same sort of chant that those rehab clinicians sang to me? Let him hit rock bottom, they said. He'll soon learn, and he'll stop. Tough love, tough love, remember?

But I would have chosen to have my eyes gauged out over witnessing my little boy's suffering, so once we are home I make sure that his beating heart is next to mine. Night and day. Day and night.

People bring presents – books on sleep training are the most popular, and I wonder if there's a universal conspiracy going on. They boast how 'they've cracked the sleep thing by putting their baby at the far end of the house. Thought this could be useful,' they say, patting the book, smugly. 'Vital to get him on track.'

Outnumbered and under duress, self-doubt gnaws at me – I am clearly doing it all wrong – and I cave in. I follow the book's instructions, forcing myself to listen to him cry – to leave him, not touch him, call a few soothing words from his open door, then leave him, not touch him, call a few soothing words... But still he cries. Every nap, every night is reduced to misery. Me crying. Him crying. What am I doing? He's a new-born baby, for God's sake! Not a fledgling soldier. None of it makes sense to me. In Africa, a baby sleeps with his mother so that he can feed from her breast at will.

I throw the books away and when he cries I put him back into my bed at night. In the day I carry him in a sling strapped to my front, with his little head, as soft as a rabbit's, just under my chin. I kiss it several thousand times a day and his nick-name quickly becomes Rab or Bun or Rabbity-boy.

But stray thoughts puncture my bliss. Is it fear that makes him cry when separated from me? And if so, from where did it spring? Did my anxiety handicap him even from the safety of my womb? Did I transfer it to him, blotting his unadulterated record even before he got going?

Is the damage reparable still? He's so little, surely it must be? But how?

Will love do it? Will it fill up the cracks made by fear? If I were to teach him the language of emotion, as if it was his mother tongue, he'll surely learn to identify, and express how he feels, so that the rot doesn't get the chance to grow. He'll learn the different ways that other people feel, and compassion will follow. He'll learn to have a healthy internal dialogue and healthy external one, and he'll understand that the prism through which he looks at his life, will ultimately dictate it, and that neither background or colour or status will alter it. He'll learn his worth and learn to believe in it. He'll learn the difference between good and bad relationships, and with his solid sense of self will know to set boundaries. He'll learn the importance of supporting others and accepting their support, and he'll learn the business of living and dying, and nothing will be left unsaid. Won't all of that help repair those cracks, and prevent a crisis in mid-life, which could lead to years of unlearning everything that he'd already learned?

It'll be easy. Surely. Already the rush of love I feel consumes hours without me noticing, lost and carried along as I am in a fuzzy cloud of euphoria. I marvel at him: at the tiny fingers gripping mine, soft plump leg across my stomach, huge innocent eyes – and my heart melts with every smile, and moment of understanding between us. It has never felt so alive or full, nor has it ever had to work so hard, with the overflow of love surging through my veins.

But. He is so vulnerable, my baby, so dependent on my protection, so dependent on my survival.

And with that thread of thought my old childhood phobia of my mother being taken from me bursts up again like a geyser. This time round it is about him losing *me*. I find myself sucked into the same old hyper-vigilant loop and precautionary rituals. Driving becomes an issue. If I drive I am sure to crash, so I stay at home and Charlie does the shopping. Night is again filled with footsteps and looming shadows. If I dare sleep 'a baddie' will come for me. Rip me away from my little boy. Instead, I lie awake, alert for any unusual sound, fully clothed, set to jump from the window with Theo in my arms. I keep a baseball bat under the bed, and I fill a notebook with poems, love letters, my moral code and life rules: A backup just in case my parental care is lost. A testament to my love.

How can I have let myself get caught in this spiral again? After all the work I have done? Damn. Damn. Damn.

For my parents and theirs before, fear had to be squashed into corners of their souls, and with nowhere else to go, its toxic vapour diffused outwards, mutating into mental illness, and from there into alcoholism, gambling and other addictions. I know one thing: fear is a bit like snake venom. If it isn't drawn out before it enters the bloodstream, life is immobilized, with paralysis and cessation of breathing. Fear tyrannizes when trapped and hidden, and its power swells. Draw it out, talk about it, and its power shrinks.

So, in this notebook, I write about it. Over and over again. Because, no matter what, I cannot permit it anywhere near my child.

Chapter 41

Today, I accept that the Big Bad Wolf's shadow is part of me, his hostile voice hides in the corridors of my brain, and the only result of the years spent trying to assassinate him, is my surrender. In my next life I will come back without him, and I look forward to that. But for the time being he is here. We muddle through together; I work my life around his caprices and, as if he were a corrupt cousin, I have given him a spare room in the far corner of my house. His repetitive voice bores me to death, which has toughened my shell and made me impatient. Nowadays, I can anticipate its level of noise and nastiness long before it goes up a notch. It is not mine, I tell myself. It's a habit of my own making. Every task or action remains, however, a bit like a hurdle race. I know that the hurdles – or taunts – are there, and I must jump them to get to my goal, but sometimes my only feat is to pull myself over the first one, such is the effort required to ignore them. I know his patterns now, though, for finally I know me. I accept that his absence and presence still determine my accomplishments, big or small. I am powerful, strong and able in moments of his absence, but defeatist and ineffectual in his presence.

When I am facing catastrophe, he absents himself. Crisis, catastrophe, and drama in every shape I am good at, and his taunts don't get to shoot at me. He knows how attuned I am, how strong-shouldered, how calm and methodical I prove to be when another day, week, or month is sucked up by the shredded emotions of a calamity, and particularly someone else's. He knows there's no point even tapping on my window then, to tell me how rubbish I am.

Nor do I hear him within the frames of my friendships. I am strong within them. I am good at being a friend. Good at loyalty and commitment. There are no hollows in there for him to shout down.

But as I write this manuscript, his soundtrack is on repeat. He ambushes every sentence, outwitting me. 'You can't write.' 'Not good enough.' 'You're second-rate.' 'Why are you bothering? No one's interested.' 'Give up.' 'You'll humiliate yourself.'

The ghost of catastrophe is in there too. 'You'll hurt people you love. Bad girl. Bad girl. Bad girl.'

So I give up, time and time again. And his winning streak endures. Off and on for thirty years.

But. Periodically, I dare to scream. I dare to drive back his judgements and prophetic doom, to withstand him and mow him down. 'I've had enough! You're dead! Over! Finished with! It's a duel to the death! I can't let myself down. I must not capitulate. To hell with failure, fear and doom! You can't stop me this time! The truth will out. My truth. That was why I started this, wasn't it? For *truth*. No more hypocrisy. No more pretence. No more chaos. No more confusion. You're dead, do you hear?' And for good measure I scream just one more time.

In motherhood, he spoils my joy at bath-time, when Rab's little body swims on mine. 'Smothering him.' 'Over-protecting him.' 'He won't have a chance.' 'You're co-de-pendent, remember?' He prevails, and I bathe him in a plastic tub until anger of my acquiescence gets the better of me and I reinstate our original routine. My burning de-sire to be right for my child makes me vulnerable to the Wolf's taunts – makes me question myself at every turn. Conscious of there being nothing lax about my maternal instinct, my inclination to believe him becomes quickly ingrained. There is a governing force that holds me back though. I am bound to health nowadays. Healthy mind, healthy body, and unequivocally so, for my child. Part of that is to keep myself in check, part is to provide a strong emotional core, and part is to shape a framework of values up which he can grow.

In my wifely duties he also goads me. Mostly when Charlie is tired, sulky, or bad-tempered. 'You're getting fat.' 'Not sexy enough.' 'Not fun enough!' 'He won't fancy you soon, and he'd be right.' 'It's him that needs attention, not your child!' 'You want him to run off with a newer, prettier, more entertaining you?'

I am inherently untrusting of a man's love. The Big Bad Wolf convinced me long ago of its fickle nature and taught me the means to regulate it: not only keeping in shape, but by consenting to his every whim. So I make up my sleepless eyes, squeeze into tight black jeans, cook Charlie's favourite dinner, and stay awake long after I want to.

Chapter 42

The walk uphill to the Marquis de Sade's old chateau is steep and slippery. The old cobbles in the strips the sun doesn't reach are icy, and I pull Theo and myself up by gripping the craggy edges of stones that bulge from the adjacent wall. A fig tree snakes out from them, last summer's shrivelled figs still clinging to its bare branches. Bobble trots on ahead of us, her nose to the ground. Smells of coffee and detergent waft out from open shutters. A radio plays *Joe le Taxi*. I remember how much Will loved the song. Or was it just Vanessa Paradis who appealed to him?

Once at the top we sit down on the hard earth. Below us tumble the slanting terracotta roofs of Lacoste, butting one up against the other like a cubist painting, and the valley beyond is hazy with plumes of smoke zigzagging south-wards from chimney pots. High up here, the Mistral's speed is stronger and its sting razor sharp. It whistles through the openings in the castle walls where once there were windows and over the craggy parapet where now an oak stretches its branches towards the light. I zip up the collar of my little boy's fluffy jacket. A messy tangle of branches jumps wildly in front of us, and through them I can just about pick out our house.

There is a man-made order to the linear design of vineyards, orchards, and fields, and an underlying continuity in the woolly prehistoric hills cradling it. The light is clear and sharp. The Mistral flutters the leaves of the olive trees, and the silver undersides glint like electric lights.

There is nothing so perfect as nature, I think. It doesn't try to be, it just is. It doesn't need to work harder and harder to be more beautiful, bountiful or acceptable. With every season, it just is. It breathes and grows and dies. Punished by frost and disease, it does its best to survive in symbiosis with other organisms. It draws from the earth and atmosphere only what it needs to grow. It is perfect.

Rab gasps suddenly and snaps me out of my thoughts. He has pulled off his hat, but it is caught by the wind and carried over the walls of the castle, which resemble a toothless maw. His fine hair is blown across his face. He totters and stumbles. I fold him in my arms and roll over onto my back, pressing my face against his soft cheek. Wild thyme grows in the dry dusty soil, and its scent is released in the air. Bobble's whiskery muzzle and wet nose trace our faces and we blow her away, giggling. Her tail wags and dirt whips over us. Hoping for a ball game, she barks playfully, but a sudden gust of wind knocks her over, and as she scrambles to get up we are submerged in a sandstorm. The swirling grit rushes across our skin and into our hair and threads of wool. Laughing, we snort it out from nose and lips.

The earth is compressed and stony. Pebbles knead my shoulder blades like acupressure. I look upwards, beyond Rab's warm head. An aeroplane trail wanes in the sky, and the little puffs of separating cloud look like a white feather on a bright blue canvas. White feathers are the calling cards of angels, to remind us they are near. Three weeks ago today I attended my dad's funeral. Did he cast the feather in the sky? I wonder. If I close my eyes and concentrate, can I connect to him? Can I catapult my thoughts up beyond the blue, and God's pearly gates? Through energy, can I message him?

Dad? Are you there?

I squeeze Rab's tummy. 'How hungry are you, my bun? What shall I make for supper? What about baked eggs? Shall we have buttery soldiers or baguette with them?'

A hawk soars upwards over the castle. From where we lie, its broad wings and wide fanned tail appear still, as it hovers on an air current. Rab's arm darts up, pointing at it. 'Whoosh' he cries, mimicking its flight. It swoops down, gaining speed, and its pale under-feathers and belly are revealed. Rab turns quickly to bury his head in the fur of my coat collar.

'Mum! No!' His little body trembles suddenly with fear, and his eyes are tightly shut. 'No Mumma! Not me! Please no!'

I kiss the top of his head and sit him up. I think of the Big Bad Wolf. The threat he poses of danger and doom.

The hawk heads towards the sweep of the hills, over the vines and olive groves. Its silhouette melds with their shadows and is nearly lost. Softly, in his ear, I sing a song that I sing daily on our walks together. 'He'll Be Coming 'Round The Mountain When He Comes…', and slowly he brings half his face out from my collar, and turns his eyes upwards – hesitantly – ready at any moment to dive back in.

'Look, my darling.' I point towards the village. 'Look at where the hawk is now! Do you see him? Hmmm? Look – there he is, all the way down there, swooping towards the old goat gate. Got him?'

Under my hands the tension drains from his ribcage and his breathing steadies. Between kisses, I whisper into his ear.

'No need to be scared, my baby. He's no threat to you. He's just getting on with his life in the sky. Just a beautiful bird doing his thing. He's looking for air currents, not small boys. All is well. Take a deep breath, come on!'

The bell chimes from the clock tower. We count. Theo extends his fingers to mark each number, one… two… three… four… five… six.

Then all of a sudden, I hear a voice, *his* voice, and with it, a familiar chuckle, and the sense that somewhere up there an eye is winking.

'It's got to be six o'clock somewhere in the world.'

Ah! My dad! There! There he is!

I knew it! I knew he was there!

My head jerks upwards and his old nervous tic transfers itself to me. For a split second I feel his feelings and see through his eyes again, as if his spirit has slipped into my own. In a sudden shifting of shape we are interwoven once more. He is here after all and we are connected: he hears, feels, and sees me – and me him.

Down in the house in my bedroom cupboard I have a small tortoiseshell box filled with a handful of his ashes. We'd scattered them in his requested corner, high on the beach in Jersey, 'but for Gawd's sake, do *not* let me get washed away by the tide.' Not being able to completely let go off him, I'd smuggled some crumbs of bones into my shoe, and had hobbled back home to France with them. In a short steady stream, they'd tumbled out from the heel and into the box – each white, gritty grain sweeping the soft grey ash along with their weight. It is only a small box, one in which my great grandmother kept an impressive necklace, but when I pick it up, its heaviness surprises me. My dad. There was a lot to him, I always knew that.

I wonder if now is the time to scatter them, to let him go forever. Yes, I think. It's time. After Rab's supper I will take them into the garden. I will sit under the almond tree where Dad would sit when he visited to take in the vast view of fields, hills and shadows. Ice in his whisky glass would chink with the movement of his arm while his big tanned hand beat out the rhythm of 'Raindrops Keep Falling on my Head'.

'Reminds me of the Rift Valley, darling. Just more houses. Awfully nice.'

I will empty out the ashes and let the Mistral take them south towards Africa. I will let him free, to be reunited with the happy pieces of his soul left buried there – in the stable-yard, the fields where his cattle grazed, and the club bar where he and his chums 'always had a good laugh.'

Rab has wriggled off my lap and pottered behind me where Bobble, on her back, rolls in the dry dirt. Her legs are open wide and her tail wags vigorously. His mittens, dangling on strings from his sleeves, are tossed upwards by the wind in another whirl of dust that clouds them both. He laughs and pats the dog's tummy. Her tail wags faster.

All is finally well.

'Come on you two,' I call. 'It's six already. You must be hungry. *On y va* my darlings!'

Introduction of Two Souls

Where we are heading I don't remember now.
I remember the sun through the boughs
Of the trees, the cow parsley, the light spring breeze,
I remember the ease between you and me,
And the sign on the road spelling his name
And I exclaim, 'Shall we go see – you and me –
The burial place of my lost love?'
And you, sweet child, agree, to the undreamed of
Plea, with curiosity and care for me.

I remember soft dappled light on the down hill road,
Driving slow through the brook from the Cam,
Crows from doves, an early rose, smiles from an elderly
man.
I remember the church – St Michael's – it is,
Holding the cycles of life in its earth,
And your distance at first – your offer of worth
To the veil of loss crossing the years,
While from his grave I clear the moss,
The dirt, the memories and earth.

I remember your gaze, when I beckon you come
And as my son, to say hello,
And though you know it is just a show,
You bow your head, and tread with careful steps
Towards his grave. And in your address
There's grace on your lips – what a heartfelt caress –
'I am so pleased to meet you Will, hello', and you show
A smile – so near and new – that I know then
That our souls renew. Amen. Amen. Amen.